HEADFIRST

HEADFIRST
The Olympic Success Story of Skeleton

© 2006 Robert C.Vaughn

Written by Robie Vaughn with Mike Towle

Grateful acknowledgment is made to various photographers and individuals for permission to reprint their photographs.

Cover image: Jim Shea, Jr. begins a run during the 2002 Olympic men's skeleton competition.
CRIS BOURONCLE/AFP/Getty Images

Manufactured in the United States of America.

For information, please contact:
Brown Books Publishing Group
16200 North Dallas Parkway, Suite 170
Dallas, Texas 75248
www.brownbooks.com
972-381-0009
A New Era in Publishing™

Hardcover ISBN: 1-933285-08-7
LCCN 2005932907
1 2 3 4 5 6 7 8 9 10

HEADFIRST

The Olympic Success Story
of
SKELETON

BY ROBIE VAUGHN WITH Mike Towle

Headfirst is dedicated to
Fallon, Robert, and Browning

Much Love

Table of Contents

Foreword IX

Preface XI

Chapter One
Downhill Texan 1

Chapter Two
Meet Bob Skeleton 7

Chapter Three
Good Ol' Boys at 80 Miles Per Hour 17

Chapter Four
Mountain High 51

Chapter Five
On a Wing and a Sled 65

Chapter Six
Red Tape and Black Eyes 79

Chapter Seven
Samoan Odyssey 97

Chapter Eight
A Slippery Slope 107

Chapter Nine
Olympic Ideals . . . and Back Room Deals 147

Chapter Ten
American Sliders 165

Chapter Eleven
The Countdown to Salt Lake City 185

Chapter Twelve
Sprint to the Olympics 201

Chapter Thirteen
The Olympics 215

Afterword 231

Acknowledgments 241

Foreword

Everyone with pride in America owes a debt of gratitude to Robie Vaughn of Dallas, Texas, for being the main driving force behind the USA Skeleton team's becoming number one in the world during the February 2002 Olympic Winter Games in Salt Lake City, Utah (Park City). Unbelievably, he and a few other dedicated participants and supporters accomplished the unlikely, in only thirty months leading up to the Olympics, when heretofore the U.S. skeleton sliders had been the international laughingstock of the sport. This was an Olympian feat and is what *HEADFIRST* is all about. I've never read a more breathtaking and gripping story of perseverance.

I'm awed by Robie's passion and focus—despite his extremely busy life— on the sport of skeleton in general and the underfinanced, seemingly makeshift U.S. team in particular. Through his and his wife Fallon's participation in the sport (in itself quite remarkable), and their patient, though repeatedly frustrated efforts, they facilitated the organizational leadership and monetary support to the relatively few athletes who had been racing domestically—where the sport is hardly known—as well as sometimes in skeleton's European meccas, where champions enjoy true celebrity status.

Nothing rankles so much in the minds of men as the thought of neglected opportunity. I kept thinking of this phrase as I read *HEADFIRST*, because I regret I was completely unaware of skeleton and had no idea of Robie's involvement, prior to being told shortly before the 2002 Winter Olympics by my son, Dan Bass (a classmate of Robie's in elementary and high school), that the sport was going to be added to the Salt Lake City Olympic events, partially as a result of Robie's efforts. In a way, I've often considered a number of my two sons' friends from their Dallas school days as somewhat surrogate sons, even though I haven't seen some of them for over thirty years. Robie, however, was one whom I did see from time to time—not only socially in Dallas, but also at my Snowbird resort in Utah, where Robie owned a condo. Most memorably I spent time with Robie, when together we climbed Denali (Mt. McKinley, Alaska, at 20,320 feet the highest peak in North America) in June/July 1983; and in the fall of 2004, when we trekked to 18,000 feet in Nepal.

Robie probably requested I write this foreword because of our mutual adventurous spirit and the fact that my being the first to climb the highest mountain on each of the world's seven continents (in my fifties) has been considered by many to be recklessly risky and even completely crazy. As far as I'm concerned, that seems like child's play compared to the sport of skeleton. I was mentally scared to death as I read the detailed descriptions of the sport and imagined myself as a human projectile hurtling down an icy track at breakneck speed, headfirst on my belly on a tiny sled, with my chin bobbing only an inch or two above the track. This breathless, adrenaline-rush, teeth-chattering, seemingly out-of-control ride lasts only approximately one minute, but I can't imagine that my mind or heart could handle it—and neither did Robie when a good friend of his first urged him to try sliding. Even the description of the way any beginner works up to a full-course, top-to-bottom run hasn't changed my mind in the least that the sport is only for those with a definite death wish. I'll get my skeleton thrills by being only a spectator, thank you, but I understand watching it is well worth the effort.

Another aspect of *HEADFIRST* that makes it so impressive and uplifting is Robie's family's history and his emphasis on his parents' and others' influences that have shaped his values, perspectives, and purposes. From having a close relationship with Robie, when I was a grade school "volunteer parent coach," and later following his Culver Military Academy and University of Texas at Austin continuing education, I've seen him grow and develop into an outstanding person of integrity, ability, and ambition to do worthwhile things for his family, his business, his country, and his Creator. In short, he is a lifter, not a leaner. He is one of his generation who gives me faith that "the world is [not] going to hell in a handbasket!"

In summing up, I want to pay tribute to the God-given human choice to live one's life with ENTHUSIASM. The word enthusiasm comes from the Greek *en-theos,* which, loosely translated, means "God's spirit in each of us," and which I consider to be the Holy Spirit part of the Christian trilogy concept. Enthusiasm doesn't manifest itself in all its facets automatically, but it is there for those of faith who believe that humans are endowed with a meaningful degree of our Creator's imagination, creativity, and productive capabilities. So Robie, I salute you with the conviction and appreciation that your skeleton pursuit is a tangible testimonial to Emerson's stirring maxim: *Every great and commanding movement in the annals of the world is the triumph of enthusiasm. Nothing great was ever achieved without it.*

Dick Bass
Dallas, Texas
January, 2006

Preface

One thing is certain: our lives are a blink of an eye when we hold them next to universal or geological events and forces. From our human perspective, the universe and earth seem fairly constant and static. In fact, they are actually evolving in constant, steady, and mostly predictable ways. There are parallels to evolutions in our cultures, societies, businesses, and lives in the sense that growth and change are ongoing givens. And so it is that each of us is challenged with the struggle of how to grow and change within our lives into interested, passionate and valuable individuals.

As a child, I was exposed to and recognized the accomplishments of astronauts, athletes, businessmen, explorers, politicians, and others. It was the combination of these characters and their chosen occupations and subsequent challenges, failures, and successes that caught my curiosity and riveted my interest—the romance of the Mercury, Gemini, and Apollo space programs and those memorable views from space and on the moon; the excitement and intensity of downhill ski racing and bobsled in the Olympic Games; my father's diversified business pursuits in banking, oil and gas, printing, radio, television, and ranching; the motivation and inspiration emanating from fictional characters such as "Rudy Matt" in *Banner in the Sky,* real-life personalities such as Sir Edmund Hillary, Tenzing Norgay, Chris Bonnington, and leadership traits of Barry Goldwater, Richard Nixon, Ronald Reagan, and George W. Bush.

By observing and experiencing the accomplishments and dramas of these individuals and their pursuits, I began to discover and develop my own passion, focus, and determination that have inspired and motivated me in life. One thing I have learned is that a life lived without passion and inherent risks is a life unfulfilled. There is something to be admired about those willing to step outside their comfort zone in order to risk making a difference in someone else's life as well as in their own.

I am thankful for the numerous opportunities I have had over the years to wander outside the envelope of everyday experience and try something different, something that breaks new ground for me and for others. Atop that list of unique experiences is my involvement with the sport of skeleton, beginning as a neophyte slider—almost petrified of such sheer speed on ice—and evolving into my filling a needed role. This was a sport lacking vision and leadership, and I took it upon myself to fill that vacuum in a way that would benefit others and elevate the sport to its rightful position—on the Olympic Winter Games docket.

For thirty-five months, I was the first program director of USA Skeleton, charged with nurturing an infant program into one that in less than three years would become a world challenger. This book is the story of what turned out to be one of the most challenging, exciting, fun, and successful activities in my life (so far), and it involved something as simple as a sled and something else as treacherous as a twisting, ice-laden, downhill track. Working with skeleton was a pure experience in that it was one in which I had a passion for the sport as well as for the athletes. The challenge seemed so simple: courage, determination, and physics. It required a commitment to achieving excellence and reaching for the pinnacle of success, and it offered an opportunity to set an example that would involve putting the athletes first and making the right choices to benefit them. It was an opportunity of purity—right in front of us, just waiting to be done, but done right.

This is a story about dreams, but not just mine, and about a bond between athletes, staff, and a team leader, all committed to pulling off what cynics might have considered the improbable, if not the impossible. I'm talking about those unmitigated dreams we have as children—to be an astronaut, a firefighter, or an Olympic athlete. In living our lives and chasing our daily pursuits in the working world, especially as we grow older, we often lose sight of those dreams. There are many distractions and a lot of stress with which we have to deal, making it difficult to be creative and pursue those dreams.

Remember this, though: at the same time we're viewing those dreams, fantasizing them, we're also intuitively learning the very basic lessons that form the principles for the rest of our lives, the fundamental lessons of right and wrong that don't need to be justified or nuanced.

If we take those fundamental values and principles and apply them to our families, our friends, our work, or our athletic pursuits, we might one day find ourselves back on track for those dreams, even if we take a roundabout way to get there. We might be so fortunate as to find we can achieve those dreams after all. As I found out firsthand, that's a life lesson in itself.

Human beings are of such a nature that we should have spiritual sustenance as well as material facilities. Without the spiritual component, peace of mind can be especially elusive. The Dalai Lama once said that the very purpose of life is to be happy. We desire contentment from the very core of our being. I have an addendum to that: the more we care for the happiness of others, the greater our own sense of well-being. Cultivating a close, warmhearted feeling for others puts the mind at ease. It helps remove whatever fears or insecurities we have and gives us the strength to cope with and the ability to see beyond the obstacles we encounter. Contentment is the principal source of success in life. It is a mistake to place all our hopes for happiness on external development alone. Inner peace is the key.

Through skeleton, I touched the peace of which I believe the Dalai Lama spoke. It all started with a personal curiosity and challenge of and to myself, evolved into a desire to reach a personal, self-oriented goal, and culminated as I dedicated myself to helping a team of others achieve their goals. The dream I realized was much more gratifying than the dream I had started chasing in the first place, one that had been in the back of my mind since childhood.

This book is not only my story of how a dream was birthed and then realized, it's also an account of what a small group of people can achieve against all odds. We came a long way in a short period of time. I hope this book will touch you and perhaps even change you in some way, lighting your own path to whatever your definition of achievement, success, and happiness happens to be.

CHAPTER ONE
Downhill Texan

It is only in adventure that some people succeed in knowing themselves—in finding themselves.

—Andre Gide

Standing at the top of the nearly mile-long bobsled, luge, and skeleton track at Lake Placid, New York, one of only two such tracks in the United States, I am uncomfortably anxious and fearful. The entire track is contained within a quarter-mile of terrain, encompassing a vertical drop of 344 feet. The track crisscrosses the mountainside, its layout highlighted by sixteen steep curves and banked from seventy to ninety degrees, sometimes more. I will encounter these curves, on average, about every two to three seconds.

I'm going to slide down this mile-long track on a sled that, at first glance, looks not much bigger than a cafeteria tray. And I'll be traveling at seventy to eighty miles an hour.

I'm a Texan, in my forties, an oil and gas executive, and I've taken on the responsibility of making skeleton an Olympic sport and a success.

And I must be out of my mind.

They said that hard work means putting your nose to the grindstone. In the case of skeleton sliding, it's really about putting your chin to the hard ice. My nose—practically my whole face—is safely ensconced inside a face-shielding helmet and visor. This leaves only my mouth and chin perilously vulnerable to contact as I dip down the icy chute. Once I start moving, my chin will bob along barely an inch or two off the ice, as G-forces bear down on my head and neck, relentlessly trying to push my chin onto the ice, where friction can burn flesh.

1

I am about to jump onto the razor's edge of danger. One false move or even a twitch can send me careening off concrete walls partially covered in rock-hard ice, leaving a red trail of blood to mark my route. Gert Elsasser, Europe's top-rated slider during the early 1980s, summed it all up this way: "Ze nize sing about skeleton sledding is zat if you do it right, you can smell ze ice."

Piloting a skeleton sled, headfirst on my belly down a twisting track of glaring ice, at speeds that would buy me a speeding ticket in a red Lamborghini, is a serious dance with fear. And it will all be over in sixty seconds. The slightest mental lapse or physical wobble going into or out of one of the curves beneath me can result in a cracked-helmet concussion, a broken arm, a torn ACL, or worse.

This truly isn't a sport for everyone, I tell myself, as I hold my sled tight and prepare to take the running start, the leap onto the sled, and the downward plunge. Truly world-class skeleton racers number only in the dozens, while more established sports like bobsled or luge count hundreds or even thousands at the top. This sport requires every ounce of my focus, determination, perseverance, stamina, and courage.

An extra pint of blood can't hurt, either. Dave Graham, the former president of the Alberta Skeleton Association, once lost his spleen and six pints of blood when a tiny mistake in a training session nearly cost him his life. He had been preparing for a World Cup event in Oberhut, Germany. According to the chap who cleaned it up, Dave left a trail of blood 128 meters long on the track. Talk to Graham today and he'll insist that skeleton is no harder, mentally or physically, than driving a truck off a cliff.

My sled, a smooth slab of steel and fiberglass with slick, rounded iron and carbon runners, provides enough velocity to fulfill my need for speed. Don't bother looking for brakes. There aren't any. I'll just keep picking up velocity, reaching 130 feet per second at top speed, which is a lot like being shot out of a cannon, especially if that cannon is Nolan Ryan's arm.

Jim Torrico, a veteran slider, once described the experience this way to *U.S. News and World Report*: "Your adrenaline is really flowing. The gravitational force through the turns pushes your body into the sled, and you can't hold your head up off the ice. The first time I got to the bottom, I could not wait to go back up. I just wanted to feel that wind and speed again."

Sometimes people ask me how skeleton compares with the other sliding sports like two- and four-man bobsled and single and doubles' luge. Bobsledders seem to nestle themselves in the cozy confines of their protective vehicle. Lugers ride on a sled, like skeleton sliders, but they start off seated, their feet out in front of them. Lugers ultimately lie back on their sleds while steering with their feet, lifting their heads just enough to see where in blue blazes they're headed.

Skeleton, on the other hand, is kamikaze-style, all-out sledding. Once it's my turn to go, I'll sprint as hard as I can, leap chest first onto the sled, tuck my arms into the sides, and duck my head to create an aerodynamic position. From there until I reach the finish line, I'll steer with subtle movements of my head and shoulders, my chin practically shaving ice on the way down. The downward pressure I will exert with my knees and the subtle dragging or touching of my toes on the ice will help keep the sled in check and "on line." I guarantee you I don't want my toes touching the track for too long.

Vermonter Tim Rath, a pioneer in the American resurgence of skeleton in the early 1980s, described a run down the mile-long track as the equivalent of electroshock treatment. "You are so focused all the way down," Rath said, "that when you get to the bottom, all the tension is drained out of your body. That explains why I used to say that one of the reasons I did skeleton was to relax, because my work in the field of explosives has such a high stress level."

Just how fast will I be going once I start moving? Terry Allen, skeleton athlete and advocate, shares the following: "If you enter late into turn six in the Park City, Utah, track, you go from zero Gs to five Gs in .2 seconds. An F-16 fighter jet can take 2.5 seconds to hit five Gs. At five Gs, your normally eight- to ten-pound head now weights forty to fifty pounds. Again, this change happens in .2 seconds, faster than it takes to blink your eyes. Is it any wonder that this spot in the track is where a lot of chin, teeth, tongue, nose, neck, and skull damage can occur? Many a friend has had to wait a few days for the swelling to go down before they could get their helmets back on."

Maybe this whole thing is crazy.

As a competitive racer, I've already taken careful measure of the course before I slide it. Ice conditions can change from day to day, necessitating a track walk from top to bottom, the better to memorize every nook, cranny, angle, rut, bump, and even puddle. One racer, Jimmy Shea, repeated to *Sports Illustrated* what the Europeans told him—that a good slider must treat the track like a beautiful, curvaceous woman. "If you don't give her a lot of attention," the Euros told him, "she will break your heart and a few bones along with it."

It's almost as exciting to watch skeleton sliding as it is to perform it, even though watching can be somewhat repetitive. You don't always have enough context to process what you just saw. To the spectator, skeleton occurs in blink-of-an-eye bursts. Pay close attention, though. Accessible vantage points along the track afford, at best, hundred-foot segments for your viewing pleasure. Turn your back for just an instant at the wrong moment, and your only evidence of a passing slider will be the whooooosh accompanying the blur you just missed.

Enough talk. It's time to slide.

So here I go.

I'm bent over, rocking the sled as it lays on the ice, and when queued by the starter, I begin my flat-out sprint toward the brain warp. Skeleton athletes work on their overall conditioning as any Olympian would, but it all starts with building explosive power and quickness in the legs. Sprint speed is important, because as the run begins, I'm pushing the sled as fast as possible from behind and a bit to the side. I'm holding onto one or both of the saddle ridges affixed to the top of the sled. The two runners on the bottom of the sled keep the sled straight on track, sliding in a groove cut less than an inch into the ice.

I'm crouched over while sprinting, my metal spikes penetrating the ice, as I accelerate as quickly as I can, tripping the electronic timer fifteen meters from the start line. With the sled still on the almost-level, grooved track, I keep pushing for about another fifteen meters, finally diving onto the sled just as it leaves the start area, which begins the first stretch of descent, downward into turn one, which is waiting another thirty or so meters down the track.

Here at the top of the run, the corners are very subtle, yet I have to have a plan before I get to each turn—where to enter it, where to exit. I'm focused on the entry points. As I pick up speed, I start riding higher on the turns, which means that I have to be more wary of skidding as I come out of a high turn. Every time I skid, I lose time. Ditto for dragging a toe. Friction slows me down. These are inefficiencies I'm attempting to minimize.

My first order of business, once on the sled, is to settle myself physically—to become and remain calm. I've got to keep my heart rate down and my mind clear. The biggest thing when on the sled is not to be tense. At this moment in the run, the words of former national team member and volunteer coach Peter Viaciulis come into my head. "You don't want to be a white-knuckle driver," Viaciulis said. "You get all pumped up for the push, but as soon as you jump onto that sled, do an exhale and make sure your hands are relaxed. Big exhale, curl the shoulders in. Don't again think about your breathing after that exhale, and then everything goes into slow motion. You shift around just a little bit, but you have to be gentle. The trick is to look as far forward as you can while still keeping your shoulders pinned to the sled. Always try to be conscious of that contact between shoulders and sled."

I become acutely aware of every little move I make. Every twitch, every flinch. That's because I don't want to be making many movements. I remind myself to be still, just like when the dentist steps out of the room to take x-rays.

Now I'm halfway down the track, zipping along at or near top speed of seventy to eighty miles an hour. Today the track is a little bumpy, the result of how the track officials maintained it overnight and changes wrought by the weather. A bouncy track like this blurs my vision, making it all that much more difficult for me to focus my eyes. The run has quickly transformed itself from smooth to teeth-chattering, and it has given rise to the stress and strain of high speed and extra Gs. It's only going to get more intense, and quickly. If you're in the present and not focused on where you're headed, you are "behind the sled," as we say, and you'll soon be in deep trouble.

Some of the late turns near the bottom of the track are banked at angles greater than ninety degrees. Suddenly it's a real chore for me to keep my chin and toes off the ice. I force myself to use subtle knee pressure instead of toe-dragging to help steer the sled, to increase aerodynamic efficiency.

As fast as I'm going now, I will continue to compound acceleration for the rest of the run. The turns are starting to come faster and faster, and I'm going higher and higher on the embanked turns. Some of these walls can be fifteen feet off the ground. In Igls, Austria, turn fourteen is thirty feet high. My centrifugal force keeps me safe from what otherwise could be a painful two-story fall to the bottom of the icy track—at over seventy miles an hour.

My chest begins to tighten, and I grip the sled like a madman—then, suddenly, I realize the ride is over. I'm drifting to a stop, and once again, my surroundings are coming into focus. I had just spent what felt like an eternity stuck between exhilaration and trepidation, yet it felt as if I had only started the run. I found myself unable to think until my sled came to a complete halt at the bottom of the run. It took a few seconds for my wits to return. And there was only one thought in my mind: *Again! I can do it better, and I can go faster!*

* * *

This is the story of a passion verging on an obsession, first with the sheer thrill of sliding down tracks on skeleton sleds, something I tried for the first time in my life at age thirty-nine, and then with the idea of representing the United States at the Olympics as a member of the Winter Olympic skeleton team.

There were just a few obstacles to overcome.

First, many Olympic athletes are about half my age. So there was a good chance that I'd be too old or too slow to qualify for the U.S. Olympic Team.

And second, there was no U.S. Olympic skeleton team, for the simple reason that skeleton wasn't an Olympic sport. It hadn't been in the Olympics for decades. The bobsled powers that be, insecure in their control, had jockeyed feverishly to make sure that skeleton stayed out of the Olympics in past decades.

The officials figured that the Winter Olympics only had so much sponsorship appetite for sliding sports like bobsled, luge, or skeleton. To open the door to skeleton could only dilute the importance of bobsledding. At least that's what they believed. And they would fight hard to keep bobsled the paramount sliding sport.

This is the story of my quest to bring skeleton to the Olympics, so that our great American skeleton athletes would have the chance to represent our nation against the world's best.

This is the story of a quest for Olympic gold . . . the gold you mine when you slide downhill . . . headfirst through life and into the future.

CHAPTER TWO
Meet Bob Skeleton

Imagination is more important than knowledge.
—Albert Einstein

Anyone who grew up in snow country knows that sliding headfirst on a sled down a hill covered in snow or ice is at the heart of the winter sports scene. First or fastest one down the slope wins.

The full name for skeleton is Bob Skeleton. No relation to Red Skelton, but a close cousin to Bob Sled. Bob Skeleton's roots stretch back to the late nineteenth century, although it went more than fifty years without Olympic Games certification. Skeleton has been on the sports page radar only for the past twenty years or so.

The name "skeleton" traces its origins to the sliding device known in Norwegian as the *kyalke*, later Anglicized to *skele*. Another popular theory is that early versions of the Cresta sled, with its rib-like structure, bore a resemblance to a human skeleton or a skeletal frame of a sled—hence, the name skeleton.

Historical records are vague, but we do know that organized skeleton and bobsledding both date back to the late nineteenth century. Their origins were continents apart, but both felt American influence. In the late 1880s, lumberjacks in and around Albany, New York, 160 miles south of Lake Placid, would run their lumber sleds. Another account has it that the bobsled was invented when an enterprising American diplomat and sportsman named Townsend started tying together two skeleton sleds, making the second one bob along behind the first sled, creating a makeshift sliding apparatus naturally referred to as a bobsled. Yet another version says that the bob got its name from the riders' bobbing to make it go faster!

Sled racing itself is believed to have its roots in and around St. Moritz, Switzerland. St. Moritz is a jet-setter's paradise with a sustained Old World charm, evidenced in its narrow, winding streets, its ringing church bells, and its aged stone and stucco buildings. Men and women alike raced small sleds from the St. Moritz resort down to the village of Celerina, where a bottle of champagne awaited the winner. St. Moritz remains one of the meccas of skeleton and other sliding sports. The legendary Cresta Run, the forefather of skeleton, is located in the Cresta Valley just below St. Moritz. St. Moritz is to skeleton sliders what Augusta National Golf Club is to avid golfers—a historic and revered destination available for use only by the members and those specially invited. An entertaining account of the Cresta story is found in the book *Apparently Unharmed.*

The first Cresta Grand National Race took place in January 1885, and featured twenty contestants. Two years later, one of the Cresta racers went against tradition and lay down on the sled, head first. Within several years, all Grand National participants were emulating this radical approach to sledding, giving the sport a whole new look.

In the infancy of the sport, sliders steered bobsleds by pulling on ropes, and sleds didn't have brakes. Sledders had to use garden rakes to stop! St. Moritz was home to the first bobsled club, founded in 1897 and considered the catalyst for the sport's growth and popularity at winter resorts throughout Europe. Men's bobsled was among the sports contested at the first Olympic Winter Games, in 1924, at Chamonix, France. Men's skeleton, then called "Men's Open Frame Toboggan" or "Cresta," joined the Olympics in 1928 at, of course, St. Moritz. American brothers Jennison and John Heaton of New Haven, Connecticut, won Cresta gold and silver, respectively, at those St. Moritz Games.

Twenty years later, John Heaton added a second silver during the second and only other time Cresta was in the Olympics—again at St. Moritz. The sport would disappear from the Olympics, and through an unusual series of events, would return to the Olympics over fifty years later.

Various types of toboggans and sleds have found their way onto icy tracks over the years. One of the most durable models has been the Cresta sled, originally developed on the Cresta Valley track and outfitted with a sliding saddle. That saddle was necessary because the turns in the Cresta track were elliptical, convex, and flatter than the more concave turns built into the modern bobsled, luge, and skeleton tracks. The sliding position required lying down headfirst on one's stomach. On the Cresta, the slider must hang off the rear end of the sled and drag his knees and toes in order to negotiate turns—while staying in the track at race speed. Bobsledders in the 1970s began to experiment with these sleds on existing bobsled tracks around Europe, and competition ensued. The new generation of skeleton sleds was built without the sliding saddle. They are now designed to be more flexible, so that the sled may be steered while the driver maintains a consistent and aerodynamic form.

It took two months to build the original Cresta Run, a track completed in January 1885. This, of course, is not to be confused with the nearby modern-day bobsled, luge, and skeleton track used as a venue for international competition. The original Cresta Run remains in use as a sort of living museum piece. Both tracks were built from scratch each year, utilizing the natural contours offered by the lay of the land, with subtle banks of earth that comprise the framework upon which the track is laid out. The track itself is made from blocks of ice cut from the large lake just below St. Moritz. Tradition has it that for generations, local families have built certain sections of the track each year.

At season's end, the Cresta Run melts to the ground, keeping it out of sight and out of mind to summertime visitors who reach this idyllic destination. Just how esteemed is the Cresta Run? James Bond's creator, Ian Fleming, wrote it into the plot of his novel *On Her Majesty's Secret Service*. Fleming had Bond in the thrilling bobsleigh chase which ended, in the movie version, with Telly Savalas's bad guy, Blofeld, nearly decapitated in a collision with a tree.

The Cresta Run ordinarily is opened right before Christmas and stays in operation through February, with recreational riding available every morning, and more than two dozen races taking place during the ten-week season. It is a private club, although nonmembers are welcome to come by and give it a turn. There is the matter of formality and proper protocol, though. This is Switzerland! Hot-dogging competitors are outlawed from sneaking in to take a run.

Soon after the beginning of the twentieth century, formalized Cresta racing as we now know it started cropping up around Europe. By 1906, Austria was conducting its own national championships. Two years later, races were held just outside Vienna, and in the winter of 1912–13, an ice hockey and Cresta club was formed in Germany. Bad weather in 1913 and 1914, followed by the outbreak of World War I, put Cresta racing on ice in locales other than Switzerland.

Competitive sliding in one form or another made a renewed appearance in the 1920s, starting with the rebuilding of the Cresta Run in 1921, continuing with the founding of the Federation Internationale de Bobsleigh et de Tobogganing

(FIBT, the International Federation for Bobsled and Skeleton) in 1923, and culminating in the inclusion of Cresta in the 1928 Winter Olympics in St. Moritz. Italy's Nino Bibbia, the individual regarded as the greatest Cresta racer ever, won the gold in 1948, one of his more than 200 Cresta victories—and one of his first. Remarkably enough, in 1948 Bibbia, a ski jumper, was a novice slider who took the gold in only his sixth trip down a track on a Cresta sled, upsetting the heavily favored Swiss racer Christian Fischbacher, who was racing in his own back yard. That year marked the last Olympic appearance for Cresta. It would take half a century before a like event, skeleton, would become Olympic once again. And somehow I, an individual from a Texas climate that doesn't exactly favor winter sports, had made it a quest to get skeleton back to the Olympics, where I truly believe it belongs.

It wasn't so much that international interest in skeleton was waning. The disappearance from that particular world stage was more a reflection of the fact that the sport hadn't become widely known or popular. Cresta figured in the Olympic Games in 1928 and 1948 only because the Olympics were held in those years in the town where the Cresta track was located. After Cresta's last Olympic appearance of the twentieth century, twenty years would pass before skeleton regained international attention in 1969, when the first combined manmade run was opened at Koenigssee-Berchtesgaden in Germany, just below Hitler's "Eagle's Nest."

Skeleton's competition and track availability had been hit or miss for decades. Now, finally, the sport had a venue that would be open and available for the entire winter season, regardless of the weather. Training in races could be planned and carried out for a full five-month period, giving organizers and racers ample opportunity to grow the sport and refine their techniques.

While bobsleigh was still considered the most important of the sliding sports, granted top priority when it came to track time and the training of athletes, skeleton was given a place of honor in the new German training center. Incoming FIBT president Klaus Kotter's home base was the Bob Club Munich, and Kotter wanted to make sure that the new track at Koenigssee-Berchtesgaden was utilized to the fullest. Internationally renowned bob pilot Max Probst suggested that skeleton sledges be built to accommodate the newly constructed combined run, a proposal that was met with unabashed enthusiasm. Soon, another new Olympic track for bobsled, luge, and skeleton was erected on a beautiful valley hillside overlooking Innsbruck, Austria, in the village of Igls.

Throughout the 1970s, national skeleton races started to come into vogue. Soon after, the European championships came into existence. During the late 1970s and early 1980s, the occasional American was introduced to the European version of the sport. The Americans were dazzled by the sheer speed of the sliders, who rode low and hid their sleds with their bodies in a way that made them look as if they were rocket-propelled. To put it simply, it looked like fun. Soon skeleton would be a new American athletic phenomenon, one that would catch on slowly but surely.

The first time I saw an icy skeleton track, I pondered wearing some kind of padding for every body part. I quickly realized, though, that the speed suit, gloves, and helmet with its built-in visor and chin guard would suffice. On colder days, an extra layer or two of clothing under the speed suit affords added protection and warmth. Yet like most athletes, I believe in the old adage "skin to win." How cold is it? Did I mention that when you factor in the wind chill while sliding, it can be eighty below?

I was thirty-nine when I took my first skeleton run. My initiation was in January 1995, at the Canadian Olympic Park in Calgary, when my good friend, J. Taylor Boyd, fourteen other neophytes, and I took part in a skeleton school sponsored by the Alberta Skeleton Association. At the start area atop the track, the very beginning of which is composed of a wooden plank well-worn over the years by bobsledders and skeleton sliders, it didn't look that bad. Watching from behind as others pushed off, jumped onto the sled, and started sliding toward the first turn, there was little sense of intimidation. They didn't appear to be going that fast.

My real schooling came on my first run, when the sled stubbornly and relentlessly kept picking up speed, with nothing but wind resistance and the barely discernible friction of steel on ice to govern my increasing speed. I tried to keep the sled in the center on straight sections, entering the turns with as much advantage as I could to complement the shape of the turns, which dictate the amount of pressure or G-forces. A twitch of the head, I quickly learned, could change my direction for better or worse.

As I awaited my turn, I was anxious and sweating, despite the freezing temperature. I kept going over in my head the instructions that had been given me, going against every bit of common sense and need for self-preservation screaming inside me. The instructors had told us three things, and we were to follow those instructions in order: One, stay on the sled. Two, keep your form.

Three, have fun. Amazingly, I accomplished all three on my very first run from the junior start halfway up the track. As soon as I was on the sled, I got to thinking, *Hey, this isn't so bad.* Then I took that first turn, and I bumped the wall, but fortunately it was nothing serious at that low speed.

Then there was a straight leg, and my speed started increasing. Suddenly, I was reminded that there is, in essence, little friction—with no brakes. My mind started going into dark territory. Out of nowhere came that irrational fear that whispered to me that there was some sort of obstruction up ahead on the track, or that I'm about to have an equipment failure, or that I'm doing something wrong and I'm going to crash. Your mind can play tricks with you.

I stared ahead as best I could, my chin guard sometimes tapping the ice, and suddenly I saw a looming turn so sharp, somewhere in the range of 180 to 270 degrees, that for an instant it appeared to be a wall dead ahead with nowhere to go but smack dab into it. Thankfully, it's only an optical illusion made scary by the nanoseconds your mind has the chance to process depth perception. Yes, there is a curve that gives you an out from playing tag with an impenetrable wall.

I have entered the world of extreme sledding, and I am riding the human bullet train. This is a high-octane sport that requires nerves of steel, a mind properly wired for processing steady streams of instant decision-making, and a willingness to push the envelope—but not too much—in trying to shave hundredths of seconds off times. I did all this while wearing a skintight suit made out of synthetic materials such as Lycra that are less than perfect at protecting the body from cold, friction, and blunt trauma—and great at exposing every flaw of the physique.

Even now, as an experienced slider, I still get butterflies—butterflies that frequently squash themselves into a fist-sized ball in my gut. The finish-line payoff I await is the kind of euphoric exhilaration that you can only find in a breakneck sport conducted on a three-foot long contraption that weighs between seventy and one hundred pounds.

I look around me and see various other skeleton athletes going through their preparations before their own slides. It's fascinating to see how everyone deals with pressure in his or her own way. Some crank up music through headphones. Others meditate. More than a few sit alone in the warming hut, eyes closed, visualizing their run, their bodies or their heads leaning left and then right in perfect synchronicity with the mind's picture of the run. This is a common and effective process, one I've adopted as well. I can sit anywhere—on a flight, in a coffee shop—and my mind will wander to a track where I'll be sliding. I'll start the timer on my watch, picture my run, and visualize the perfect line going into each turn.

As I mentally complete the run, I'll stop my timer, and I'll try to be within seconds of how long the actual run would take. I repeat this exercise until my time and my mind meet the objective of that run. Your mind and your run, the run and your mind, melding and becoming one. It's all very Zen-like, especially for a Texan like me.

The track down which I'm about to career has a surface a lot like hockey arena ice—smooth, rock hard, and nearly impossible to get traction on, unless you're wearing skates or the metal-spiked track shoes I have on. We wear these special shoes primarily for the push starts on top of the course. There are no Zambonis to resurface the track ice between periods, as they do at hockey games. The track officials occasionally "spritz" or spray the course with water to smooth out the wrinkles and speed it up—the new layer of water immediately hardens into a glaring sheen of new ice. Keeping my face close to the ice is my goal, from the moment I flop belly first onto my sled, all the better for maximizing the aerodynamic aspect of racing. You can't help but smell the ice, as those speeds, faster than a mile a minute, produce upwards of four Gs that keep my body, and most noticeably my head, forced downward for most of the run. A good training day is one without mishap, one in which frozen sweat and a stiff neck are the only lingering physical manifestations of the intense stress and anxiety that I'll put myself through.

"Skeleton has always attracted me because of the combination of attributes that you need in order to succeed," says Terry Holland, who has spent more than twenty years as a member of the U.S. national team. "You have to have good athleticism and superior driving skill," Holland says, "and you need to be able to be very calm while also having the kind of hair-trigger temperament that allows you to deal with something as potentially catastrophic as a car wreck and then being able to go right back to being very calm again. When going down the track, there are events that can be very calamitous if you can't react instantly and then settle right back down. Immediate calm, steely nerves, no fear. And a really quick analytical ability."

Holland continues, "There is something about skeleton that is not on the immediate level of consciousness. Remember, in golf, 'See the ball, be the ball'? In skeleton, it's 'See the track, be the track.' There are moments when you get into a zone with this, and it becomes almost surreal. The first time for me was in Sarajevo in the mid-eighties. All of a sudden on one particular run, I was totally into it on my own, and everything jelled. I had one of those runs where it was 'whoooooaaaaaa!!!' when I got to the bottom. I knew right then it was something that I just couldn't go right back to the top of the hill and duplicate. Something happened—sort of like the time when long jumper Bob Beamon had that otherworldly jump at the 1968 Summer Olympics. He obliterated the world record by more than a foot in a sport where progress ordinarily is measured in fractions of a inch. His incredible flying leap came from somewhere that Beamon could not fully explain or comprehend. You wonder, 'Where did that come from?'"

When I was a novice slider, I had fleeting moments on the run where I would fight the urge to lift my head or drag my toes—anything to slow down this unrelentingly accelerating sled. When I was new, the sled seemed to have a mind of its own, as if it were in charge. But after just a few times down the track, I began to get the feel for it, and that's when I aspired for the other end of the racing spectrum. I began to ask myself the question, "How can I go faster?"

The answers fly into my brain in terse bursts: aerodynamics; toes pointed together, off the ice; shoulders down; head tucked, arms in; work on those runners; and more foot speed at the top.

"Anyone can do it," says American skeleton racing pioneer Pat Murtagh, now a bank executive in Burlington, Vermont, about twenty years removed from his sliding days. Can anyone do it? That strikes me as threatening to step over the line into easier-said-than-done generalization. "There's no big macho thing in any of these sliding sports," Murtagh adds. "However, it is a whole different ball game to be competitive and win. The exhilaration is high. Sometimes, the anxiety, the anticipation of your run is worse than the run itself."

Novice sledders, under proper tutelage, are incrementally phased into a full run of the track. Beginners start about halfway up the track, reaching speeds of about forty to sixty miles an hour, depending on ice conditions. Then it's on to about the two-thirds or three-quarters mark before the new slider eventually graduates to the full monty—the start at the top of the hill.

Skeleton today is the classic competitive winter sport. It features the kind of speed that dazzles spectators as well as thrills junkies. It is a sport that can be conducted properly only in the cold, snow, and ice of winter. And there is nothing subjective about scoring contestants. The fastest one down the track is the winner, plain and simple. Skeleton's roots pay homage to one of the most fundamental sliding activities known to man. Millions of new skeleton admirers are added each year, yet it is not one of those nouveau chic sports devised practically overnight like snowboarding and moguls (skiing down steep, bumpy terrain). Skeleton is a new phenomenon for its new generation of admirers, yet its legacy stretches back more than a century. It's a sport that, at least in America, has been born again.

Although skeleton and bobsled, or bobsleigh, as it's more traditionally and formally known, are related, they're very different sports. Bobsleigh has consistently been a part of the Winter Olympics (except for 1960, when Squaw Valley left out the sliding sports because it did not have a track, and officials opted not to spend the millions of dollars needed to build one). While bobsledders and skeleton sliders share a venue and occasionally hop from one sport to the other, the mindsets employed for the two sports differ. Bobsledders, racing in two- and four-man teams, are more like race car drivers, making split-second decisions while fairly well protected in front and on the sides in a vehicle-like sled featuring steering and braking mechanisms. Don't get me wrong—an inverted bobsled is a very dangerous thing, but hopefully does not happen too often. Skeleton sliding, on the other hand, is an individual sport and functions in more of a minimalist environment, where the only thing between the slider and the elements are the heavy sleds beneath them, with no movable parts other than an arched eyebrow, a hand, or a toe to assist with steering or braking. Out of winter, bobsledders might do well segueing into a sport like NASCAR, truck racing, or heavy duty track and field events. Skeleton sliders by nature would be more into bungee jumping or skydiving.

The demographics are different, as well. Generally, many bobsledders have pedigrees rooted in football (think Herschel Walker, the football great who turned to bobsled to compete for the U.S. Olympic team) or the military (think Navy SEALs). Skeleton sliders are more likely to be found in ski racing, entrepreneurial activities, or busing tables. When American skeleton sliders started coming out of the woodwork in the early 1980s, and they were sporting the space age, skintight racing suits provided by sponsors, one bobsledding old-timer took one look at the glistening suits and said, "That stuff is so slick that if a fly tried to land on it, he'd slide right off and bust his ass."

Just like a true skeleton slider.

CHAPTER THREE

Good Ol' Boys at 80 Miles Per Hour

*He who doesn't risk
never gets to drink champagne.*
—Russian proverb

In the afterglow of the U.S. Olympic men's hockey team's upset of the Soviets in 1980 at Lake Placid, en route to a gold medal, another miracle on ice was underway in the Adirondacks. It involved a handful of thirty-something gents, weekend warriors of a different sort. They were taking what had been an age-old winter sport for kids and turning it into an extreme sport for grownups. And this was happening before there was such a thing as extreme sports.

Lake Placid, its name newly synonymous with American hockey gold, was about to become the place of rebirth of American skeleton. Several locals were emerging as a new generation of sports pioneers. They were flying well under the radar. Their mission was totally unknown to hundreds of millions of Americans not living in the northwest Vermont corridor that connects Burlington to Swanton, two hours east of Lake Placid, across Lake Champlain. Their names were Tim Rath, Pat Murtagh, Chris Leach, and John Thoren.

Outlined against a cold, gray January sky, legendary sportswriter Grantland Rice might have given these Four Sledmen of the Apocalypse the same appellations he had famously given four members of the Notre Dame football team: Famine, Pestilence, Destruction, and Death.

In truth, these men were all respectable family men, working steady jobs during the week—Rath, an explosives expert; Murtagh, a businessman; Leach, an engineer for a weapons manufacturer; and Thoren, a pharmacist. Come the weekend, however, they stepped into a phone booth, or least into the backs of their cars, to shed their business apparel and buttoned-down personas to become ice-bound adventurers. It would be an uphill battle for respect for these downhill enthusiasts, however. Skeleton was their thrill ride in life, a chance to climb out of the relative safety of bobsled and plow the ice as speed demons mounted on exposed flatbed contraptions that offered neither security nor serenity. The skeletons were coming out of the closet.

Rath, a recreational bobsledder who had also given luge a shot, led the way as the first of the four to give skeleton a try. He had been a sliding romanticist ever since childhood, when as a St. Albans youth in the early 1960s, he would listen to Lake Placid bobsled races over the crackle of AM radio. One time he found a magazine that included drawings of the old bobsled races from the 1930s. He was hooked, although he wouldn't get a chance to slide until after he was out of high school.

Rath's eventual introduction to sliding was one part innovation, one part peril. Instead of bobsled, it would involve luge, which he had discovered as a sliding alternative in a book previewing the 1968 Olympics. What ultimately sold him was seeing luge on a Wide World of Sports telecast. Home for Christmas break from his archeological studies at Northern Arizona University, Rath asked around. He found his way to a Canadian bobsled racer who sold Rath a Piltz luge for about fifty bucks. Rath then had it shipped to Flagstaff.

"There's a ski area out there called the Snow Bowl," said Rath, "which rises to an elevation of over twelve thousand feet, about five thousand vertical feet above Flagstaff. The Snow Bowl road would get covered with snow and then packed down by cars. I'd go up there at midnight and slide the luge down the road, my friends following behind me in a Dodge four-wheel pickup truck with the lights on so I could see where I was going.

"It would get kind of hairy when I went around the curve and had to wait a few seconds for the truck's lights to catch up with me. During those moments, it would be all dark, but I could see the trees on either side of me and look up and see the stars whizzing by. The truck was reading about forty-five on the speedometer, which is a little over half the speed lugers go on a real track nowadays, but it was fast enough. We took turns, although I was the one most interested in it."

Rath earned his bobsledder's license at Lake Placid that same winter. Ten years later, in 1978, he was introduced to the sliding sport that would steal his heart forever: skeleton.

"Of the three sliding sports," Rath said, "I always thought of Cresta, skeleton, as the most elegant, the most pure sliding sport of all, the human body becoming a projectile on runners."

Rath got his introduction to skeleton from veteran Austrian skier Dr. Horst Passer, who in the role of skeleton emissary brought a sled with him to Lake Placid in 1978, his mission to check out what the United States had to offer. Skeleton racing, of course, was already popular throughout much of Europe, but Passer knew that if the sport were ever going to make it into the Olympics, the United States would have to be involved, and in a big way. At that time, an American skeleton program was nonexistent.

Rath would become the first to step into that void. Back in 1978, Passer still had hopes for getting the United States on board. Passer took his sled down the old Lake Placid bobsled run, the track built for the 1932 Olympics, at which bobsleds had reached speeds of about sixty miles per hour—and lived to talk about it. As you can imagine, there were plenty of bobsledders and officials watching with amusement, curiosity, and anticipation of something horrifying. He didn't have much good to say about the antiquated track. The side walls of Lake Placid's track in those days were made of wood; by the time Passer got to the bottom of the course, he had splinters all over, and he hurt like hell. As a result, international skeleton officials were prepared to write off Lake Placid as a site for future World Cup races. On top of that, Lake Placid's construction of a new track, adjacent to the old bobsled track, was built especially for luge, so it failed to offer much of a solution for skeleton. This new track was tough, too steep at the top for skeletons, followed by an early turn considered too extreme even for skeleton extremists.

"There was always a fear that those straight walls weren't exactly square," said Murtagh, familiar with the track because he had been doing four-man bob at Lake Placid on and off during the 1970s, with a brief foray into luge before making his first go at skeleton around 1979. "Even though there is some bite on the back of the skeleton's runners, our concern was that the runners on the skeleton sled were rounder than they are on a bobsled or luge, meaning that the sled tends to drift more easily going down the track. Things could get dicey, and we weren't out there just to get ourselves all diced up. There was no honor in getting your face smashed or elbow shattered, especially with no one around to watch us in those days."

Still, while Rath, Murtagh, and friends weren't exactly enamored with the old Lake Placid venue at Mt. Van Hoevenberg, they didn't have much choice in the matter, not if they wanted cherished track time. And track time was hard to come by, in part because bobsledders and lugers had priority due to their Olympic status. There was nowhere else in the United States to practice, let alone to compete. Even if there had been another skeleton site then, it likely would not have helped the Green Mountain Boys. Back then, there was no such thing as a travel budget, so thrill seekers came to Lake Placid as often as they could in order to get whatever runs track officials would permit them.

It was left to the engaging Rath to negotiate track time for his fellow Vermonters. In Joe McKillip, a former bobsledder and superintendent of the Mt. Van Hoevenberg track near Lake Placid, Rath found an ally. Rath was able to get McKillip to bend a bit and allow the skeleton sliders onto the track each morning before it opened for the bobsledders. In the winter of 1979, Rath, using a skeleton sled, unofficially became the first man to slide from the top of the new luge track that had just been completed.

That was a story in itself. During final preparations of the luge track, a welder working on the track would take breaks and join Rath and a couple of the other sliders, taking his Flexible Flyer down the track from as high up as the ice went, while the track was being iced from the bottom up.

"When we got three-quarters of the way up the track," Rath recalled, "this welder guy, outfitted in insulated coveralls and rubber boots, jumped on his Flexible Flyer and really got going. When he hit the Omega Curve well down the track, the Gs nailed him and his runners just flattened out to each side, sending him sprawling down the track. To his credit, he returned the next day, having straightened and reinforced his runners by welding metal rods across them."

Rath was eventually joined on the track by fellow skeleton daredevils Murtagh, Leach, and Thoren. All were devoted to the sport, although it was pretty much left up to Rath and Thoren to convince skeptical track officials to allow them a little more practice time. Their best bet was early to bed, early to rise, often leaving home by three in the morning so they could be at the track at sunrise, giving them a couple of hours of track time before the bobsledders arrived.

These were all guys who loved the outdoors and outdoor activity. For six months out of the year in Vermont and Upstate New York, that meant making the best of the snow and cold. Alpine skiing, cross country skiing, skating, and hockey long had been staples in this winter wonderland, with the more obscure sports such as bobsled and luge left to the few willing to make the trek over to Lake Placid, a winding journey best done by crossing on one of the Lake Champlain ferries. For the skeleton men, the most convenient route was the ferry linking South Hero, Vermont, to Plattsburgh, New York.

There were no sliding manuals available to study between runs, no instructional videos. Basically, the skeleton men were left to their own devices. They learned what they learned through trial and error. The important thing was that skeleton racing was novel—it was new and exciting, and there was lots of speed to go around. "Give it gas and get there fast" long has been a mantra echoing throughout the winter hills of Vermont. Now here was a really cool way to do it without having to bug mom or dad or get gas money for the Chevy.

"At that point," Murtagh said of his early skeleton days, "I wasn't particularly good at anything. All I was doing was participating and trying to compete, although there wasn't much of that. Things started to pick up right after the 1980 Olympics. There was another fellow around by the name of Bob Terwilliger, a restaurant owner whose daughter, Erica, had been a very successful luger. Bob was doing whatever he could to help us get the sport off the ground. Our only recognition was amongst ourselves and the good times we had, all the time being careful we didn't step on anybody's feet. We cherished whatever track time we could get, and we were in no position to make a lot of demands."

By the time the 1980 Winter Olympics were over and hockey's miracle had been played out, Murtagh and his sliding buddies were hearing more frequent reports of how skeleton was taking off in Europe. If skeleton was going to get anywhere in the United States, it would have to get more track time on the bobsled run. That meant kissing up to the United States Bobsled Federation, which would eventually add skeleton to its name and become the United States Bobsled and Skeleton Federation. But that was in name only, for skeleton, as a non-Olympic sport, would remain for years the USBSF's bastard child, last in line for track time, attention, and funding.

The double jeopardy of politics and pecking order did little to dampen the spirit of the early sliders. They loved spending their winter weekends at Lake Placid and racing against one another, often with the winner being the last one who could stand on his own two feet without having to lie down on a stretcher or a gurney and get shoved into an ambulance. These guys got banged up a lot, but they never gave up. They kept going back up and coming back down as fast as they could go and as many times as they were able to finagle track access.

"It wasn't so much a matter of spills," Murtagh recalled. "We were just getting beat up fairly substantially. Part of the reason was that the ice didn't hold well. You banged concrete coming out of a curve, and those curves weren't perfect like they are now at some of the newer tracks. It was like being a battering ram. I broke an arm. A wrist, too, although that was just your typical bang-the-wall kind of thing. No biggie. I wasn't aware of any catastrophic injuries."

The old Lake Placid track was built for bobsled speeds of up to sixty miles per hour, and these guys were going more than seventy miles per hour on skeleton sleds with little protection. There was a lot of banging in and out of the turns. Leave it to the gentle, bearish, six-foot-one, 210-pound Rath to break the ice with the Bobsled Federation. He mixed TLC with gift bottles of wine and beer, whatever it took to loosen things up. By 1981, Rath and crew were starting to make a powerful impression. In that year, Bobsled Federation president Bill Hickey went to Europe for a meeting of the FIBT. There, Hickey ran into Passer, an FIBT vice president. Passer used the occasion to implore the United States to join the Europeans and thus help turn skeleton into a global—therefore potentially an Olympic—sport.

His plan was for the Americans to send a team to the World Championships at St. Moritz the following year, 1982. Two years later, the United States would hold its first-ever national qualifying races, with Murtagh winning all three runs. A year after that, in 1985, America would move up another rung on the international skeleton ladder, hosting a World Cup at Lake Placid that drew thirty sliders from around the world, although it would be another three years before an American would finally be competitive in World Cup competitions.

When Hickey returned to the United States in 1981 after meeting Passer, he called a meeting of skeleton veterans and told them of his plans, promising that the U.S. Federation would provide financial assistance to the strapped skeleton team. It was clear to the racers that practically all expenses would have to be out of pocket. Rath, Leach, and Thoren were the three most active of the U.S. sliders, with Murtagh, less experienced than the others, tapped to be a fourth. Their manager would be New Hampshire resident Bill Hunt, and together these five men would make up the first U.S. national skeleton team. In February 1982, *Sports Illustrated* ran an article featuring the five men, titled "Boning up on the Skeletons." The article served to introduce the sport of skeleton to a new generation of sports fanatics. The skeleton piece appeared in 1982's swimsuit issue, adorned on the cover by none other than Carol Alt, a sports-minded supermodel who would go on to marry a national hockey league player.

Only seven nations entered the first World Championships at St. Moritz in 1982, which explains why the event did not become an annual competition from the start. Subsequently, championships were limited to continents, with North America still lagging behind on the global front. There was good reason for picking St. Moritz as host venue for the first skeleton World Championships. This was the ancestral home of skeleton, most closely associated with the legendary Cresta Run. If Lake Placid is the birthplace of American skeleton, St. Moritz is the skeleton capital of the world.

Although St. Moritz's original Cresta Run is something of a cathedral, worthy of a slider's genuflection, it doesn't mean you can't have a little fun with it once in a while. Skeleton sliders in those days were more fun-loving than medal-obsessed. When the Yanks went to Switzerland in 1982 to compete for the first World Championships of skeleton, they were accompanied by a couple of Canadians, including one Peter Fowler, known for his adventurous spirit and willingness to try just about anything at least once. During a break from the championship races, Fowler paid a visit to the Cresta Run. Visitors were allowed to slide once they had been properly introduced and indoctrinated by the keepers of the track, who frowned on foreign hotshots dropping by without proper respect for their beloved course.

"The Cresta Run," Murtagh said, "very much has that kind of pomposity, the arrogance, you might associate with British aristocrats. You had retired admirals or some such running the place, including this one gent by the name of Digby Willoughby. They didn't like these real smooth skeleton sliders coming by to use their precious run, even though one of their own riders was competing in the Skeleton World Championship that year.

"Anyway," Murtagh continues, "Fowler just shows up there one day, telling them he's visiting from Canada and that he doesn't really know much about what all this is, that he's just a curious onlooker checking things out. So these guys made a big deal out of telling Peter all he needed to know about how to handle a Cresta sled and what to do on it going down the run. They took him up to Junction, a secondary start about a third of the way down from the top. When they got Peter up there, he just grabbed the sled, jumped on it, and started hauling down the run. He ended up setting a new track record for a first-timer, but when they found out he was a skeleton racer competing in the World Championships, they threw him out of there. They were mad as hell."

Going into the 1982 Worlds, the American team, as hard as it tried, remained a motley crew compared to its European counterparts. With the U.S. sliders lacking refined training, ample track access, and financial backing from the national governing body, the Americans were nothing more than neophytes in a sport dominated by Europeans. Beating the Americans would be a sure thing for the Euros, a given opportunity to boost their egos. In between training runs at Lake Placid, the U.S. national team members—a description that sounded grandiose in light of their true sliding ability—called on friends and small-time local business sponsors for fun and assistance. They put together fundraisers such as spaghetti dinners to buy equipment and the slick, skintight racing apparel that was years ahead of what other amateur athletes around Vermont were wearing in those days. They had the look, if not the push, the driving skills, and the know-how to make the subtle adjustments at warp speed needed to compete internationally.

Dig out that *Sports Illustrated* article from February 1982, and see the evidence for yourself. There, in an article that begins on page eighty-six, is an action shot of a skeleton-borne Murtagh hurtling full tilt down the track, his legs splayed behind him with pigeon toes dragging the ice, his shoulders and head raised much too high in front, looking as though he's trying to peer over the dashboard to spot any potholes in front of his vehicle. When Murtagh pulls out the clipping to show an observer, he still shakes his head, cringing, as he eyes the photo, displaying him as the poster boy of how *not* to drive a sled.

He had plenty of company.

"Well, we're still learning," Rath told *Sports Illustrated* at the time. "We're desperately trying to master the techniques—and here the World Championships are just a few days away. I think it's fairly safe to say that, with nine or ten [sic] countries and some ninety sliders entered, that we're not going to come home with any gold medals."

The Americans didn't win any gold in St. Moritz, but they didn't embarrass themselves either—no goofy belly flops onto the ice at the end of the push, no sled crossing the finish line without a slider. And they did get some help getting there. In a gesture of good will as generous as any ever likely to be seen in the wide world of sports, Austria sent over Gert Elsasser, Europe's top-rated slider at the time, to help the eager Americans with their sliding technique. Or at least help them enough to keep them from killing themselves once they got to St. Moritz.

Elsasser's instruction/demonstration session was helpful, but not overwhelmingly so. His English was just okay, the participants reported. He also had a streak of arrogance and at times was difficult to deal with. This was especially true for Murtagh, a genuine novice who still didn't own his own sled and wouldn't be able to buy one until he got to Europe (and then only after Leach got a credit card advance to lend Murtagh the $300 he needed to purchase the sled). In addition, Murtagh had been able to make only a total of three runs from the top at Lake Placid before flying over to Switzerland as the third member of the three-man team. Rath couldn't make the trip because of work commitments. It was all Elsasser could do not to insult his pupils as he explained to the talent-thin squad how to perform the basics like keeping their feet off the ice, their hands tucked into their sides, and their chins close to the ice.

When the Americans arrived at St. Moritz, they found the track daunting. From their perspective, the St. Moritz track appeared to be a notch or two above Lake Placid's in terms of difficulty. Even the names of various aspects of the course were foreboding. Starthus Dracula greets sliders at the top of the course, which also offers up frightening landmarks with names like Snake Corner, Horse-shoe, and Devil's Dike Corner. These names created tension that more lighthearted names like Sunny Corner and Shamrock failed to dent.

"I was scared to death when I saw that track," Murtagh recalled. "Three runs from the top??!! An argument could have been made right then and there that it was premature for us to be taking part in the World Championships. After two or three runs, I was starting to wonder if I was going to make it out of there alive. But we did okay, considering everything. Our technique wasn't great, but we survived the week."

Those pioneering American sliders in 1982 won the hearts and minds of other adventurers who had seen the *Sports Illustrated* article and felt compelled to try the sport for themselves. It was just a trickle of newcomers to skeleton at first in the early 1980s. But they were eager and energized to find out for themselves what skeleton was really all about.

Among those in this new wave of skeleton men was Eastern New York State resident Danny Bryant, a veteran bobsledder who had caught a glance of the likes of Leach and Murtagh up at Lake Placid. Intrigued, Bryant shopped around for a skeleton sled, eventually finding an Austrian-made sled in town for which he paid $300. Over the next fifteen seasons, Bryant went to Europe to compete about a dozen times as a member of the U.S. national team. Back then, it wasn't that hard to do. All that you needed was about $2500 a year to cover travel expenses and entry fees, both of which should have been covered by a national governing body, namely the U.S. Bobsled Federation. Such support was still years away.

It might have been a drain on one's pocketbook to run the race, but the actual race was a physical pain as well. Bryant once slammed so hard into the side of the Lake Placid track that the print of a metal bolt was branded into his knee. "I was taken to a hospital for an x-ray," Bryant remembered, "and the doctor about freaked out when he saw what he thought was the actual bolt lodged inside of me. That's how deep the impression was. He asked me, 'You wouldn't be Herman Munster by any chance?' It hurt like crazy, but it was nothing that a couple of beers couldn't take care of."

Other newcomers to skeleton in those hand-to-mouth years included fellow Easterners Orvie Garrett, Don Hass, Jr., Terry Holland, and Peter Viaciulis. They all entered the sport during the 1980s, and they all remained closely affiliated with skeleton in one capacity or another, in addition to racing, for more than twenty years. Skeleton sorely lacked an infrastructure. It was up to the sliders themselves to wear two hats—a racing helmet and an administrative cap. The inmates were indeed running the asylum and they knew it and had fun with it. All kept sliding and competing well into their forties, mixing in along the way administrative stints ranging from coaching the U.S. national teams (Holland and Viaciulis), to serving as a USBSF officer (Hass), to toiling as FIBT jury officials (Garrett and Viaciulis). Along the way, the U.S. Bobsled Federation could have been said to have embraced skeleton, at least in name, as it became known as the United States Bobsled and Skeleton Federation. And yet, as a non-Olympic sport, skeleton would continue to get the short end of the stick, across the board.

"We got the system down pretty well," Bryant recalled, "when it came to car rentals, the cheapest hotels, and finding the least expensive places to eat. We did whatever it took—sharing hotel rooms, maxing out the credit cards, hitting up friends and relatives for contributions. We would pool our money together, and that's what we came up with for a system to fund all this."

Eventually, with a minimal amount of help from the USBSF, the U.S. sliders were able to work out small sponsorship deals with travel-related companies. Pan Am, for instance, would cut deals for the sliders, offering reduced fares on flights and transporting their bulky sleds for free. There were times when sliders had funds earmarked for them by the USBSF, only to see the money disappear at the most inopportune times. Holland remembers an occasion when the USBSF had budgeted $10,000 for the entire U.S. team to travel to Europe for three weeks of competition. On the night before the team was to depart, Holland received a phone call from the treasurer of the USBSF informing him that the ten grand was gone, more likely siphoned off for bobsled-related uses.

"For years," Holland said, "I put my own money into skeleton to cover certain administrative things, and it added up over the years. We were able to find a few sponsors, and the USBSF found some money here and there, as did the United States Olympic Committee, but at that, they were always scraping just to keep bobsled operating at an internationally competitive level."

For the remainder of the 1980s and into the 1990s, American sliders learned much by watching their more skilled European counterparts, experimenting with, say, a slider's push technique at the start of a run in much the same way an amateur golfer might try to mimic Tiger Woods or Freddy Couples after watching them on the driving range. The rumor that motivated those early sliders was that skeleton was about to be made into an Olympic sport. Too bad it was more wishful thinking than anything else back then. The sliders were men, mostly in their thirties, with full-time jobs, some with wives and families back home. These sliders were exploiting skeleton and the availability of international competition as one last vestige of the wild days of youth. None of them had ever achieved greatness in sports in high school or beyond. Now they had this unique opportunity to excel at something that might even have the Olympic five-ring logo at the end of the rainbow. Even as early as 1982 and 1983, these vagabond skeleton racers were starting to catch wind of rumors that skeleton might soon be admitted to the Olympic agenda, perhaps as early as the 1984 Sarajevo Games.

After Sarajevo came and went, skeleton-free, talk turned to 1988 in Calgary.

"We thought for sure we were going to get in for Calgary in 1988," Holland recalled. "We were hearing this from some folks at the FIBT, one jerk in particular who would then turn around and tell the IOC another thing—that skeleton wasn't yet ready for the games. He was an old bobsledder, probably threatened by the idea that skeleton would upset the apple cart and maybe take away from bobsled. It was absurd."

To bolster their Olympic case, sliding proponents like Holland hammered away at FIBT officials, trying to convince them that adding skeleton to the

Olympic agenda would pour more money into the IOC coffers while increasing utilization of a track facility costing $25 to $30 million. Now, three sports would be using the track, not just two. At the 1988 Winter Games in Calgary, Holland even tried to get on the track to run a demo for spectators and the TV audience, but race officials repeatedly denied his overtures. The trip wasn't an entire PR failure—Holland was able to slip past security near the finish line for the bobsled races, making himself as conspicuous as possible within range of the TV cameras, doing everything but a rain dance to get his U.S. skeleton sweatshirt on screen.

"Some bobsled guy said 'You're getting more coverage than bobsled,'" Holland remembered.

Okay, how about 1992?

"By 1992," said Orvie Garrett, a Mt. Washington, Massachusetts, native who in 1985 had headed straight to Lake Placid after his high school graduation, "we all knew that by the time skeleton finally did get into the Olympics, guys like us would be out of the picture." Garrett had gone to Lake Placid, figuring that he would get the equivalent of a college education on the track at Mt. Van Hoevenberg. Garrett started out in luge but would occasionally get shoved into a bobsled when somebody needed an extra 130 pounds to get the bob down the track as quickly as possible.

"My hardest day in all this was the day I quit racing," Garrett said. "My last race was at the 2002 U.S. Olympic Skeleton Trials in Park City, Utah, where I finished eighth overall out of sixteen racers. When I got to the bottom of the track that day and knew it was over, I cried. Other than my wife and kids, it's been the greatest part of my life. I made some great friends out here."

Indeed, skeleton racing was like one big frat party, with enough shenanigans and free-flowing alcohol to go around. Three weeks at a time on the road in Europe could do that to a man. (There was no organized skeleton racing for women in those days.) On many of the overseas flights, it was free booze for the sliders, coming and going. When Bryant was stopped for speeding one time in Europe, he finagled his way out of a ticket by handing over some skeleton pins and paper souvenirs that looked an awful lot like U.S. currency. Another time, Bryant found himself on the ground at three in the morning, an Uzi pointed at his head, the result of his running an Austrian/Swiss border-crossing station when he saw the Austrian guard apparently asleep in his post.

"I drove through, figuring it was no big deal," Bryant said. "By the time I got to the Swiss side, a roadblock had been set up. They got me out of the car and put me on the ground. Then they tore the car apart. Needless to say, I never did that again."

Holland was one of the newcomers to the sport who had seen the 1982 *Sports Illustrated* article, picking it up at a dentist's office. He had no trouble finding the article—all the swimsuit photos had been torn out. Holland tracked down the sliders mentioned in the article and told them he wanted in, and they showed him the way.

"They asked me what my credentials were," Holland recalled. "I said, 'Credentials? I don't know. I played some soccer in high school, did some skiing, and did some ski jumping.' They said, 'Ski jump?! Why, that's crazy! You can do this, for sure, then.'"

The tall and lanky Holland made his way to Lake Placid. Once there, he discovered he would have to earn his way to the top. One of the prerequisites at that time was that beginners had to start at the halfway mark and slowly progress up the hill. All told, Holland made forty-three runs from the beginner's start before he was given clearance to go all the way to the top. On the last day of sliding for the 1982–83 season, Holland made his debut run from the top of Mt. Van Hoevenberg and covered the course just .33 seconds off the track record.

Holland also gave the American sliders something other than innate talent— he gave them innovation. Not content to stick with the standard equipment and tactical advice issued him, he set out on his own to find ways to go faster and to increase his aerodynamic efficiency. Holland quickly surmised that the U.S. racers knew relatively nothing about the mechanics and physics of operating a skeleton sled, and he knew that everyone else in the world knew those things.

"We were comic relief," Holland said twenty years later, his face reddening slightly as he recalled those early days. "We were learning things the hard way, all through trial and error. That's always stuck with me, and I vowed then and there that as long as I had a say in things, I would never let an athlete go through what we had to go through. Now I can teach a skeleton athlete in three weeks as much as I learned in my first three years of racing skeleton. So I guess you could say there were some good things that came out of it, too."

Necessity was the mother of invention in skeleton racing. When everyone else was still using the old-fashioned goggles worn as a separate accoutrement beneath the helmet, Holland was the first to use an enclosed helmet with visor attached. Better for the aerodynamics. Then he turned his attention to the sled, trying different techniques to fit his body to the sled better and reduce drag coming down the track. As Holland developed a reputation for pushing the envelope when it came to testing rules regarding equipment, the Europeans stopped laughing and started paying close attention.

"I believe in doing something different," Holland said, "until somebody comes along and tells me I can't."

One time, Holland grabbed his sled and headed to Louisville, Kentucky, to visit a manufacturing plant that built transmissions and body parts for the U.S. Army's newly unveiled Bradley Fighting Vehicle, which was being phased in to replace the old armored personnel carriers that were the trademark of infantry units. Holland hooked up with a plant engineer who showed him how to apply a special type of foam that would shape to the contours of his shoulders at the front of the sled, making the sled an even better fit for his body and giving him yet another edge when it came to streamlining man and sled. The foam technology was quite similar to the approach used in ski boots, in which foam was injected into boots to shape them to the skier's feet.

Soon thereafter, Holland went to St. Moritz and finished fourth in a race there, the highest finish an American had ever achieved in a major international contest. After the first run, he had been in second place, and skeleton officials took note. By the next summer, the FIBT rule book for skeleton had been revised to outlaw Holland's foaming technique.

"It's been fun doing that," Holland said. "Rules are strengthened by testing. I would never, ever purposely break the rules, and I have a very strong opinion about the people who do. The best way to determine the strength of a rule is to defend it—explain why you have it. You want to have a sport with clear rules that are easily followed, inexpensive, and which put up a very light barrier to new sliders, to new nations coming into the sport. This makes the sport more broadly based and therefore more likely to succeed. It remains more of a sport and less of a technology race, more dependent on athletic ability and driving skill on ice, which is the way I've always thought it should be."

Peter Viaciulis had been introduced to the sport in the early 1980s as a bobsledder. "Don't get in with those skeleton guys," one of his fellow bobsledders warned Viaciulis back then. "They're crazy, and you don't want to do anything like that." Undeterred, Viaciulis one day sauntered over to some skeleton racers and asked what he needed to do to get involved, what he had to do to become part of a sport that looked really cool to him the first time he saw a slider streak by (with clothes on, that is).

"They said, 'get on a sled and go down,'" Viaciulis recalled. "Next thing you know, I'm a skeleton racer." For the personable Viaciulis, once a promising ski racer whose career was cut short by a motorcycle accident, this was the beginning of a love affair with a new sport. For skeleton, it was the beginning of an association that would give the sport one of its best and most loyal proponents for decades to come. By 1984, Viaciulis was sliding, trying his hand at local races. He lived in Westport, New York, about thirty-five miles east of Lake Placid.

By 1985, more budding sledders were turning out, and competition was increasing for spots on the U.S. national team. With a skeleton sports infrastructure still in its infancy, it was hard at times to determine the pecking order of American sliders. Case in point: When someone happened to ask him what day he was leaving for Europe, a baffled Viaciulis stared back at his inquisitor and asked him why in the world he would be asking that.

"'Because you're on the national team,' he told me," Viaciulis said, shaking his head in wonder twenty years later. "I had figured all along that I would just do these local races and then go back to work. At the time I had a construction business with fifteen employees, and I couldn't just up and leave. That's why I missed the first season in which I could have slid internationally for the U.S. team."

Viaciulis would get plenty of additional chances in the coming years, once he figured out how to keep his construction business humming while he was away for weeks at a time. Most of Viaciulis's business was residential, with some light commercial work. One week it might be a hotel kitchen, and another project might involve a restaurant renovation. At first, he could only get away for a week or two, three weeks tops. Before departing, he would work overtime to line up enough jobs to keep his guys busy. He kept in touch with them over the phone as much as he could.

Viaciulis, yet another member of skeleton's thirty-something crowd, continued to race until 1991, when he answered a call to become the volunteer coach—they were all volunteers back then—for the national team. As before, skeleton's continued omission from the Olympics precluded any significant support from the USOC, and no one was holding his breath waiting for the USBSF to change the meaning of its first two letters to Uncle Sugar. The USBSF was top loaded with former bobsledders who treated bobsleigh as the sacred sport worthy of their full attention and support. This was despite the fact that thirty-five years had passed since U.S. bobsled had garnered a single Olympic medal. It was as if the USBSF was stuck in a time warp, still trying to market the Edsel while the rest of the sliding world was marveling at the snazzy new sports car parked right beneath the USBSF's noses.

In the late 1990s, Viaciulis wrote a personal check to pay for a $3,000 video camera he needed for training purposes, so that he could videotape sliders and offer technical analysis. Until then, guidance from coaches could be processed only by what the naked eye and sober brain could fathom. The key word in that sentence is *sober*. Keep in mind that for years, skeleton, at least from an American point of view, was little more than *Animal House* on ice, a fraternity on runners. A martini on the rocks, if you will, shaken (on the track), but not stirred.

"Skeleton in the '80s had just been good ole boys having a lot of fun," Viaciulis said. "Go to Europe and have a super time while doing some sliding in between. We drank some good German beer, did some skiing in Austria and Switzerland, all the while paying our own way. It was that way with everybody, and that included the Austrians, Germans, and Swiss. After a race, we would all go into town and sit and drink beer all night, telling stories and slapping each other on the back. That's the part of the sport that has gone, now that it has become an Olympic sport."

Another member of the new wave of sliders in the mid-1980s was David Kurtz, a Philadelphia attorney introduced to skeleton almost by accident. At the invitation of a buddy going to Lake Placid to work on a magazine piece comparing bobsled to race car driving, Kurtz tagged along. That's when he saw a skeleton sled for the first time.

"There were only a handful of guys doing it," Kurtz recalled. "Doug Tyler was the coach at the time, and it was obvious he was interested in just getting bodies onto the track. He told me if I could go up to the top and finish the course, I would be something like the sixteenth guy who had ever done it. Who could resist that?"

Not Kurtz. He completed a run and soon volunteered to be another of Tyler's track bodies, vying for World Cup pointers more than the points. Kurtz and other sliders were offered a deal hard to refuse—if they agreed to be the ballast for the four-man bobs in practice, they would get free skeleton training.

"We all broke bones in one way or another," Kurtz said of those rough-hewn days of skeleton. "The Lake Placid track was still pretty dangerous. Its curves hadn't been engineered for current-day technology and speed. It really was scary. You had guys vomiting in back of the start building before a run, asking, 'Who's going down next?' I remember this time so vividly because it was at the same time that Willie Gault of the Chicago Bears was trying to make the U.S. bobsled team.

"The turns weren't the only problems with the Lake Placid track. Another was the scheduling. It wasn't opened until December, putting the U.S. sliders at a competitive disadvantage against their European counterparts, who were a month or two out in front of the Americans. In going to the races, we'd get off the plane, put our sleds together, and go down a track without any training," Kurtz said.

"But we saw it as a chance to keep the sport going, and part of what kept us going was the dream that it would be introduced as a demonstration sport at the 1988 Games in Calgary. We *knew* we had the hot sport, but in 1988 they came out with curling instead. To this day, when I hear someone mention curling, my toes curl."

A spot alongside the five Olympic rings was all that serious skeleton riders wanted, even more than another Heineken or another glorious day schussing down the slopes of St. Moritz. Kurtz would end up playing a key administrative and lobbying role in the effort to get skeleton into the Olympics. So, too, would Paul Varadian, another 1980s skeleton slider who would rise into a prominent international administrative role. Kurtz and Varadian were up against the old bobsled mentality, which said that if a new sliding sport were to be added to the Olympics, another would likely be dropped. Frankly, bobsledders were worried and were out to protect their own.

"It was very difficult," Varadian recalled, "and it took a lot of politicking to make it happen, but one day we would succeed."

By the mid-1990s, American skeleton racers were occasionally winning World Cup skeleton medals. America had hosted World Cup events, and television viewers were enthralled when ESPN carried a World Cup skeleton race in 1992 in Calgary. Still, back when discussions of getting skeleton into the Winter Olympics had been all talk and no action, there was no one in America with the clout to make it happen.

It was about this time that I became interested in skeleton, even though I had no idea of the inner workings of the USBSF, the efforts of trying to get it reinstated in the Olympics, or how I would become involved. I was simply a guy following a friend's bidding to come try something really cool.

An early day's start from the top of the
Cresta Run, St. Moritz, Switzerland.

Vintage sliding on the Cresta
Run, St. Moritz, Switzerland.

Lieutenant Commander J. Taylor Boyd, a.k.a. "YTB"
(Young Taylor Boyd) in his F-4 cockpit, 1983.

Terry Holland negotiating the "finish curve" of the old Lake Placid track, 1984.

Author's first run from the junior bob-sled start at the Calgary Olympic Park, Calgary, Alberta, Canada, 1995.

Anxious author with fellow oilman and skeleton slider, Clay Roark, at the top of the Calgary track, 1995.

Author's first run from the top begins—with a little help
from Bill Sheard—at the Calgary track, 1995.

Taylor Boyd, following
another "bleeding" at the
Calgary track, 1996.

Louis Carrasco (during his first visit to the Calgary track), future Mexican Olympic skeleton athlete, interviews Taylor Boyd and Dave Graham for an extreme sports program, 1996.

Author, Coach Peter Viaciulis, and Fallon Vaughn (with black eyes from sliding), 1998.

1998–1999 National Team selections. Bottom (l to r): Cindy Ninos, Babs Isak, Tricia Stumpf, and Marta Schultz. Top (l to r): Lea Ann Parsley, Fallon Vaughn, Tristan Gale, and Juleigh Walker.

Ryan Davenport, 1996 and 1997 Skeleton World Champion, with Davenport sled and a Texas Longhorn.

Taylor Boyd: climbing out of bed, or in search of cardboard for protecting a skeleton sled during shipment?

Ryan Davenport in the wind tunnel at the University of Texas at Austin's Balcones Research Center, 1997.

Author and Taylor Boyd trying out aerodynamic "Landingham" helmets, 1997.

Start area at the top of the St. Moritz-Celerina, Switzerland, Olympia Bob Run track, 1998.

World Champion Ryan Davenport driving through "Horseshoe" at the St. Moritz–Celerina track, 1998.

Coach Peter Viaciulis and author at 1998 Skeleton World Championships in St. Moritz, Switzerland, 1998.

Jim Shea, Jr., author, and coach Peter Viaciulis on the slopes of Corvatsch, following the 1998 World Skeleton Championships, 1998.

Neophyte skeleton slider—sporting ski helmet, goggles, and golf shoes with spikes—with skeleton school coach Clay Roark at Utah Olympic Park, 1998.

Early skeleton school participants at Utah Olympic Park, 1998.

Slider exiting curve too late.

Friction burn at over 70 mph.

The skeleton sled usually makes it to the bottom of the track, with or without its owner.

Taylor Boyd, Ken Tupua, and author in front of the American Samoa Olympic Committee offices, 1998.

Author and Fallon Vaughn in Park City, Utah, before the opening World Cup race for the 1998–1999 season.

Fallon Vaughn pushing in Park City Skeleton World Cup competition, 1998.

Author pushing in Igls, Austria, Skeleton World Cup competition, 1999.

Fallon Vaughn and Kevin McCarthy, FIBT jury member, monitoring competition from the Krisel at Koenigssee, Germany, World Cup competition, 1999.

Martin Rettl, Jim Shea, Jr., author, and Toshinari Miyamoto
following the Stubai Cup in Igls, Austria, 1999.

Injured author and Canadian coach
Markus Kottmann at St. Moritz, 1999.

U.S. contingent (Jim Shea, Sr., in center foreground) at 1999 Skeleton World Championships parade in Altenberg, Germany.

Assistant Coach Dave Graham, author, and Coach Peter Viaciulis at 1999 Skeleton World Championships at Altenberg, Germany.

Jim Shea, Jr., 1999 Skeleton World Champion.

Mitt Romney, chair, Salt Lake City Olympic Organizing Committee; Jim Shea, Jr., the first American Skeleton World Champion; and Utah governor Mike Leavitt, 1999.

World elite skeleton slider Chris Soule, with Vaughn Petroleum sponsorship on helmet, 2000.

Courtesy of DUOMO Photography

American Samoa bobsled team of Oa Misifoa and Taylor Boyd, 2000.

Fallon Vaughn pushing in competition.

CHAPTER FOUR
Mountain High

Men achieve a certain greatness unawares,
when working to another aim.
—Ralph Waldo Emerson

What would you do if someone you really respected, a mentor, the man who was practically your surrogate father, called you one day and invited you to take three weeks off from work and climb a mountain in Nepal with him?

If you have the slightest spirit of adventure in you, you would say yes without thinking twice.

That's how it was for me when the phone rang in early autumn, 2004. Dick Bass is a fellow Dallas businessman and outdoor adventurer. He called to tell me that he was headed to Nepal. That's Mt. Everest country, where climbers earn the right to peek into and sometimes above the clouds. The dictionary definition of "hale and hearty," Bass had decided he was going to Nepal to climb Gokyo Ri. At just under eighteen thousand feet, Gokyo Ri is dwarfed by its neighbor to the east, Everest, but it still lurks as a stern, oxygen-light test of fitness and endurance. It's a great way to find out if you've got the juice to attempt the brutish and dangerous 29,028-foot Everest. When Dick called me, he was just a few months shy of his seventy-fifth birthday. At that age, most people are fervently praying they will get a free ride into heaven—instead of having to hike there, as Bass intended to do.

Bass had some unfinished business in Nepal, and it all had to do with Everest. Back in 1985, at age fifty-five, Bass had made it to the top of Everest, becoming the oldest person ever to accomplish the feat. He was joined on that climb by, among others, his good friend the late Frank Wells—then, he was the retired vice chairman of Warner Brothers and future president of Disney—and the mountain-climbing filmmaker David Breashears. Breashears would become a witness and, ultimately, an unwitting hero in the ill-fated 1996 expedition on Everest in which five climbers died in a terrible storm, the story of which was recounted in the best-selling book *Into Thin Air*. Bass and Wells collaborated with Rick Ridgeway on their own book *Seven Summits,* chronicling their unprecedented feat of climbing the highest peak on each of the seven continents. By the way, at the age of twenty-seven in 1983, I was a member of the Seven Summits expedition climb up Mt. McKinley in Alaska.

Dick Bass, at seventy-five, is twenty-six years older than I am. He has a photographic memory. His energy is tremendous. He's amazing. I don't generally use the word respect when I talk about Bass, but I don't need to. When I talk about him, I think the respect just shines through.

Both Bass and I thrive on endeavors that can become accomplishments in relatively short periods of time. Such victories occur regularly in the world of mountaineering, as opposed to business projects in which we typically find ourselves—situations that can take years and years to develop and complete.

When Bass called me that day in the fall of 2004 to say that he was going to Nepal, his intent was obvious. My wife, Fallon, was the one who actually picked up the phone message from Bass.

"Robie," she said, "he's asking you to go with him. You ought to go with Dick! Nepal's the quintessential climber's dream—go check it out for yourself."

I carved three weeks out of my work schedule to accompany Bass to Nepal. Once in Kathmandu, we hooked up with the rest of the contingent that once again included Breashears, along with three other climbing acquaintances from out west. The purpose of the expedition was for Bass to determine whether he still had the ability to scale a mountain rising nearly six miles above sea level, where few people can survive, even while resting, without oxygen bottles. Bass was hardly an old codger with delusions of grandeur. He is an amazing physical specimen. Not a natural athlete, and certainly not someone who craves three hours a day of exercise back home, he was blessed with a powerful heart and lungs and an unbending resolve. His cardiovascular mechanism is an object of marvel. He has a resting pulse rate that stays consistently under sixty beats a minute and the kind of low blood pressure that gives him a built-in advantage for high altitude climbing. In fact, mountain guide Phil Ershler once labeled Bass a "freak of nature" due to his unusual stamina in high altitudes.

Bass had a powerful incentive to give Gokyo Ri a try. In May 2002, two years earlier, Japanese climber Tomiyashu Ishikawa, sixty-five, had made it to the top of Everest, breaking Bass's seventeen-year record for eldest summiteer. A year later, in May 2003, Yuichiro Miura, also of Japan, an old friend of Bass's known as "the man who skied Everest," reached the Everest summit at the age of seventy years and 222 days. The climbs by the two Japanese men spurred the indefatigable Bass to give Everest one more look to see if he wanted to try to win back his world record.

"When I made my climb with David Breashears," Bass said, recalling his 1985 Everest climb, "we were not roped together. So all the way to the top, I climbed with the realization and the anxiety of knowing that if anything happened to me, I was not tethered to anyone else. Also, when I climbed Everest, it was set up to where we had to do twenty-eight hundred feet on summit day. Nowadays, all you have to do is fifteen hundred. That makes a big difference."

Gokyo Ri was routine for me. For Dick, it took him hours longer, but he did make it. Afterwards, my Sherpa guide and I continued on, traveling four days on foot to nearby Island Peak to climb successfully to the top of that 20,300-foot, snow-capped mountain before returning to Kathmandu to rendezvous with Bass and the rest of the team.

In Bass's own words, he likes to "push the envelope of human capability," to conquer "the inner mountain. The life is in the mind, and it's all about attitude. You're not a champion unless you come off the mat." From there, for Bass and me, it was back to Dallas, a world away from the thin air and thick lungs characteristic of Nepal. The trip to Nepal clearly had been a Dick Bass Production, but it became an epiphany of sorts for me as well, an opportunity to confront some of my own hopes and dreams. It made me reflect on who I was, where I came from, and what I still hoped to accomplish with my life.

So let me try to answer this question for you: who exactly is Robie Vaughn?

* * *

There's a lot of Texas in me, and you can translate that any way you want to. You can take me out of Texas, but you can't take the Texas out of me. Generations of Vaughn blood, sweat, and tears have dripped over the decades into the Texas soil, underneath which has bubbled the source of much of the family's assets. Our roots run deep in oil and gas, natural resources that have long been there for man to find, although the discovery phase involves trial and error, financial risk and reward.

My grandfather, Grady H. Vaughn, was a self-made pioneer in oil and gas who went broke three times during the Depression. He suffered a stroke in 1947, at age fifty-seven, that left him somewhat incapacitated for the last eight years of his life, until his death in November 1955, less than two months before I was born. Jack C. Vaughn, my father, the younger of Grady's two sons, also made a run at oil and gas and branched out into other industries as well, looking to hedge his investments with a varied portfolio that included broadcasting, printing, real estate, and ranching. In an oral history compiled and published as a dissertation by a University of Texas graduate student, my father, affectionately known to friends as "Cadillac Jack," said that his success in business had been the result of a combination of an intense desire to see tangible results from his efforts and a willingness to assume some reasonable risks. He was following the example set up by his own father, who held a respected position in the Dallas banking and business community, and he was also blessed with luck and good timing. Cadillac Jack made his living in the oil business, but he diverted profits and some of the oil and gas capital into real estate development, in the process becoming one of the sweaty, dusty builders responsible for many of Texas's rising skylines.

Despite his own deep pockets, Cadillac Jack had to roll the dice with bank loans to bring his dreams to fruition. He was a self-made financier skilled at convincing banks to lend him money beyond his collateral, and at the same time negotiating settlements of long-term leases with tenants before he could begin demolishing buildings to make room for the new.

"A good learning experience," he called it. "When I started out in real estate, I was aware that I knew very little about the business, but that did not particularly worry me. I thought I could feel my way along and teach myself what I felt would be adequate to get me through it."

My father fancied himself a creative thinker as well as a builder of small companies, admittedly selfish in his desire to be his own boss. In today's terminology, Cadillac Jack was an entrepreneur, one who spent all of his time chasing his dreams. He and his wife, Mary Josephine, passed along their business acumen to their children, Jack Jr., Sharon, David, and me. I inherited my entrepreneurial spirit from my mother and father and from my grandfather Grady, and that entrepreneurial spirit served me to help lead the family business after my father died suddenly of a heart attack in 1977. I was a senior at the University of Texas at Austin at the time of my father's death.

At age twenty-two, I was suddenly learning the ropes of running a business concern with many related entities. I was surrounded by grizzled oil and gas veterans twice my age or older. The geology, oil and gas, and real estate law class lessons from the University of Texas were immediately relative.

I was listening and watching, and my instincts were decent, but I didn't always have the confidence to say, "Look, we need to take all these properties and all these different entities and just roll them up into one entity." The fractured inter-company ownership that existed at the time resulted in inefficiencies in both time and money. I was unconsciously allowing our advisors to maintain the status quo.

I was at best a B student in college, but I seemed to be somewhat business-savvy for my age. I had interned for my dad for several summers. One summer, I worked in the printing business. On several other occasions, I worked on the fence crew as a roustabout on our family's New Mexico ranch. All of these experiences helped to toughen me and to help me develop self-reliance and the steely confidence to trust my instincts.

Around the house in Dallas, when I was a boy growing up, I would often overhear my parents talking about stocks and investing. My mother, Mary Jo, founded an investment club at Southern Methodist University. Whenever the club would receive annual reports of companies, she would pass them on to me and I would sit down and study them, learning how to decipher balance sheets as well as profit/loss and cash flow statements. For most teens, this would be boring beyond comprehension, but I soaked it all in. I was fascinated by the numbers but even more by the business strategies revealed between the lines. By the time I was a high school sophomore, I had come to treat my schoolwork as a necessary nuisance. My interest then was investing in stocks and monitoring information flow. During my college years, I continued to study and buy stocks.

I was further indoctrinated in the ways of leadership at Culver Military Academy, an outstanding private secondary school founded in 1894 in Indiana, whose alumni include, among others, shipping magnate and New York Yankees owner George Steinbrenner; Bill Koch, founder of the Oxbow Corporation and America's Cup yacht race winner; CEO of Abbott Laboratories Miles White; and Hal Holbrook, actor. When my parents offered to send me to Culver, they gave me the kind of well-rounded education that transcends the traditional classroom of globes, chalkboards, and wooden desks.

The ethos of Culver is described on its Web site: www.culver.org. Students are encouraged to try new things, to test themselves. If they fail, there is no ridicule, only support to get up and try again until they get it right. Whether one wants to learn to fly airplanes, participate in crew, fencing, theater, or ride in the renowned Black Horse Troop, Culver can help develop the discipline, the skill, the confidence to do whatever one wants to do. If a student applies himself, he will leave Culver with a clearer direction and confidence about his life goals than he ever thought possible. Subsequently, I found that discipline truly is freedom, and that the choices I make now take on a deeper, more satisfying meaning.

I made good use of my time at Culver, and the school viewed me as a natural leader. As a senior, I was promoted within the ranks to captain and squadron commander of the Black Horse Troop, which put me in charge of 160 cadets and made me one of the four highest-ranked members of the cadet corps. Founded in 1897, the Black Horse Troop remains the largest mounted cavalry unit in the United States and has participated in many Presidential Inaugural Parades.

One thing I learned at Culver was that you can't expect to lead if you don't know how to follow. All the cadets begin as equals and then have to decide for themselves, without parental intervention, whether to learn and grow or resist and struggle. It takes structure, discipline, leadership, and organizational ability to motivate other fourteen- to eighteen-year-olds to make their beds, shine their shoes and brass belt buckles, sweep the floors daily, and rise at 6:30 each morning to march to breakfast.

I didn't meet my wife Fallon until after I finished high school. She now knows enough about Culver to understand the role the school had in shaping me for a future that would extend well beyond oil and gas. Both our children attend Culver; Robert is a member of the class of 2006 at Culver Military Academy, and our daughter Browning is a member of the class of 2008 at Culver Girls' Academy. The Girls' Academy was founded in 1971 for the purpose of encouraging young women to attain the highest degree of self-development.

"Culver, for Robie, was all about teaching him a lot of his leadership skills," Fallon said. "It's all about God, country, family, and honor—being a leader and setting the example. That's how Robie has lived his life. There are people who talk the talk and those who walk the talk, and Robie does both in being a father, a husband, and a businessman. Anything I've seen him do, this is the way he does it. And he doesn't look for people to pat him on the back about it. He's admired a lot by his friends as someone who means what he says. You can count on him. He won't bail on you."

My youth was not all spit and polish, stocks and bonds. All work and no play was not the Vaughn family motto. Ski trips to Colorado were fairly common, and by seven, I was already learning to negotiate slopes at Vail. By twelve, I had hiked seventy miles of the Appalachian Trail along the North Carolina and Tennessee state lines. In the late 1960s, I went to the Teton Valley Ranch Camp outside Jackson Hole, Wyoming, where I ratcheted up my hiking and backpacking skills. At one point, we climbed one of the smaller mountain peaks in the Tetons, near the south end of the mountain range. I climbed the Grand Teton itself while in college, with three school friends, as we were guided by renowned Yosemite "big wall" climber Chuck Pratt. I have now climbed the Grand four times, the last in 2003 with my son Robert, when he was sixteen. During the summer of 2005, Robert, my brother David, and I climbed the second highest peak in the Tetons, Mt. Moran, a long and dramatic climb that requires patience.

Back home in Texas, and during my days at Culver, I excelled in other sports as well. I could easily think of a half-dozen activities I would rather do than splash around in water. Still, I was an accomplished swimmer as a youth, winning trophies and ribbons by the dozens. At Culver, I developed into an excellent equestrian, adept at handling horses and experienced in jumping them. I also was a pretty good marksman. For these reasons, by the time I graduated from Culver, school officials were encouraging me to pursue junior modern pentathlon, an established Olympic sport for which I lacked expertise in just one of the five disciplines—fencing—but I never pursued this. I also had shown promise as a soccer player and had taken up golf and tennis. Like most young men born and bred in Texas, however, my strongest athletic ambition was to play football for the University of Texas Longhorns. At six feet and a shade under 170 pounds, I was a bit light and a tad slow to play, though. At least that was my perception.

Also, I'd rather try to run through somebody than run around them. That's why I was never really too good. My instincts were to hit the other guy as hard as I could because I knew I wasn't quick enough to go around him. I really enjoyed flattening a guy. I would visualize running through someone and be energized for that eventuality.

There would be no serious pursuit of athletics at UT for me, however. I was always fit and active through my high school years. In college, though, I slacked off from physical activity. Some racquetball and jogging was about it. When I did think of sports, my mind took me back to the snowy winter lands, where I could see and feel the smooth knee-deep powder of Vail or Snowbird. I would fantasize about schussing my way down the beloved slopes that beckoned in Colorado and Utah. This Texas boy relished his roots, but the Walter Mitty side of my existence always took me back to the mountains.

I had thought about the Olympics, both summer and winter, quite a bit over the years. It had always been an unspoken, passionate dream of mine growing up, watching the Olympics. I was totally into skiing. I learned to ski at Vail in 1963 and then really learned about how to ski well beginning in Aspen in 1967. Every Christmas and spring break in high school I went to Vail. I just loved the mountains and loved winter. The downhill was the ultimate concept for me. I can still see Franz Klammer, nearly out of control as he pushed the envelope, winning the 1976 Olympic men's downhill. Before that, the highlight had been watching Jean-Claude Killy win all three men's alpine gold medals at the 1968 Winter Games.

I dreamed of being involved in skiing in the Olympics, but I never pursued it because my instincts told me that wasn't what my life was designed for, and I didn't even know how to take the first step. My dreams growing up included playing football for the University of Texas, being an astronaut, and competing in the Olympics. Those were my early motivational, driving passions. Yet I never realistically expected, at least consciously, to pursue any of those, which is why I never took that first step—although I did interview at the United States Air Force Academy before deciding on going to UT and pursuing the oil and gas business.

I was a really reserved kid, kind of shy, always keeping things inside. I didn't show a lot of emotion. Culver and the University of Texas changed all that. At Culver I was taught to lead by example. No more holding it in. Basically, don't screw up. At the University of Texas I learned what leadership was about in a broader community. I was a member of the Phi Delta Theta fraternity, becoming president in my senior year, and an officer of the Texas Cowboys honor organization. Staying loyal to who I was and trusting my instincts throughout the initiations, pledgeships, and rituals of those institutions taught me that leadership was in the blending of the talents of many in order to benefit all.

When my father, Cadillac Jack, passed away at fifty-one, my plans didn't change. While many of my UT classmates were gearing up for graduate school, a trip overseas, or a job hunt, I already knew I would be returning to work in the oil and gas business.

I felt a tremendous obligation to my family to do so. And as soon as I went to work, I was dealing with people. This was something I had been prepared to do. My instincts were more in line with the oil business itself—how to put the prospects together, packaging them, and selling them. Even though geology had been one of my favorite subjects in school, I wasn't really a science guy. Yet I was coordinating the technical guys and the land men, and the more I knew about science, geophysics, geological, and engineering, the more I would be able to ascertain the risk in any particular deal. I would accompany the exploration manager who would present the prospect, after which I would handle the business side of it. I was in the upstream segment of the industry, the exploration and production side. I never really felt comfortable selling, but I did it because I had to.

I was neither an expert salesman nor a technician, so I had to discover and exploit my strengths as best I could and make the best possible use of my drive and passion. Frequently, I was faced with the prospect of having to meet men my father's age to try to convince them to partner with Vaughn Petroleum on a new prospect to be drilled, perhaps somewhere out in West Texas. Dealing with these established businessmen was at times a challenge, a test to see if I could convince these skeptics to risk hundreds of thousands of dollars to buy into my deals. This wasn't my preferred way of spending my working days, but the experience would serve me well nearly two decades later when I became involved in diversified pursuits including the U.S. skeleton team and the USBSF.

My view of leadership and vision can be summed up in this equation: one plus one equals three. It's all about the creation of value. I have a hunger for knowledge and a love of being able to put together a team and a plan that can accomplish more than others believed possible. Many times we fail, but the only real failure is failing to learn from such experiences. As Rudyard Kipling noted, triumph and disaster are often imposters that have to be treated the same.

Some of the oil-and-gas vets I went up against were self-anointed J. R. Ewings, perhaps spurred on by a certain TV prime-time soap opera making its network debut around the same time I moved into my dad's office. One such antagonist who headed a company could have been respectful when we approached them. Instead, when my technical team and I tried to make our presentation, we were second-guessed and shot down, and every point we made was defiantly criticized.

Obviously, this individual was doing all this on purpose, just to see how I'd react. I admit that I'm a serious type-A guy, moderately aggressive, someone who wants to make things happen, but it was important to me that I always stay calm. Using cuss words or showing anger is a weakness in one's ability to communicate. You have to accept the fact that sometimes there are people who are just going to be that way, for whatever reason. Most times, too, there are prospects which refuse to cooperate, leaving a drilled well high and dry. But that's the nature of the oil and gas business, built on performing due diligence and exhausting all drilling efforts before moving on to the next one. One project in particular demonstrated the determination and perseverance with which Vaughn Petroleum pursued the exploration side of the oil-and-gas business. Beginning in the early 1980s, my close friend Carter Montgomery and I began screening prospects in Alaska. This was after intuition tempted us to go after Alaskan prospects capable of producing one hundred million-plus barrels—strikes the size of which are rare finds in the lower forty-eight states. In the industry, these are known as giants.

Alaska offered the kind of oil reserves usually found outside the United States. And yet, in Alaska, we would be speaking English, dealing in American currency, and working under U.S. laws with which we were already familiar. No translations needed; no exchange rates called for; no political red tape or tricky import rules with which to wrangle; and no nationalization risk. There was a lot to like about exploring this relatively untouched region, which many competitors hadn't bothered seeking out. Eventually, we selected a prospect adjacent to Prudhoe Bay, the largest U.S. oil field, with more than ten billion barrels of reserves.

Montgomery and I reassembled the old Atlantic Richfield Oil and Gas Company (ARCO) exploration team that in 1969 had discovered the super-giant Alaskan oil field. This team consisted of skilled and savvy exploration geologists, geophysicists, and engineers, plus a land man. Together, they helped give us the added clout and credibility needed to convince major oil companies operating in Alaska that we were for real. We needed to show them that it would be worthwhile to finance, operate, and drill in what was a fragile environment on the North Slope of Alaska. This was in 1986, when the oil industry was mired in a severe depression that had slammed into Texas like some fiscal hurricane, sending many newly bankrupt oilmen and businesses scrambling, with the cost of oil slumping downward to less than ten dollars a barrel. In such a depressed climate, few companies were willing to drill new prospects. We were willing. Naturally, I like buying when no one else is interested, and then selling into demand.

Montgomery and I drilled Gwyder Bay for about one-third the cost that major oil companies had been spending to do the same in the region. We utilized an internal mud system, which facilitated our drilling for the first time on the North Slope. This had been a major undertaking of exploration and a cobbling together of unlikely partners, but Montgomery and I, barely thirty at the time, pulled it off . . . almost. The well itself was unsuccessful. But the fact that a junior independent oil company could put all this together on its own surprised the industry. We inspired other independents, demonstrating that this remote Alaskan environment could be safely and effectively worked at a fraction of the cost that had been borne by the majors. Other independents soon began chasing projects in Alaska with renewed interest.

The Alaskan deal was one of the experiences that reinforced in me how learned traits such as motivating others, communicating often and well, and making capable decisions, along with inherent traits such as intuition, personal values, and an aptitude for risk-taking, are so important for achieving success. You need to be able to analyze people and situations instinctively in order to assess risk and produce a positive experience. That's the common ground when it comes to leadership in the worlds of business and amateur sports.

My father's death had been a wake-up call for me in more ways than one. It not only forced me to exert my intuition, it inspired me to take running more seriously. The year before my father died, I had picked up James Fixx's best-selling new book, *The Complete Book of Running*, and I had resolved to start running, like it or not. Three years of the relatively sedentary lifestyle of the college student had softened me somewhat. I needed a healthy outlet for my energy. I also had to be concerned about my family history: my grandfather's stroke at fifty-seven, and the deaths of not only my father but my uncle, Grady H. Vaughn Jr., who succumbed to a heart attack at age forty-seven. Beginning in 1977, around the start of my senior year at UT, I laced up my running shoes.

Running in those days was not a labor of love for me. I *hated* running. But in the summer of 1977, while home from school, I forced myself to go to the track at nearby St. Mark's School of Texas, which I had attended prior to Culver. With temperatures consistently in the nineties and above, I would complete four laps around the quarter-mile track—an even mile. This was my daily routine. While not a long run by any stretch, it was a torturous test of endurance—to see if I could stave off boredom long enough to complete the eight-minute workout. I remember telling my dad about it, saying I was going to keep on doing it for as long as it took to get used to it.

By that fall, I was seriously into running, reading Fixx's book, getting back in shape, and burning pent-up energy. Within a couple of years I was running in 10Ks, starting with a chili cook-off event in San Marcos, Texas, that I ran in just under fifty minutes. In that race I averaged about eight minutes a mile. It was the first time I had ever run that far in one shot, and it felt like a marathon. I ran my first actual 26.2-mile marathon, the White Rock Marathon, in December 1980, in Dallas. I fed off running, and running provided a venue for me to push myself beyond what I had previously perceived as my mental and physical limits. Running was no longer laborious. It also gave me an outlet from the stress and rigors of long meetings and the long time frames inherent in waiting for business deals to come to fruition.

Running became a building block for activities that were bigger, better, and more adventurous. I would continue to run the occasional 10K and marathon during the 1980s. I eventually segued into triathlons, heli-skiing, and once again, mountain climbing. In 1989, I completed the vaunted Hawaiian Ironman World Championship Triathlon, a supreme test of endurance that includes a 2.4-mile open ocean swim, a 112-mile bike ride, and a 26.2-mile marathon. My goal was to complete this challenge in fewer than thirteen hours. My time was eleven hours, seventeen minutes. The Ironman was the culmination of a goal I had set years earlier, but it would not become an annual avocation. Since then, I've ridden my bike only on random occasions, keeping it tucked away in my garage for some possible future use when the riding bug strikes again.

As much as I enjoyed running and, to a lesser extent, triathlons, I felt most invigorated when in the mountains. My running and triathlon cross-training became as much preparation for mountain climbs as anything else. With my companions I have climbed in Argentina, Chile, China, France, Mexico, Nepal, Switzerland, and the United States. Several of the climbs have been up peaks of twenty thousand feet or more, including Mount McKinley in Alaska, Aconcagua in Argentina/Chile, Island Peak in Nepal, and Mustagh Ata in Western China, the latter a twenty-four-thousand-foot peak on which I was accompanied by my wife Fallon. We spent three weeks living at fifteen thousand feet—Mustagh Ata base camp—or higher, after it had taken us a week to get to base camp.

I would later see parallels between climbing in foreign countries and my experiences with skeleton. In climbing, you go to a foreign country, hook up with a guide, and find you have something in common. It's the same way with traveling around the world with skeleton. You go to Europe, and you're in a community with common bonds. That's what is great about sports—an instant connection between people from different cultures. It doesn't matter that your background and beliefs differ from those of the people you're meeting. You're all in it together.

So now you know me pretty well. A businessman, an athlete, an individual who had bidden farewell to his Olympic dreams . . . until one night in 1994 . . .

CHAPTER FIVE
On a Wing and a Sled

No matter how tough we think we are,
we can't do it alone.
—Tiger Woods

The Park Cities, more specifically known as Highland Park and University Park, are where much of Dallas high society and old money mix with the nouveau riche and young professionals, all comfortably nestled in their sprawling homes, some partially hidden from view on one of the tree-lined streets that crisscross in this north central area of Dallas.

Yet there is little about the Park Cities that could be construed as snooty or snobbish. Few of the homes are surrounded by the massive privacy walls, guardhouse gates, or moats that you might find in other private neighborhoods in large cities. Here in University Park, at least, the usual attire, day or night, is nice and casual, even preppy. Neighbors think nothing of strolling across the lightly traveled streets or down the sidewalk to visit one another for Saturday afternoon pool parties for the kids or Sunday night neighborhood dinners. Many send their children to private schools, some of those in faraway places, but a fair number allow their future collegians to attend the local public school.

And Highland Park isn't exactly teeming with restaurants on every corner—it's not that kind of area. But when folks want to go out and dine in a swanky restaurant that caters to the kind of clientele that doesn't need to see prices on menus, they often go to Café Pacific, one of Highland Park Village's most popular havens. Its convenient location makes Café Pacific an easy choice for the locals. They can go there and share a romantic evening, have a serious business meeting, or just hang out over drinks with friends.

Café Pacific's black-and-white-tiled floors and the white linen-covered tables evoke a sense of 1940s' New York City, although it is the contemporary and innovative seafood selection that gives diners an eating experience that never grows old. On Valentine's Day 1994, my wife and I arrived at Café Pacific, looking to savor a rare, cherished night out on the town, while a sitter back at the house looked after the kids—Robert, then six, and little Browning, four. Of course, there was a touch of romance in the air, almost a sense of expectation that we were about to embark on an adventure, although it was nothing we could put our finger on.

Upon arriving at the restaurant and making our way to the bar for the traditional wait on a table, Fallon and I spotted our good friend J. Taylor Boyd. There was no missing or mistaking Taylor, six years my senior. The thick, dark hair, athletic build, and highly engaging personality were a few of the traits that for years have served the boyishly handsome Boyd well. He's a man's man, and a ladies' man as well, all in one. Boyd is one of those men best described as the kind of guy other men aspire to be and women aspire to be with. If the prequel to *Top Gun* ever gets made, Boyd at least gets an audition to be Tom "Maverick" Cruise's fighter-pilot dad. Boyd is certainly qualified for the part—he was a Navy F-4 Phantom pilot, a true-to-life member of Top Gun.

Even in his fifties, Boyd has an indefatigably boyish, rakish charm, a playful and openly gregarious contrast to my more reserved and buttoned-down personality. I tend to play things close to the vest—I'm friendly, polite, and able to let part of my guard down in the company of close friends, but I'm usually in control and it can be difficult for me to depart from the programmed itinerary. Boyd, on the other hand, is the life of the party, hopping from one conversation to another and telling jokes with a self-deprecating, borderline ribald sense of humor. No doubt, Boyd and I see a way to complete ourselves vicariously through the other, which helps explain why we have been close friends half our lives.

Our tastes in women run much the same course. Years ago, Boyd met a strikingly attractive and athletic young woman named Fallon Browning, only to learn that her friendly relationship with me was getting more serious by the day. Boyd had the news broken to him by Jack Vaughn, my older brother, and that was that. When Boyd realized that I was indeed serious about Fallon—we would become man and wife, in fact—Boyd left well enough alone.

Born in Chattanooga in 1950, Boyd belonged to the early generation of

Baby Boomers who would be subjected to the draft lottery starting in the late 1960s. The government put 366 balls into a hopper, each one representing a birthday, and drew them out one at a time, establishing the order of those eligible for the draft. Boyd's birthday was picked number sixty-one, a good number only if your name happened to be Roger Maris.

"I was making good enough grades to stay in college, but with this lottery thing all bets were off," Boyd said. "I remember sitting in the TV room of our frat house. The guys in the two-digit club went out and got drunk because they knew they were going to Vietnam. The guys in the three hundred club went out and got drunk because they knew they weren't. And the guys in the middle went out and got drunk because they didn't know what was going to happen to them."

A "double-digit midget," as the expression put it back then, a drunken Boyd then loaded up his motorcycle to prepare for the getaway run to Canada. By the time he sobered up, he realized his dad Lamar would not look favorably on the idea. Lamar Boyd had been a spy behind the Russian lines during World War II—in Iran, no less. "Stuff that was being shipped to Russia, our allies at the time, was turning up missing as it passed through Iran," Boyd said. "So Dad and a small group of guys were shipped over there to figure out what was going wrong."

Okay, so Taylor wasn't really going to bolt north of the border, after all, but he wasn't too keen about waiting around to get shipped off to Vietnam, either. His solution was to apply for and then earn a Navy ROTC scholarship, giving him a reprieve from the beans-and-bullets life of a rice-paddy grunt, at least until he finished college. If all went well he would be a commissioned officer, giving him more career choices. First, though, he had to go to Montgomery, Alabama, for an interview with a naval officer to get his future sorted out.

"I was only nineteen or twenty years old at the time," Boyd recalled, "and this officer looked me straight in the eye and asked, 'Mr. Boyd, what do you think of the war in Vietnam?'

"To this day I have no idea what possessed me to say what next came out of my mouth, but I looked right back at him and said, 'Sir, it says in the *Battle Hymn of the Republic*, "As He died to make men holy, let us die to make men free."' Even as the words were leaving my lips, I was asking myself, *What the hell am I saying?*

"I was awarded a full scholarship, which meant I didn't have to go to

Vietnam right away. In fact, each year I changed my curriculum just a little bit so I wouldn't graduate on time. I managed to extend a four-year course into five years, figuring out that with any luck they'd have pulled out of Vietnam by the time I had to go there."

These best-laid plans didn't quite pan out. After completing college and then flight training in San Diego, Boyd went to Vietnam as one of the last group of fighter pilots to be sent there. The good news? He got to see another side of the world without getting himself killed.

There's a part of Boyd that reminds me of Frank Abagnale, Jr., the chameleon-like guy who wrote the autobiographical book *Catch Me If You Can* (in 2002 it became a movie). Just as Abagnale did, Taylor, while in college, once impersonated a professor, almost making it through an entire lecture before his cover was blown. An inveterate charmer, Taylor has squired Dallas socialites, while carving out a nice niche in real estate sales.

When our Café Pacific table was ready on that Valentine's Day in 1994, we invited Boyd, there alone as a bachelor dad—he was between marriages—to join us for dinner. We persisted with our invitation over his gallant objections, and he joined us for what would turn out to be a life-changing dinner for us all. A couple of hours, a few wine bottles, and at least a dozen navy stories later, the cheery talk turned to aspirations we had dreamed of in our youth and of roads not taken. These included becoming an astronaut, playing college football, getting a degree from Harvard, or even being in the Olympics. This was February 1994, remember, and another Winter Olympics was about to begin, the one in which figure skater Nancy Kerrigan came back from a knee injury inflicted by a metal baton wielded by a thug hired by the ex-husband of rival skater Tonya Harding.

The Winter Olympics. Lillehammer. Snow. Ice. Medals. The pageantry. The patriotism. The people. The more we talked about it, the more animated Boyd became. He was always selling, a veteran in a profession in which you are taught to "always be closing." By now a savvy and successful real estate agent, the retired Top Gun pilot was trying to close a deal that would mean more than just getting on an airplane and zipping over to Norway for the Games—his bigger goal was ultimately to compete in the next Olympic Games. Simple: pick a sport and become one of America's best.

"C'mon, Robie," Boyd said. "We're not as young as we used to be. Why shouldn't we go to the Olympics while we can?"

"As a spectator, sure," I said, by now figuring that all that wine and those years of slam-dunk landings on ocean-borne carriers had jumbled Boyd's mind beyond repair.

"As athletes!" Boyd responded fervently. "As Olympic athletes!"

Me, by now in my late thirties, and Boyd, in his mid-forties, competing in the next Olympics? *Are you nuts??!!*

"Oh, c'mon, how hard can it be?" Boyd countered.

Deciding to play along, I said, "Okay, here's the deal. The Summer Olympics are out—too many countries, too many athletes, and way too competitive. Ah, but the Winter Games. Maybe there's something there that we can do. After all, we've got four years to get ready. That should be enough time. Learn a new sport, get really good at it, win some events, and in a couple years we'll be representing the USA. Sounds like a plan to me."

How hard could it be if we really applied ourselves and took up a sport that wasn't already overcrowded with elite athletes, at least not American athletes? Curling, perhaps? Nah, too much of an old fogy's sport, we thought initially. Our natural athleticism, notwithstanding our own age factor, would not be advantageous in a sport resembling shuffleboard but played on ice.

In curling, one team member, a skip, "bowls" a large round game piece known as a "rock" and another member of the "rink" (team) uses a broom to sweep a path ahead of the sliding rock, hoping to get it to the "house," which is comprised of target circles at the end of the rink. Not exactly a goose-bump sport for the ages. Just the *aged*, in my opinion. Still, we *did* talk about curling, going so far as to discuss the idea of converting an old Quonset hut in Dallas into a little curling arena complete with bar and tables. It wasn't until sometime later that we discovered that curling was more than just a sport for wannabe retirees—it has been an intensely competitive sport in Canada for decades and in some border states, and it certainly was no sport for some young-in-spirit bucks figuring it would be their Easy Street to Olympic glory.

In short, curling was out.

So, how about one of the sliding sports? We both were avid, experienced skiers, accustomed to high speeds over snowy and sometimes icy surfaces. Plus, the United States hadn't had much international success in either bobsled or luge for decades. Maybe, just maybe, a lot of hard work and some good coaching could help us make up a lot of ground between then and 1998. If a ragtag team of Jamaican bobsledders could make it into the Land of Five Rings, and if a woman our age could compete in luge for the Virgin Islands, why couldn't we—Taylor

Boyd and Robie Vaughn—trip the ice fantastic for a few good moves come Nagano, Japan, four years down the road?

A lot of wine- and pride-induced talk went down that night. As I returned to work the next day, I thought little of what had been discussed. I was still in the slight haze of a mild wine hangover, if there is such a thing. Being around Taylor had always been so much fun, and now it was time for me to get serious once again. No more playing around with such foolishness. Boyd, on the other hand, couldn't get the Winter Olympics out of his head. Within days of that fateful dinner, he was boarding a plane for a series of connecting flights that would take him to Lillehammer. He landed there two days in advance of the opening ceremonies for the 1994 Olympic Winter Games.

"I was able to put the whole trip together at the last minute for like five or six grand," Boyd said. "I got plane tickets at the last minute and then once I got there I stayed in a chalet out of town. One day I was getting on the bus to go into Oslo and see the sights, only to realize that I was a couple krones short to cover the bus fare. I was able to bum what I needed off another American. Get this—the guy turns out to be Duncan Kennedy's brother, and Duncan was the number-one luger for the United States. So he and I get drunk and had a great time down there."

Boyd soon met all of the Kennedys, including Duncan's mother, whom he spent much of the rest of his time in Norway escorting around in the unofficial role as her "walker." They got VIP passes to some of the events. Whenever Duncan was being interviewed by television crews, Boyd was positioned nearby, just off camera. When Duncan Kennedy was going into his third and final run, he was within striking distance of a luge medal. Boyd was standing by at the top of the track while Kennedy prepared to make his last run.

"Duncan looked over at his mother and said, 'Mom, I'm going to bust it.' Sure enough, he busted it—he shot it so fast that he wiped out going into the third turn from the finish line and was disqualified," Boyd recalled.

Later, Boyd asked Kennedy to help him learn the luge. Duncan explained to the Texan the finer points of luge: how the luge has edges on its runners and a center of gravity that is nearly a foot off the ice; how the luge was very light, can be over-steered very easily, and is prone to flip-overs; and how it takes a luger almost a full year of diligent practice, bumps, and bruises to become adept enough to navigate the luge all the way to the bottom of the track; how those who are any good at it have already been racing luge since they were kids. If there was going to be any hope of making it into the Winter Olympics in 1998, let alone 2002, Boyd figured out quickly it would not be on luge. Not in this lifetime, anyway.

"At some point as I'm talking to Duncan, he tells me about the skeleton," Boyd said. "I had no idea what it was. It wasn't an Olympic sport. But I find out that there's going to be a skeleton school later that year in Calgary, so I go up there for the school, still oblivious to what it was all about. I showed up knowing only that I needed some shoes with cleats, so I brought some golf shoes, some blue jeans, and a sweatshirt. And with that, I was ready to take on skeleton."

By now it was fall 1994. When Boyd got to Calgary, he met Dave Graham, president of the Alberta Skeleton Association and director of the three-day skeleton school Boyd had signed up for. Boyd had come to the right place. A bear of a man with an outgoing, friendly demeanor that suited Boyd to a tee, Graham let the skeleton's newest maverick borrow his sled and helmet for what would be, in all respects, what you could call a "crash course" in skeleton. It wasn't that bad, actually. Calgary was then known for having one of the easiest tracks in the world, a venue where sliders could tweak their techniques and put the hammer down without constant fear of bone-jarring crashes and skin burns. By the end of the school, Boyd had made it from top to bottom in one piece, further buoyed by the scuttlebutt going around that skeleton would likely become part of the 1998 Winter Games in Nagano, Japan.

Boyd was in the right place at the right time, for soon he would get to meet some of the top sliders in the world, and this is a sport where good things can rub off. During his second week in Calgary, the track also hosted an America's Cup race. The U.S. contingent that showed up included volunteer coach Peter Viaciulis and a slew of sliders that included Terry Holland, Chris Soule, and Jimmy Shea.

The American sliders quickly took to Boyd, intrigued by this daring Texan flaunting a healthy bankroll and cruising around in a large van, perfect for road trips over to Lake Louise for some partying. For much of his second week in Calgary, Boyd slid alongside the American racers, becoming "one of the boys" while improving with every trip down the track. One thing he already had mastered was the ability to count to ten, and he discovered that where the Canadians had ten sliders entered for the America's Cup event, the United States had only nine.

Boyd went straight to Viaciulis. Like the solo golfer who walks up to the first tee and finds a threesome ready to tee off, asked the coach if it was okay for him to tag along, to suit up for the race later that week.

"Well, you now have a skeleton slider's license and you're an American, so sure, let's go," Viaciulis told Boyd.

ESPN, televising the event, conducted pre-race interviews with all the American racers, making sure they had enough feature video in the can to cover all race contingencies.

"They're interviewing me," Boyd said, "when they go, 'So, Taylor Boyd, how long have you been doing skeleton?' And I said, 'Oh, twelve days.'"

"'You mean twelve years.'"

"'No, twelve days.'"

"I've still got the tape from the telecast. While I'm racing down on one of my runs, you can hear one of the commentators saying, 'Well, here we have Taylor Boyd from Dallas, Texas. He's a real estate broker, and he likes to be on the edge.' Of course, I came in dead last. But it was great. In what other sport could you in twelve days' time be able to compete internationally, and on national TV at that?"

Is this a great sport or what?

Boyd was driven when it came to sliding, a veteran adrenaline junkie fighting off the onslaught of age. He was in his mid-forties, quite possibly on the cusp of a mid-life crisis, or maybe not. He was determined to do something significant with his life. While jockeying a Phantom had fulfilled his need for speed, it hadn't quenched his thirst for life.

"You're constantly reevaluating yourself as you go through life, and I'm one of those people who always needs to be moving on and progressing in some direction," said Boyd, who shares an Oak Lawn townhouse with his teenaged son, Kitt. The main living area, open and airy, includes only three pieces of furniture, each personally commissioned to unorthodox specs by Boyd. On the walls are several paintings, each one his interpretation of an existing work or works. Included is a wall-sized, paint-dipped rendition of a work obviously inspired by the renowned artist Jackson Pollock. The townhouse's previous owner had a prized painting hanging on the same wall, which he offered to let Boyd buy for $70,000. Boyd passed on the offer, reasoning he could do something on the cheap that would have a lot more meaning to him. The result is a highly credible piece of art to which even Pollock might have given a second glance. A second rendition of the "Taylor Pollock" now hangs in a local restaurant as a commissioned piece.

The chase for a spot in Winter Olympics was part of a great plan Boyd had fashioned for himself, based on the YMCA motto of "Body, Mind, and Spirit." He was seeking an extraordinary means to fulfill each of the three goals as a renewed quest for self-actualization. The Body part would be the Winter Olympics. For the Mind, he had committed to earn a degree from Harvard. He found that Harvard offered a master's degree in real estate that would take only nine months to fulfill. For Spirit, he turned to a buddy of his, a transcendental meditation guru, to teach him the ways of TM.

"I had done a little bit of meditating when I was young," Boyd said. "My TM buddy did the whole thing where he lights all the candles and that sort of stuff, and he came up with a mantra for me. As for the Harvard thing, I made some connections. This would have been around 1991. When you go to Harvard, I was told, they ask you stuff like 'What are you going to do with this degree if we let you come?' At my age I was trying to think of a good reason, maybe something to do with urban revitalization or Habitat for Humanity—I've always been a strange thinker, so I had some concepts there, some angles to try. But it was going to cost me something like seventy grand, and I would have to take a whole year off to focus on it, and I ended up not doing it."

Of course, there was still the "Body" aspect of the Body, Mind, Spirit trifecta. And what could be better to do with one's body than hurtle it headfirst down an icy track?

After returning from Calgary in late 1994, Boyd called me at the office and insisted we get together that night. He wanted to stick some skeleton photos under my nose and pique my interest in learning more about the sport. It was late in the day when Boyd called and I had already made plans for dinner with the family at home that night.

I was skeptical, but I invited him to join us. Fallon adored Taylor, and I knew she wouldn't mind, just as we had enjoyed Taylor's company during that dinner at Café Pacific back in February. He had even reminded me of that dinner when he called to arrange this latest get-together, and I could tell that this was really important to him. Besides, this would be a great opportunity just to catch up with each other. There's never a dull moment when you're around Taylor.

When we got together that night, Boyd launched into a breathless rehash of the Lillehammer trip and followed it up with details of his skeleton training and racing that followed later in the year at Calgary. He regaled us with his tales of meeting Duncan Kennedy and picking his brain about skeleton, of escorting Kennedy's mom around Norway, and of then learning how to negotiate the icy track at Calgary, culminating in the America's Cup race televised by ESPN. By now, knowing a sales pitch when I heard one, I realized this was more than just looking at photos from my buddy's vacation getaway. Boyd started with his first close, pulling out the Calgary photos and placing them on a table, each one with another plot twist behind it.

I stared at the photos, shaking my head. The gesture was as much about disbelief of the premise of skeleton as it was my first sign to Boyd that I wasn't biting. Skeleton was not my cup of (iced) tea. No way was I going to put myself in harm's way on one of those so-called sleds at seventy-plus miles an hour. Yet, as I looked at the pictures, I was reminded how my younger brother David had recently returned from a skiing trip to the Canadian Rockies, a trip that included a day's detour for a bobsled run down the track at Calgary. I, too, was familiar with the area. On several occasions, I had driven right past the Canadian Olympic Park just west of Calgary, on my way to ski vacations in the Purcell, Selkirk, and Monashee mountain ranges west of Banff, Alberta; one of those trips was during the 1988 Olympic Winter Games. Small world. Hey, there's a connection, but no way was I ever going to load myself onto one of those lunch trays.

Boyd wasn't finished. Even as I continued to shake my head, Boyd had his presentation carefully researched. He knew, for example, that I had already arranged to return north for a helicopter-skiing trip in the Canadian Rockies as part of a Canadian Mountain Holidays trip in January 1995. Sensing an opening in the conversation, Boyd leaned across the dinner table. His eyebrows turned upward and his gaze piercing through me, he beseeched his dinner host to remember the Winter Olympic prospects we had discussed at our wine-soaked February dinner. Not only that, but Boyd, thanks to his budding friendships with North American skeleton insiders, had it on good authority that skeleton, finally, *would* make it into the Winter Games for 1998 or 2002. This would be our big chance to make it as Olympic sliding buddies, and our window of opportunity, age-wise, was rapidly closing.

All I kept thinking about at that point was how misguided Taylor had been in this pursuit. Even Fallon, laughing, told Taylor she, too, thought he was crazy . . . this coming from someone who herself had been a fearless athlete. Fallon is someone who enjoys life and relishes every challenge that gets thrown her way. We enjoyed some more wine over dinner and, as we had in February, chatted the night away with Taylor, discussing his adventures and misadventures into the wee hours. Still, even as mutually adventurous as we are, I agreed with Fallon—this whole business looked a little out of whack.

Later that night, though, I couldn't help but ask Fallon, "Okay, maybe it is crazy, but do you think I could do it? Is it possible?"

"'Robie,' she replied, "as long as I've known you, there are two things I can count on with you: One, you always do the right thing, whether the stakes are large or whether it's something as simple as what you eat every day for breakfast. And two, you've always accomplished anything you set your mind to. But let's be honest—do we really have the time for one . . . more . . . hobby around here?"

Our children were seven and five at the time. And I admitted wryly that she was right. As I drifted off to sleep that night, though, I realized that this was not the last I had heard about skeleton, and it dawned on me that somehow, somewhere, I would probably be giving skeleton a shot myself. One try, just for the challenge of it.

In the days that followed that second fateful dinner, the determined Boyd kept working his mojo on me. Did I mention that Taylor is the kind of person who usually gets his way when he sets his mind on changing someone else's? The man could wear down the mountains themselves with his bull, charm, and perseverance.

Eventually I absorbed Boyd's vision as well, relenting to give up the last three days of an upcoming heli-skiing trip so I could rendezvous with Boyd at the Canada Olympic Park on January 20, 1995, to check out skeleton for myself. It just so happened that another skeleton school was scheduled for that week. Boyd took care of the logistics, making reservations for the two of us to stay at the Bob Niven Olympic Training Centre in the Olympic Park near Calgary. Our accommodations put us, literally, within a one-minute walk of the track's finish line.

As soon as we arrived, Boyd wasted no time. He walked me to the track, where a junior luge training session was in progress. When the first luge whizzed by, its runners a shrill whisper against the slick ice as wisps of frozen crystals blew by, I, startled, had to fight the reflex to jump back. It was the most terrifying sporting activity I had ever witnessed up close and personal. Immediately I began to wonder what I had allowed Boyd to talk me into. Just like that, my nerves were frayed. I just couldn't comprehend the pure, silent speed I had witnessed.

I grasped it a lot better while making my first run down the track from the junior start, the speed increasing relentlessly, like a runaway train. Then, suddenly, it was over, as I drifted to a stop after crossing the finish line. There was only one thing I could think of: *I have to go again, and I know I can do better.*

I did both of those things. I had the fifth-fastest time among the skeleton-school neophytes on the first run and improved to fourth on the next. Between runs, sliders were critiqued via radio by instructor Denny Simon, who mixed humor with his insightful analysis of our respective sliding techniques. We novices needed all the laughs we could get to help stave off the waves of fear creeping around in the back of our heads, knowing that we would soon be leaving the lower starts behind and going to the top of the track.

After the sliding sessions were over, the skeleton students went indoors and were treated to video reviews of our run, which like the radio critiques, were one part hilarious and another part educational. Replays of amateur sliders imitating games of pinball by bumping into the frozen walls helped break the tension. It became apparent, however, from watching the videos that while forty-five miles an hour from the junior start felt like a death-defying thrill ride while on the sled, it appeared like nothing more than a leisurely descent when viewed onscreen.

The really scary part was yet to come. The next day, the sliders' two runs would begin at the women's luge start ramp, about 80 percent of the way up the track. The top speed, forty-five miles an hour a day earlier, would now be in the sixty range, a startling change that made the previous day's runs pale by comparison. Counter-intuitively, though, I found the extra speed advantageous. The faster I went, the easier it was to steer my sled with subtle body shifts or a gentle toe drag. This time, I placed third against the field, and then first.

The night before my school cohorts and I would make our full-track runs, Boyd and I went out to dinner with some of our new Canadian sliding friends who couldn't resist teasing me about my first few, albeit incomplete slides. Among the roasters were Houstonians-turned-Calgarians Clay and Rhonda Roark, both of whom were sliders who had competed internationally as well.

I didn't sleep well that night. The self-perceived savvy businessman who didn't wilt in the risky business of multimillion-dollar operations, the world traveler who had conquered some of the world's highest peaks and schussed some of the scariest black-diamond slopes accessible only by helicopter, I found myself trying to stave off the cold sweats, envisioning what would be nothing more than a sixty-second dash down a chute of ice.

The next morning, prior to my first run, I gazed down the sloping hillside to the finish area in the distance and realized just how scary this sport really is. I hoped I would make it down there in one piece . . . although, either way, I'd be at the bottom.

My first run began easily enough through the first two turns, but then the speed thing hit me again. I was going faster and faster, my speed compounding, until all of a sudden I hit the left wall of the straightaway coming out of turn eight. My left shoulder took the brunt of the impact, and all I could see were lighting bolts. The pain was so intense that I no longer was aware of any fear. All I felt was a dull pain as I dearly hung on through the finish. Once I stopped, all I could feel was the pain from my bruised left shoulder, and I could not raise my arm above my shoulder. The impact had left a gaping hole in my speed suit. But I needed to complete one more run from the top to successfully finish the school and get my license. After that, I would be certified to slide from the top of any of the two tracks then in existence in North America (Calgary and Lake Placid—Park City, Utah, was not open yet).

On my second run, I turned it up a notch on concentration, focusing intensely while visualizing my steering through turns six and seven, which in turn set up my entry into and exit out of turn eight, my nemesis from earlier in the day. I managed to make it all the way down this time without mishap. I'm not sure what the prognosis would have been had I banged my left shoulder again.

Part of me felt a little cocky about it. I was already getting pretty decent, that I knew. And yet another part of me was stuck in a state of anxious terror—a feeling that would stay with me through another thirty or so runs in later years. I didn't know it at the time, but I was only just beginning to pay my dues physically. And the wages were going to be pain on top of more pain.

It didn't matter. I was hooked.

Hooked on skeleton.

CHAPTER SIX

Red Tape and Black Eyes

*Even if you're on the right track,
you'll get run over if you just sit there.*
—Will Rogers

At the same time the Texas twosome of Taylor Boyd and I were discovering skeleton, the sport was beginning to emerge as a legitimate international enterprise, complete with network TV coverage and skilled sliders on both sides of the Atlantic. It helped that the United States had now become competitive and was winning the occasional medal, starting with Orvie Garrett's bronze during the 1991–92 World Cup season in a race at Cortina, Italy.

Skeleton was achieving the kind of credibility that was attracting attention from both the International Olympic Committee and the United States Olympic Committee. A true world championship event was being held every year, and the United States had moved well beyond the curiosity stage to the stage of taking the sport more seriously.

The American emergence was evident in international events. Where once it had been considered significant to slide to a top-ten finish, U.S. racers were actually beginning to win medals. Three years after Garrett won his bronze, Jimmy Shea took silver in a World Cup race at Lake Placid. Sure, the trips to the podium still were few and far between, but at least the Americans were mining medals instead of generating guffaws everywhere they went. If skeleton was going to make it onto the Olympic docket, it would need for the USA to be a world-stage player, and that was starting to happen. Some money started to trickle down to the skeleton sliders, but even that usually required some major squeaking of the wheel. Sliders still were having to pay their own way, and most of that time that meant pulling out the plastic, over and over. Most of the money came from private support of athletes' families and friends.

One sure sign of skeleton's increasing competitiveness and worldwide popularity was that cheating was becoming a bit more sophisticated. This is usually a sign that a particular sport's status had moved from low visibility to high stakes. The sport was able to slide by through much of the 1980s with few rules and regulations. Things started to tighten up between the late 1980s and early 1990s. Steroid and growth-hormone use wasn't a problem, as far as we know, but sliders were getting increasingly sly and subtle in trying to sneak things past race juries.

Rules, in turn, were becoming stricter. By now, Peter Viaciulis was a Federation Internationale de Bobsleigh et de Tobogganing jury member as well as the U.S. coach. His first jury duty came at the World Championships at La Plagne, above Albertville, France, in 1992. Viaciulis was at the top of the hill, tasked to check the temperatures of the runners on each slider's sled, and it was apparent that not everything was legitimate.

"Christian Auer, an Austrian and good friend of mine, got to the start line," Viaciulis recalled, "and we found that his runners were about fifteen to twenty degrees centigrade too hot. They were just about glowing red. At the time, the rules said you didn't have to have your sled to the start until just twenty minutes before the race. Someone mentioned that his runners had been kept in a pizza oven all night.

"Auer still took his run and won the race, and then we got the protocol sheet with the temperature information on it down to the jury president at the bottom. We had a meeting and disqualified the winner of the World Championships. That didn't go over too well. Auer understood it, but his coach was in tears, crying.

"I felt bad for the guy and really blame the coach, although there's no excuse for the athlete not knowing that something like that is going on. The following year the rule was changed to where the sleds now had to be at the start line a full hour before the race. For several years they called that the Christian Auer Rule."

David Fay, president of the United States Golf Association during the 2005 U.S. Open, said, "In the healthy sports, athletes are getting faster, quicker, and stronger." This is also happening in skeleton today more than ever as more "world class" athletes are coming into the sport. Even China, it is rumored, has been filtering thousands and thousands of its population to see which have the attributes required to compete in skeleton.

While skeleton was getting better at policing itself, it was missing the mark in trying to promote itself to the Federation Internationale de Bobsleigh et de Tobogganing and, subsequently, the International Olympic Committee. If the former wasn't going to vouch for the skeleton, then certainly the Olympic folks weren't going to go over the FIBT's head to pluck skeleton from its below-the-radar status. The best skeleton could hope for was to bide its time and patiently work the FIBT and Olympic officials behind the scenes, lobbying with carefully written letters and even in person whenever they got the chance. Fighting city hall was out of the question, at least from the outside, but perhaps they could work their way into key positions to make a difference—to educate the FIBT and IOC while selling softly along the way. It would take time, but there really wasn't anything to lose but time.

Advocates central to skeleton's future, themselves familiar with driving sleds down icy chutes, began to emerge with self-built bases of lobbying influence. Two of skeleton's most influential campaign chairmen would turn out to be Massachusetts native Paul Varadian, a skeleton slider of Armenian descent, whose heritage would play a pivotal role in his growing influence, and David Kurtz, a Pennsylvania attorney and, likewise, a veteran skeleton slider who understood well the mechanisms of back room deal making. Both men, in their different ways, knew how to negotiate the corridors of politically charged organizations such as the FIBT and the IOC. They both knew that it all boiled down to a people business. Varadian and Kurtz, in their own unique ways, understood the art of the deal, even when it meant, as in the case of Kurtz, fending off the alleged threat of physical violence.

They knew how to manage the delicate balance of pulling strings while at times pushing their luck. Their biggest obstacle, at both the U.S. and international levels, was the bobsled aficionados firmly entrenched in their almost unassailable positions of power in both the USBSF and with the FIBT.

"To be able to work with these people, you had to understand their motivations and why they do what they do," Varadian said. "There are cultural factors, and there are financial factors. Selfishness was at the root of it all. Financial resources were already scarce in bobsled—they hadn't had an international sponsor for years, and it was a relatively expensive sport. So what you have are these people clinging to their good-ole-boy network, going to all the competitions, staying at the hotels, drinking and socializing together, doing this and doing that, and that's their life."

In 1989, skeleton supporters such as Varadian petitioned the FIBT to ask the IOC to make skeleton a demonstration sport for the 1992 Games in Albertville. They were confident that once sports fans saw the sport's speed and technical expertise of its sliders, the sport would be viewed as Olympic-worthy. Getting demonstration status would be a good stepping stone to full Olympic status, and it would allow room on the calendar for skeleton to further build its international legitimacy in time for the 1994 Lillehammer Games. But the FIBT refused to budge, arguing that skeleton wasn't yet well-enough established as a sport around the world. Reading between the lines, Varadian and others in his camp figured it was more a matter of territoriality, that the FIBT saw skeleton as a potential threat to the self-interests of bobsled. Skeleton would be in line to overshadow the spotlight and siphon off whatever financing they did have in pocket.

"There was a lot of grumbling that we would break off into a separate federation, and just the thought of that ruffled a lot of feathers," Varadian said. "Now you can see why sports such as this tend not to attract the long-term supporters. That's because there's no financial reward in dealing with this kind of operation, one in which any attempt made to evolve only gets dragged down. What happens, therefore, is that most of the people who do gravitate to administrative roles in these nonprofessional sports are usually former athletes in the sport or locals in the communities where these sports, in this case bobsled, are big, and they have risen through the ranks sort of like the Peter Principle. When they feel challenged, they get extremely clingy, and they fight back."

It got rough at times. Kurtz, a former U.S. skeleton coach and slider, learned that during the 1994 FIBT congress in Calgary. A year earlier, Kurtz, too, had petitioned the FIBT to act on behalf of skeleton in getting the sport admitted for Olympic status, this time as a full-fledged sport because demonstration slots were no longer available. That 1994 petition also got shot down, when FIBT president Klaus Kotter, a renowned former Austrian bobsledder, did what he could to influence FIBT members into giving a thumbs-down to skeleton, according to Kurtz.

Kurtz and the skeleton community got revenge at the 1994 FIBT congress. That's when Kurtz aggressively campaigned behind the scenes to round up the votes necessary to oust Kotter as president. His candidate: skeleton ally Bob Storey, a Canadian who had earlier approached Kurtz to ask for U.S. assistance in the voting process.

"He promised he would do his level best to get skeleton into the Olympics, and so I told him he had our support," said Kurtz, who by then was vice president of the United States Bobsled and Skeleton Federation. "Bob was elected by a margin of two votes, making it the first time that a FIBT president had been unseated for reasons other than death or retirement."

Kotter did not take his ouster well. It was no secret that Kurtz had been the main force behind his electoral loss, and later during the congress, Kotter stalked off toward Kurtz's hotel room, according to Kurtz. Kurtz claims he fended off Kotter, although his work to get skeleton into the world of the five rings was far from finished. This had only been the tip of the iceberg.

"We found out later," Kurtz said, "that when the Germans figured out before the election that Kotter might lose, they started offering gifts like cars and TVs to delegates. They asked the guy from Trinidad and Tobago what color BMW he wanted. And they thought because of my surname that I would support them. After all this, I went to Storey and reminded him that I expected him to be a man of his word."

All the U.S. skeleton community now needed was a man of leadership, and business and organization savvy to get things done on the home front. That's assuming I could weather the bumps and bruises of my novice skeleton days and move on and up to a more instrumental role in building up the sport.

My January 1995 sliding experience in Calgary had ended on a "low" note— I had made it all the way to the bottom of the hill twice on the full-run last day. That certified me as a skeleton slider, albeit one with a very painful and bruised shoulder bone. It would be almost two years before I resumed sliding. That would happen in December 1996, when I returned to Calgary to participate in a second skeleton school. It was like riding a bike. I picked up right where I had left off, except this time I had decided I would stick with it for a while.

Although we owned no skeleton equipment, Boyd and I started competing in club races in Calgary, further bruising our extremities, suffering cuts to our heads and chins, and even cracking a few ribs on occasion. The bruises and cuts would become scars testifying to our perseverance in this extreme sport. On one occasion in Calgary, Boyd left a red trail of blood down the lower half of the track, the result of excessive G-forces in a turn that slammed his head to the ice, slicing open his forehead and ultimately covering his visor and the front of his speed suit with blood. Boyd finished the run sprayed with his blood. All this was caught on film by a Mexican TV crew onsite for a piece they were doing on extreme sports. Interestingly, the host of the program was Luis Carrasco on his first assignment to a sliding track. Luis ended up as a skeleton athlete in the 2002 Olympics, representing Mexico.

"That night," Boyd said, laughing, "I got some coaching from the Canadians there, including one guy who walked the track with me, analyzing how I had done. There were drops of blood all along the track. 'Now see where this blood is here,' he said, 'that shows you were a little high coming into the turn. But as you came out of it you were looking pretty good here.' He was able to critique my run by the trail of blood."

I also failed to make it down the Calgary track unscathed. There was the time when the Calgarians set me up to go first down the track after it had been snowing all night before. The track had been swept well through turn one, but from then on I ran into plenty of snow, hitting a bank that forced a bunch of snow up between my face and visor, effectively blinding me and making breathing difficult the remainder of the run. I was just gasping for breath, all the way to the bottom. Everyone who had seen this from the top was laughing, telling me that all they saw was this big puff of snow that shot up when I went through that turn.

After each sliding excursion, the two of us would return to Dallas reenergized by our joint adventure. Now if only we could get Fallon and some of our friends to join us. It would make the trips to Calgary all the more fun and would introduce everyone to all our newfound friends from skeleton. Fallon, athletic and daring, willing to try about anything that involved keeping score and challenging personal limits, would have none of it, even as we kept pulling out photos and spreading them on a table for her to look at it. We also returned home armed with videos as well as new and endless stories of our exploits. Still, Fallon wasn't moved.

"It was the craziest thing I had ever seen," Fallon said. "It wasn't even an Olympic sport then, and I was like 'You're going to go down and kill yourself, and for what?'"

Undeterred, Boyd and I were determined to share with others this unique sensation of sliding down a bobsled run at more than seventy miles an hour. It would take more than photos, videos, and a lot of hot air about this ice-cold sport. Eventually, we decided we had the skills and moxie to put together our own skeleton school. We started in January 1998 at the newly opened track at the Utah Olympic Park in Bear Hollow near Park City. In organizing the school, we outlined an agenda and calculated what the cost per student would be. Here we were, two years after our first school in Calgary, and now we were organizing our own in Park City.

We modeled our Utah school after the Calgary school, complete with educational discussions, track walks, and coaching at the start, finish, and by radio over the course of the track, with video sessions at the end. Clay Roark, a retired U.S. World Cup slider, was hired to coach this first school. It was a good fit. An American in love with skeleton, and living and working for an oil and gas company in Calgary, Roark had more than one thing in common with me. He also had a deep well of skeleton experience and knowledge to draw on. He knew the sport, was familiar with all the skilled American and Canadian sliders, and he was a walking, sliding encyclopedia of all that there was to know about their European counterparts. Roark also had inside knowledge of another subject that would be especially useful for me over the ensuing years—the structure and inner workings of the United States Bobsled and Skeleton Federation. I came to learn that the USBSF had no budget, no personnel, and no plans or programs for the skeleton athletes.

Before I could even think about changing the mindset at the USBSF, though, I needed to convince Fallon that she was cut out to try skeleton. And I knew that if Fallon gave it a thumbs-up, more of our friends would go for it as well. We needed to grow the skeleton community and, hence, the opportunities for contributions. In order to get enrollees on board for the first skeleton school, we hosted a recruiting party at our home, and the event took on the ambiance of what you would end up with if you held an Amway party at a frat house. The pitch would have to be a convincing one, and we would have a lot of fun doing it.

We convinced a number of our friends to drop by at least to hear us out. Eight signed up, to include Fallon and my younger brother, David. Fallon was the only Dallas woman to actually make the trip to Utah. Once in Park City, though, she was joined by a handful of Park City-area women who had decided to give it a shot.

"I remember how the Dallas contingent all flew up there together on American Airlines, drinking Bloody Marys and laughing all the way," Fallon recalled. "Taylor and Robie were kind of the leaders of it. We rented a condo in Park City, and we all stayed in it together. Clay Roark was there. Peter Viaciulis, too. We were all having a ball, but then all of us beginners went out and looked at the track after we got there, and that's when it was like 'Oh, forget this. I'm not going down that thing on a cafeteria tray.' We're just laughing, laughing, laughing."

Not for long.

We didn't have to wait long to get out onto the track. Their first night there, the Texas contingent prepared for their initiation, layering themselves in standard ski clothing that included baggy warm-up pants, parkas, and tennis shoes. The well-lit Utah track is a scene of hustle and bustle at night during the winter months. Most sliders who lived in the area had full-time jobs, and their only opportunity to slide during the week came at night.

That first night, the skeleton school sliders were transported in trucks up the track, although they didn't have far to go, and were dropped off at the track more than halfway above the finish line. After everyone fumbled around to find a helmet that fit, they received a brief explanation of how the sled worked; then, one at a time, they were placed on a sled and given a shove to begin their way down the track. So much for bringing along the students gradually. What better way to learn the sport than to get right to it? The sensation was equivalent to a theme park roller-coaster ride, with the novices pulling little in the way of Gs. Still, it was fast enough to make it a blast, a rush, for the newcomers. Roark and Viaciulis proceeded to move the school sliders up the hill in increments, with the students' anxiety levels rising along with their starts. After a couple of days of this transitioning, they would be moving to the top.

Full speed ahead.

"I'll never forget waking up that morning," Fallon said, "thinking *I don't know if I really want to go from the top.* That other stuff was okay, but now we were going to be moving really fast. Taylor and Robie had already left to go to the track, and the rest of us were sitting around in the condo feeling really nervous."

Not only were they nervous, but the condo was becoming neglected as dirty dishes stacked up in the sink, and there were no more clean cups left. The night before we had stayed up late watching a risqué comedy on video while drinking wine out of the only clean dishes we could find—some soup bowls stashed away in a side cupboard. Symbolically, the soup bowls were replaced with silver bowls and became an immediate tradition. (The tradition was later adopted by the Texas Sliding Society, a nonprofit organization that Boyd and I founded in March 1998, as a support entity for skeleton. The silver bowl became a symbol of excellence we engraved and presented to worthy sliders.) On this January 1998 morning, however, the sliding novices were feeling anything but a sense of excellence. It was almost time to go out to the track, but no one seemed particularly eager to make the first move. The morning-after cobwebs didn't do anything to give them much courage, either.

"All of us were sitting around in David Vaughn's room," Fallon said. "They were telling me, 'Fallon, if you don't do it, none of us have to do it. But if you do it, then we all have to do it.' Well, that's all I needed to hear, and I stood up and said, 'Okay, I'm doing it.'

"Not that my apparent act of courage really solved anything. As we were riding up in the truck that takes sliders to the top, we were all feeling sick to our stomachs. It even dawned on me that I might kill myself. I started to think that my head could get caught under the sled because of how it hangs over the front edge, and on top of all that you have all these G-forces bearing down on you. Maybe the helmet would get stuck down there, and your head could be ripped off. Those are the kinds of things—dark thoughts—that go through your head at a time like that."

The school participants who had stuck it out to the end got to the crest of the track. Roark met them there and handed out the speed suits emblematic of what they were about to do—the real deal, the first full run down the track. Each slider would get two runs down the track, although once they had made it down the first time, they were home free. It had gone well. The pre-run jitters and nausea were gone, pushed out to make way for an adrenaline rush that was almost overwhelming, with Fallon and others whooping it up, scrambling to pick up and tote their heavy sleds back to the truck for the return trip to the top.

Times were kept for the full-track runs, and David ended up as fastest man, Fallon as fastest woman. For Fallon, it would be the start of a trek on the fast track to skeleton success, eventually taking her onto the U.S. national team and World Cup competition. Both of us had been reluctant to even try sliding in the first place, and now we had demonstrated not only an ability to get down the track but the potential to possibly compete at the international level. It was as much a testament to our athleticism as it was the relative dearth, still, of qualified skeleton sliders in the United States.

Buoyed by the success of that first school, Boyd and I organized a second skeleton school later that year, in October, also in Park City. As had been the case with the first skeleton school in January, the October 1998 school would graduate several topnotch sliders, to include future Olympian Tristan Gale. The developmental aspect of skeleton was progressing nicely, breeding new talent, but there was so much more to be done. U.S. skeleton was still in desperate need of an infrastructure capable of supporting and driving the sport. This was something certainly not provided by the cash- and vision-starved USBSF at the time. Now Boyd, I, and others were able to make a difference by providing schools that would recruit and nurture the kind of talent needed to compete, with numbers, at the international level. Plus, I now had Fallon on board, making this a family enterprise with husband and wife competing and leading side by side.

Fallon, despite her initial disbelief and dismay, couldn't stay away once she'd tried it. Part of that I'd like to think was because of my own sales skill. Part of it, too, I'm sure, is because I don't think she could live with the idea that she couldn't even try something I was enjoying so much. She began beating me at tennis about this time, and she now gives me a run for the money on the golf links.

Her indomitable will and competitive spirit are, in part, why I love her. It is also part of the reason why our relationship has stayed so strong in the years that would come, as skeleton began to dominate much of my life, and our lives as well. The final piece of the puzzle was that thrill I got when I slid. Nothing really compares. Once Fallon tasted it, she knew she wanted to continue. And let's be honest, hanging out in a ski town during ski season is a blast no matter where you're from.

Fallon was improving on almost every run. She slid well and caught Peter Viaciulis's eye. He persuaded her to attend a World Cup race in Calgary in February, where she slid some during the training runs and helped out with the races. Though she did not compete, her training times were good enough to show she definitely had potential in the sport. Following additional training runs, Fallon decided to go out for the national team in that fall of 1998. The trials were to be held in Park City, so I decided to race as well so that I could further compare my times to those of the accomplished American sliders such as the truly "old man" of the sport, Terry "Grandpa" Holland, and the young Jimmy Shea. This also was my first time to try out my new Davenport sled that Ryan Davenport had crafted and customized for me in his Calgary shop.

Fallon, like me, has had her share of spills on the track. You can flip, scrape the walls, and you can get deeply bruised. Just among Fallon, Taylor, and me, we have cracked and broken bones (usually a toe or finger), cut open foreheads and chins, suffered heavy bruises, and had our eyes blackened. Speaking of black eyes, there was the time that Fallon and I were in Park City, where Fallon accepted Dave Graham's offer to try using his helmet, a bit too big for her. On her first run that day, while slightly turning her head to each side, she bumped the side of her forehead hard on each side. She wasn't severely injured, but by nightfall she had two shiners.

We went out to dinner at our favorite Park City restaurant, the River Horse Café, and I soon realized I was getting all these nasty stares from people. Then it dawned on me: there is a fairly high rate of spousal abuse in Utah, and the restaurant patrons were drawing the apparent conclusion. Fallon and I put two and two together, and we couldn't stop giggling. But just to show you the difference between cultures, when we go back to Dallas, Fallon was getting unsolicited sympathy for her assumed plastic surgery because two black eyes on a woman in this town often implies some modification. For us, it was just another round of chuckles.

Ryan Davenport, the sled builder, had himself been a crack slider, a world champion at that. He would become one of the central figures in the Americans' rush to Olympic gold at Park City in 2002. Davenport won consecutive World Championships in men's skeleton in 1996 and 1997, only to retire from active sliding soon after to devote himself full-time to building and conditioning skeleton sleds and runners, which he had been doing on a part-time basis for four years. He preferred working with his hands to breaking them.

A Canadian and former auto machinist and drag racer, Davenport had only begun sliding skeleton in November 1992, and he would retire from racing with an impressive list of accomplishments that included, in addition to the two World Championships, seven Canadian titles, five North American crowns, one World Cup overall championship, and a total of fifteen medals earned in World Cup Championships, representing 48 percent of all such races he had entered.

By digging further into the world of skeleton, first as a competitor and then a national team administrator, I would continue to forge new relationships with skeleton experts who would play pivotal roles in the continued development of U.S. skeleton. Davenport was one such key individual, a relaxed intellectual with a keen grasp for science, statistics, mechanics, track analysis, and sled design that complemented whatever vision and leadership I brought to the table, in much the same way that engineers and geologists had with my business enterprises back in Texas. Unfailingly straightforward, deadpan, and logical, Davenport came to be regarded by members of the sliding community as their own Mr. Spock, eerily reminiscent of the Vulcan character portrayed by Leonard Nimoy in the original *Star Trek* TV series.

"He even walks like Spock," slider Tristan Gale said, "complete with the long arms hanging at his side, barely swinging when he walks. It's like he's always carrying two heavy suitcases. He sleeps about two or three hours a night, surviving on a diet of Twinkies, Oreos, Doritos—anything that has nothing but trans fat in it. He's logical and lives for his computer. The man is wonderful with numbers. He has equations for everything."

Boyd and I had met Davenport in 1996 during our skeleton travels, many of which provided their own memories and madcap comedy. On one occasion we found ourselves, outside the training center at the Canadian Olympic Park where we had been staying, at seven in the morning, contemplating how we were going to transport our newly purchased sleds back to Dallas on the airplane. We needed something that would serve the purpose of protecting our sleds for baggage check-in and handling, as golfers use travel bags for transporting their golf clubs. But we had nothing to cover and protect our sleds, and that wouldn't work. Our prayers were answered when we found a nearby dumpster. Within seconds, Boyd was up and over one of the dumpster's sides, rooting around inside for pieces of cardboard that could be taped together into a makeshift skeleton sled travel protector. It was one of skeleton's ultimate necessity-is-the-mother-of-invention moments. It was also hilarious.

During our occasional excursions north to compete in club races, Boyd and I would experiment with different kinds of sleds and runners, looking for the right combination of equipment that would serve us well in our attempts to become faster and more competitive. Thankfully, for us, we met Davenport, who likely would never have taken these two Texas humans seriously had he ever spotted us anywhere near that dumpster.

Ryan's intelligence is vast, cool, and not easily swayed by emotion. He's exceptionally well organized, his logical mind filled with engineering and mathematical talent beyond that of mortal men. He's a competitor and engineer without formal training but also without peer. Although never a natural racer, he wasn't an adrenaline junkie, either.

From behind his mild manner and unremarkable glasses, he seems to look at the world with a bemused detachment. He runs mathematical formulae through his head while others use calculators, and he does it flawlessly. There's an episode of *Star Trek* where Spock is standing impassively behind the transporter control, staring straight ahead, his hands behind his back, Captain Kirk off somewhere in danger. Dr. McCoy angrily fumes at the science officer, asking Spock why he isn't running his complex spatial formulae and calculations so as to get the captain back. Spock, taken aback at the question and with one eyebrow raised, says matter-of-factly, "I am." That's Ryan to a tee.

Moved by a desire to find a faster sled, one that maximized aerodynamic efficiencies, and inspired by the newfound influence of Davenport in our lives,

Boyd and I sponsored (at a cost of more than $5,300) a wind tunnel test of skeleton equipment and body positions through a University of Texas at Austin Aerospace Engineering Department summer class. The sixty-page report that came out of it was titled "Aerodynamic and Mathematical Testing for the Redesign of a Skeleton Sled" and was written by students Greg De La Rosa and Dennis Jones, aka the "Skeleton Crew." Davenport volunteered to be a test subject as well as a contributor of helpful ideas. Ironically, the bulk of the study of this ice-cold sport of winter was conducted during a four-day stretch in August 1997, traditionally the hottest time of the year in central Texas, and it was Davenport who willingly served as speed suit-adorned (and sweat-covered) guinea pig for the tests.

The wind tunnel tests were conducted in the low-speed wind tunnel at UT's J. Pickle Research Campus in north Austin. Time constraints for use of the facility would prevent the Skeleton Crew from being able to test every conceivable combination of factors we would have preferred. Not only were we attempting to isolate the best possible design of a skeleton sled in terms of optimal weight and three-dimensional measurements—within rules established by the FIBT—but we also sought to determine the drag effects for factors such as optimal body position, speed suit material, angle of the head, and different types of helmets. The tests were conducted using a wind force of eighty miles per hour, closely simulating the top speed of world-class skeleton racers.

Time limitations kept us from compiling the comprehensive data of optimal-condition combinations we would have liked, but we did determine some interesting, or as Spock might say, "fascinating," conclusions. One of our findings, as explained in the Skeleton Crew's final report, was that the maximum-weight sled minimizes racing time. This analysis was accomplished with experiments that determined the coefficient of static friction between the runners of the sled and the ice, and a study of a mathematical force balance of the sled. Since the coefficient of friction increases with pressure, however, the test determined that the sled's runners should be as long as possible without exceeding the length of the sled. Of course, the optimal sled design was one with the minimal allowable length and width dimensions.

The optimal head position for the slider, we learned, was the "turtle neck" posture, with chin down and head "scrunched" down as much as possible. As for feet, the tests showed it best to keep them together with toes pointed straight back. The best body position was the aft position on the sled, lying as far back as possible with the chin positioned just barely over the front of the sled. The optimal legal helmet and suit was the Uvex helmet and the polyurethane-coated spandex suit, although they were tested independently of each other. Just for the record, Davenport also experimented with the flayed-backed helmets—the ones resembling, from the back, those helmets worn by Darth Vader and the Evil Empire's storm troopers—used by downhill speed skiers but banned for skeleton use by the FIBT. The Darth Vader helmets turned out to be the most aerodynamic of all.

Armed with the confidence in Davenport's work and the knowledge gained in the UT study, we ordered three 1998 Davenport sleds. They would be delivered with a new set of 1998 runners, which together gave Fallon, Taylor, and me a new sense of confidence and enhanced performance capability that would soon have both of us thinking in terms of sliding in World Cup competition.

Said Boyd, "I had called down to the University of Texas in the first place because I had a premonition that a lot of what determined skeleton success had more to do with aerodynamics than the actual sliding. I got Robie, who was on the development board down there, involved with the wind-tunnel tests, and then we went after Ryan because we knew he was such an engineering buff."

Interestingly, Ryan would be the first human inside this wind tunnel while operational. Getting approval to do the tests was not easy. Thanks to Taylor's selling ability, a bit of contact work by me, and the approval of the dean of the Aerospace Engineering Department, Dr. Ronald O. Stearman, we proceeded with the tests. Beaming down from Calgary wasn't an option for Davenport, and because of all the equipment he needed to bring for testing, he drove to Austin. Once there, he spent four straight days getting on and off sleds in between being buffeted by the near-hurricane-strength winds. Because of the timing requirements in turning on and off the huge fans used in the wind tunnel, Davenport usually would get only thirty seconds between tests, which was just enough time to stretch his back, arms, legs, and neck to keep from cramping up during the dehydrating processes.

"To me, what it all boiled down to at the tests is that instead of shining your runners, maybe you should be shining your helmets," Boyd added. "This was about the time that I was starting to think that maybe skeleton wasn't my ticket long term, that perhaps bobsled would be. But I wasn't about to give up on skeleton yet."

Not with me as his running partner, anyway. With the Austin wind-tunnel test results behind us and my new Davenport sled in hand, I went into the

1997–98 skeleton season determined to give it a shot at racing internationally. But I was still an outsider in a sport that, truthfully, had few insiders, and even fewer supporters in the USBSF. As fall 1997 rolled around, I still had not met Viaciulis. At the time, he was serving as the unpaid coach of the U.S. national team, squeezing whatever funds he could out of the USBSF to supplement the pocket money the sliders and Viaciulis himself were personally pouring into the sport, covering items like travel expenses and equipment costs. Here it was, as it turned out, just four years shy of what would be skeleton's debut at the 2002 Olympics, and American athletes, at the time still highly hopeful of Olympic certification, were still emptying their wallets and running up their charge cards in order to compete.

In other words, nothing much had changed from the heydays of Murtagh, Holland, Bryant, and their pioneering brethren. What *had* changed were the results in international competition. Americans were continuing to win the occasional medal and at least one of the names was a new one. At the 1996–97 World Championships held at Lake Placid, Jim Shea, a part-time bartender, won silver. Newcomer Chris Soule, a part-time Hollywood stuntman, won bronze. In 1997–98, they would follow their wins with another shining performance, this time at the World Cup in Altenberg, Germany, where Shea brought home the gold and Soule the bronze.

Later in the fall of 1997, Boyd and I returned to Park City for two main reasons: We wanted to meet Viaciulis and the U.S. national team sliders. We also intended to get a better handle on our sliding progress by sharing practice time on the track with the likes of Shea and Soule. The national team was at Park City that week for the North American Championships. What better time and opportunity to see how we stacked up against America's best, especially with our dreams of Olympic participation still intact.

When I finally got to meet the U.S. sliders, I found them much more pleasant and friendly than I had anticipated. They were all personable, fun, outgoing, and energetic. As Peter had told me in advance, the athletes confirmed to me that there was a thorough lack of focus or support from the USBSF—their national governing body. Not only were they traveling and competing on their own nickel, they were even having to pay race entry fees out of their own pockets; traditionally, entry fees were a national governing body responsibility. Further, stories abounded about subjective coaching practices, such as favoritism regarding bobsled athletes, team designations, and equipment. The spillover effect of that perception was a certain degree of paranoia and mistrust toward the coaches and USBSF among bobsled and skeleton athletes alike.

While in Park City, I sat down with Viaciulis for a lunch meeting arranged by Boyd. Viaciulis laid out for me a flow chart of the virtual U.S. skeleton program and how it interfaced with the USBSF, the FIBT, and the United States Olympic Committee, including relevant organizations and officers. While Viaciulis mapped out all of this on a paper napkin, I carefully gazed at all the boxes and lines, in my mind trying to connect the dots where inexplicable gaps popped up. I wasn't looking for problem areas; I was only trying to get a grip on how I could blaze a pathway to the Olympics through all this confusing structure and governance. I can't say for sure, but this might have been the first time that any sort of business structure had been mapped out for the program, even if only from the outside. Nor did I realize that this was the tip of the iceberg when it came to reorienting and directing a skeleton program that would do so much for so many.

At the time, Viaciulis would have been justified had he gotten discouraged while rehashing with me the problems he already knew existed. He had been banging his head against this wall for fifteen years. On the contrary, though, the more he laid it all out for me, the more animated and excited the vivacious Viaciulis became. He sensed he was sitting across from someone who cared, who not only was crazy about skeleton, but was willing and able to take the lead in giving skeleton a long-awaited boost. If I were this willing to listen, then perhaps I would be willing to act. At the suggestion of Viaciulis, I agreed to make a modest contribution to the U.S. skeleton program, starting with $1500—that went a long way for amateur athletes who, by now, were pros at stretching a dollar.

I admit that I was hoping to endear myself to the athletes to some extent. I knew I was going to need their knowledge and support if I was going to have any chance at competing at the international level. It was soon after my meetings with Viaciulis that Jimmy and Chris won medals at the next World Cup event, in Altenberg, one of the toughest tracks in the world.

Peter, Jimmy, and Chris invited me to visit them during the 1997–98 international tour. I couldn't wait! I was eager to see in person what the World Cup and World Championships were all about. At the same time, a good friend of mine, Johnny T. L. Jones III, was turning forty years old and had asked me to join him for a European ski trip to celebrate his birthday. As the World Championships were being held in January 1998 at St. Moritz—the venerable home of sliding—we quickly decided to combine the two occasions.

In St. Moritz, we witnessed the skeleton rituals of equipment preparation and practice sessions, followed by the four-heat, two-day race itself. We met many of the foreign sliders and officials and were intrigued by their diverse and fun personalities. The day following the races, Johnny, Jimmy, Peter, and I skied all day on the grand glaciers of Corvatsch, which is across the valley and south from St. Moritz. It was a beautiful, sunny day, and I remember being impressed with Peter's skiing and Jimmy's snowboarding abilities. These guys were athletes!

These were interesting days for Taylor and me, feeling out this new opportunity and hoping it would continue to grow for us. Two old fogies sliding against men—boys, really—about half our age. The sport was still primitive, too. Witness our going into dumpsters to find enough cardboard to pack our sleds for air travel, something we actually did more than once. Taylor and I also learned that even though skeleton still was a relatively obscure sport, those who were out there sliding in Park City were well ahead of the skill level we had managed thus far. But Taylor and I weren't going to be daunted by that little detail. We had something up our sleeves, a viable option that we soon would explore and which could still get us to the Olympics, assuming, of course, that skeleton was going to make it into the Olympics for 2002.

That option was about as far removed from the slopes of Park City as . . . palm trees, coconuts, outrigger canoes, and Quonset huts. It was time to take skeleton . . . to the South Pacific.

CHAPTER SEVEN
Samoan Odyssey

Only those who risk going too far
can possibly find out how far one can go.
—T.S. Eliot

Sometimes the shortest distance between two points is a straight line in the opposite direction. That's the wisdom I gleaned from an ancient Asian fable one day in the early 1990s, when my son Robert, Jr. and I attended a presentation at St. Mark's School of Texas, in Dallas. Robert, at the time, was an elementary school student there. The motivation for our visit that day was to hear guest speaker U.S. Air Force Colonel Mike Mullane, who that day would captivate his audience, me included, with tales of what it took to become an astronaut.

I was all ears, probably the most apt listener in the audience. As a boy, I had dreamed of someday becoming an astronaut and blasting into space, exploring the unknown, venturing where few men, if any, had gone before. Space travel had been one of the pillars of my youthful three-pronged Walter Mitty dream, the fantasy also including competing in the Olympics and playing football at the University of Texas.

Colonel Mullane spoke that day of how he had calibrated his course from an early age, penning letters to the pioneer astronauts of the Mercury, Gemini, and Apollo programs. The young Mullane asked them all what he needed to do in order to take his future place among the stars. Out of all the answers he received, he culled two universal dicta—to study hard and to become a leader of his peers. It was advice well received. Mullane went on to graduate from West Point and become an army officer, later to switch to the air force after earning a master of science degree in aeronautical engineering from the Air Force Institute of Technology.

Mullane tried out to be a test pilot, in essence mirroring the prototypical career track to becoming a part of the astronaut corps. Things didn't go as planned, though. Colonel Mullane flunked the vision portion of his pilot physical, forcing him to abandon his dream of becoming an astronaut. Years later, when the National Aeronautics and Space Administration began accepting applications for space shuttle astronauts, it turns out they were also looking for mission specialists—biologists, geologists, doctors, and engineers. Colonel Mullane was among those selected for the first group of mission specialists. He would fly on three space missions while logging 356 hours in space, thus—in a roundabout way—living out his childhood dream.

Although Colonel Mullane's talk was geared to young students, his message hit home with me. That day's lesson: when it comes to success in life, point A to point B is usually not traveled in a direct line. Or, if it is traveled in a straight line, it might be in a straight line in the opposite direction, as in the old Chinese fable of two villages separated by a mountain range that could not be crossed. For whatever reason, residents of the western village desperately wanted to reach the village on the eastern side. Same thing for the easterners. After many years of trying to go over, through, around, or even under the mountain, villagers from both sides finally gave up.

Finally, one morning, a western villager showed up into the eastern village and announced his presence.

"How," the astonished eastern villagers asked the visitor, "did you make it across the mountain?"

"I didn't mean to arrive here," the western villager answered simply, in Zen-like manner. "For years I tried to cross. I trained my body and mind for the task of scaling the mountain, or digging under it, or going through it. I finally gave up, turned my back to the mountain, and began walking. That was years ago. Now here I am."

Let me tell you—I can relate to that. I'd like to believe I have been successful in applying the lessons, principles, and values of my life in business. Some of my pursuits have been successful. We've done well by doing right, and by recognizing opportunities, and in doing so we've benefited our customers, our employees, and our partners. We defined our goals and accomplished them in accordance with the plan.

But all of life isn't about business. My passions are believing in God, country, and family; in living a mentally and physically active, healthy life; and in sport. I have made it a point to seek a balance between family life, business, and my own desire to pursue sport. I have evolved into a runner, a skier, and a climber. Then there's the mother of all my sports passions—golf. It's kept me sane when the other priorities in my life have seemed frustrating or overwhelming, and it's kept me young and competitive when I see age slowing or dulling my contemporaries and peers.

My passion for sports, as well as for the oil and gas business, has driven me to experience many failures and few successes. Failures are irrelevant unless you learn from them. But it is the successes that propel you forward in life. Success, measured by accomplishing your goal, is the grade you receive when completing a race or project. It's a feeling that can't be cheated, faked, or given by others. But this is an evolutionary process—change is a fact of life.

Back to that metaphor about how you sometimes accomplish a goal or a dream, not by taking the direct route, but by taking the journey of life and staying true to your principles, beliefs, and values. In doing so, you sometimes find the potential to accomplish something bigger than your original dream. What I found in a journey that took almost a decade—but which I had imagined since I was a young boy—was the truth from that ancient Asian fable about the shortest distance between two points being a straight line in the opposite direction.

My trip in the opposite direction, along with Boyd, would eventually include hopping onto an airplane, flying to Hawaii, then connecting and heading farther west out over the Pacific Ocean to a tropical island paradise—one where naturally occurring snow or ice is as rare as a Speedo-clad skeleton racer on a sub-zero day in Lake Placid.

Welcome to American Samoa, since 1900 a U.S. territory. White sand beaches silhouetted by palm trees; reefs teeming with a colorful, rich diversity of coral, fish, and other marine species; lush tropical forests dripping from recent rain showers; and island people carrying out customs and traditions thousands of years old. Located fourteen degrees below the equator, American Samoa, population about seventy thousand residents, five rugged volcanic islands, and two coral atolls, is the southernmost U.S. territory, unincorporated and 98 percent Christian. Grab a map and a pencil and draw a triangle formed by lines connecting Hawaii, New Zealand, and Tahiti. Next, jab a finger in the middle and you can almost touch American Samoa, often referred to as "the heart of Polynesia." As the bird flies, it is twenty-three hundred miles southwest of Hawaii, fifteen hundred miles northeast of New Zealand, and a whole load of time zones away from Dallas County.

It is believed that Samoans represent the world's largest population of Polynesian people, who are famously bound by family loyalties and who take great pride in an enduring culture that has survived amazingly well outside incursions from the likes of Brits, Germans, and Yanks. Not everything about American Samoa remains South Pacific virgin pure as portrayed in the touristy descriptions; much of the territory has been hastily Americanized since the 1960s, leaving behind pockets of commercial and cultural imperialism that nonetheless fail to slow down the stream of travelers who flock year round to this picturesque getaway.

The locals remain refreshingly polite and friendly to their intrusive visitors, and Polynesian customs and practices for the most part remain intact. "Add to this," said an excerpt from the *Lonely Planet World Guide* assessment of American Samoa, "the trademark Pacific islands' weather and an astonishingly picturesque landscape, and you've got a recipe for an intoxicating cocktail of rough liquor and smooth coconut milk."

This is not the first place someone would think of to pursue a winter sport that requires cold, snow, and ice. In most cases, those who do make it to American Samoa are looking to flee from those very things. Or, in rare cases, to find something much more elusive, such as the Olympic pot at the end of the rainbow. For someone with a sincere desire to make it to the Winter Olympics, even if it means a detour of thousands of miles and leaving behind the red, white, and blue, American Samoa offers an option attractive in more ways than one. To Taylor Boyd and me in 1998, it looked like a sweet-spot destination for combining a coveted South Pacific excursion with a search for an Olympic-certified entity. They just might have openings for a couple of intrepid American skeleton sliders.

The more Boyd hung out and raced against top-notch U.S. sliders like Shea and Soule, the more he realized that he and I might need an alternative plan if we were going to fulfill our shared dream of making it to the Olympics. Boyd diligently studied international eligibility rules to see what he could turn up in terms of an alternate path to the Games, still assuming, or hoping, that skeleton would get five-ring status by 2002.

Boyd turned over every rock he could to find a way in. Who did he know? What other country might be willing to let him slide for them? Then it came to him: He had buddies in the sliding world who were friends with Monaco's

Prince Albert, an avid bobsled racer who had been competing for years. Boyd asked a friend to broach the subject to Prince Albert, to see if there was any way that an American, Boyd himself perhaps, could slide for Monaco.

"Albert said, 'Yeah, but if skeleton ever gets to the Olympics, my aide-de-camp gets to do it,'" Boyd recalled. "So that was a dead end."

Back to poring through the rules and regulations. Boyd stumbled across something else that caught his eye and inspired another idea: the means to prove your citizenship in order to slide for any particular country is a passport. As he continued to burn the midnight oil, Boyd discovered something else quite fascinating: while the American territories are treated by the International Olympic Committee as separate nations, they all utilize the same passport—an American one. Boyd was as giddy as a schoolboy. Like an archeologist who had just found a long-hidden clue to the Holy Grail, he had unwittingly found an apparent Olympics opening that soon would have us flying to American Samoa.

First, though, Boyd started by contacting Puerto Rico. The good news was that Puerto Rico was open to allowing Boyd to race skeleton for them; the catch was a stipulation in their Olympic committee rule book that says in order to represent the Caribbean island, a U.S. territory, a competitor needed residency for at least three of the four years going into an Olympics. Neither Boyd nor I were about to pack up and move to Puerto Rico, despite our magnificent Olympic dreams.

Next up was Guam, another American territory. Boyd was ex-navy. Considering the U.S. Navy's close association with Guam, Boyd felt good about his chances there. Plus, he knew an admiral who knew an admiral who knew the governor of Guam. The second admiral contacted the governor, who in turn sent back word that it wasn't a good idea. Guam was squeamish about having an American represent it in the Olympics because of a snafu involving a recent Miss Guam. A young American woman had represented Guam in the Miss Universe contest. When she failed to win that title, the U.S.-bred Miss Guam flew back to the mainland and shirked her year-long responsibilities to Guam involved in wearing the crown.

So in a May 1998 fax, an official of the Guam National Olympic Committee wrote Boyd to curtly tell him that the territory now had a five-year residency rule, "with clear indication that the purpose of entry and residence is for the purpose of relocating and not for the purpose of qualifying. At this time, we are not interested in supporting or promoting your field of sport."

Disappointed but undaunted, Boyd worked his way down his short list of prospects to American Samoa. In November 1997, he faxed a letter initiating contact with the territory's Olympic officials. His biggest ally in the process would be Ken Tupua, secretary general of the American Samoa Bobsled Association. American Samoa had sent a two-man bob team to the 1994 Olympics in Lillehammer and was a member of all the right federations, including the FIBT—the international bobsled and skeleton governing body. But American Samoa didn't have a skeleton team. A door had been opened. Welcome to American Samoa, gentlemen.

"They were kind of reticent about it at first," Boyd said. "Then they said, 'We would like to meet you.' I made arrangements in July 1998 for Robie and me to fly out to American Samoa, out there in the middle of nowhere. Only two flights a week (originating in Hawaii) go out there, which is why Ken Tupua used to tell us, 'Don't send anything Federal Express because it comes on the same flight as the regular mail.'

"Samoa is this little island. It took us about nine hours from Hawaii to get there. We found one hotel there, the Rainmaker, a big Polynesian hut kind of thing. The Samoan Olympic Committee was meeting in a Quonset hut down at the beach, where all these outrigger canoes, just like the ones you see on *Hawaii Five-0*, were pulled up on the beach. We met Ken and his associates, then we went out and opened a bank account and got our American Samoan driver's licenses. We went to dinner with the VIPs and presented ourselves as normal Americans. They finally got comfortable with us. At this point, Robie and I were of the opinion that our way to the Olympics would be in sliding for American Samoa."

Boyd and I ended up spending a week in American Samoa before returning home to Texas. All of the people we met in American Samoa were so hospitable and nice. Taylor and I seemed to form a mutual bond with Ken and his associates. Further, we had decided to make annual charitable contributions to American Samoa's Olympic training program (for summer events) and to train interested men and women there in the sport of skeleton. By this time, Salt Lake City had long been awarded the 2002 Olympic Winter Games, and the new sliding track in Park City had just been opened, giving sliders a second American track to go, along with the Lake Placid venue.

There still was one hitch, and it was something that wouldn't occur to Boyd until after leaving behind the hula skirts and luaus to return to the United States.

It was a matter of simple math, and it had eluded Boyd during all these months of plowing the ground with American Samoan Olympic officials. Even if he were to slide skeleton for the South Pacific territory, and even if skeleton were added to the Olympic agenda for the 2002 Games, he likely would still be odd man out. With American Samoa being so small, circumstances portended a scenario in which it would get only one men's skeleton slot, if any, for the 2002 Games, and by this time I had clearly moved ahead of Boyd on a competitive scale. There certainly would not be room for the both of us.

"I started realizing what an idiot I was," Boyd said. "By having Robie come along with me on the trip to American Samoa, I had just cut myself out of the pattern. I would have had the straight ticket had I gone to American Samoa alone. With Robie there, he would beat me out for that one spot, and then he'd have the ticket.

"So I made a decision right on the spot, before the 1998–99 season began, to switch to two-man bobsled and try to make it to the Olympics that way. I figured I would recruit some American Samoan guys to try out to be my brakeman. Through the Pan American Society in Salt Lake City, I ended up finding this kid named Oa Misifoa, from American Samoa. He was nineteen, a recent high school graduate and football player whose family had just moved to Utah, and he was trying to get a football scholarship to go to college."

Boyd met Misifoa in October 1998. I happened to be up at the Park City track the evening Taylor sent Oa down the track in a tourist sled for his first slide. I was near the finish area and could hear Oa screaming as he slid through the bottom sections of the track and those high-G turns. It was hilarious. They were soon off to Innsbruck, Austria, to take part in a bobsleigh school in preparation for the 1998–99 racing season. They would compete in two America's Cup races at Park City in late January, and then it was on to Calgary in February for a couple more America's Cup events. They weren't winning medals, but the Boyd-Misifoa bob team was generating word of mouth. Everywhere he went, Misifoa was sought out by TV and print reporters intrigued by the presence of this American Samoa bobsled team. The attention Misifoa and, to some extent his teammate Boyd, received was reminiscent of the embrace the media put on the Jamaican bobsled team at the 1988 Games in Calgary—the same Jamaican team that became the inspiration for the movie *Cool Runnings,* starring John Candy.

One TV reporter from a local station corralled Misifoa for an interview. According to Boyd, this is how the exchange went:

"So, Oa, have you ever done the bobsled before?"

"We invented the bobsled. Have you ever been to American Samoa?"

"No."

"Well, in Samoa, the plantations are very steep, and the banana trees grow all the way to the top. When you go to harvest the bananas, you stay up there all day long and chop the bananas down. Then you put them in large bags and slide them down the hill at the end of the day. We've been doing this forever. All you guys did was add the snow."

Boyd and Misifoa, despite a thirty years' difference in age and vastly different cultural backgrounds, clicked as a bob team through 1998–99 and into 1999–2000. With their continued pace of development, they were solid picks to represent American Samoa at the 2002 Salt Lake City Olympic Games. Boyd saw the New Zealand team as their main rival for the two-man bob team that would come out of a virtual continent known as "Oceana." Under a Continental Rule established by the FIBT, any continent that participated in the World Cup competition was allowed to send one two-man bob team to the Olympics. Because no other nation under the umbrella of Oceana had accrued the points necessary for automatic qualification, an Olympic spot was available for Boyd's and Misifoa's taking, provided they could beat the New Zealanders down the road during Olympic qualifying.

For the time being, in 1998 and 1999, Boyd's Olympic dream still burned, albeit with his newfound association with American Samoa and two-man bobsled. Things would change, however, in January 2000. After Boyd's first divorce, he had been living the relatively unfettered life of a bachelor traveling the world sliding. Now he remarried. As a wedding gift, Boyd's second wife helped him buy a new bobsled at a cost of $24,000. But like many bass boats and new sets of golf clubs that over the years have seen the light of a wedding day, Boyd's wedding gift was about to start gathering dust.

"Soon after we got married," Boyd said, "I told my new wife that I would be gone for a couple of months training and racing. I soon realized that this was not a good move for the health of my new marriage and made the decision to commit myself to my marriage instead of my Olympic dream." He didn't follow his instincts and stay true to himself.

The irony of fates involving Boyd and me would again nip at Boyd following a chain of events that started occurring in early fall 1998, when he had abandoned skeleton cold turkey to switch his attention to the two-man bob for American Samoa.

The newly opened Park City track would get its first christening of major skeleton racing in November 1998 as the host of the 1998–99 U.S. national team trials. The three-heat competition would be the best two of three, with A and B teams selected for both the men and the women. Based on the previous year's World Cup nations' rankings, in which the U.S. men had finished as the world's fifth-best team, the Americans would be allowed to race four men in the 1998–99 World Cup competitions and three in the World Championships. I had assumed that the fourth men's World Cup spot was for an alternate as had been he case for the 1997–98 season. The U.S. women, who had placed sixth among the 1997–98 women's teams, had earned two World Cup slots, although there were no women's World Championships at the time.

When the three-heat U.S. trials' results were announced, the men's A team, ranked in order, consisted of Jimmy Shea, Terry Holland, Lincoln DeWitt, me, and Ralph Mirabelli. The women's A team was Juleigh Walker, Babs Isak, and Fallon Vaughn. The women's B teamers were no slouches—they included Tristan Gale and Lea Ann Parsley. The biggest news of the day was that Fallon and I had both made the first string, unprecedented in U.S. skeleton history to that point.

It wasn't until the post-trials meeting and celebration that I learned that I was more than just an alternate—I was a full-fledged member of the U.S. men's World Cup team and would be competing worldwide as such.

Colonel Mullane's words ran through my mind, and my eyes welled with tears at the prospect of representing the United States in international competition. But it was a mixed victory, too. On the one hand, I could now compete for the United States, but that would preclude the other plan Taylor and I had been working on—becoming Olympic athletes by representing American Samoa, which we had considered a good possibility. Sure, we'd be in the Olympics, but we would be representing a territory, not the United States we were from. It was a Sophie's choice—which of the two cherished possibilities do you let go to save the other?

Should I slide for the United States and represent my country in sport for what likely would be a one-shot deal for that year, or do I give that up and represent American Samoa for the next three years in World Cup competition and most probably make it into the Olympic Winter Games as an athlete? Call it old-fashioned, or maybe it was the way I was raised. Perhaps it's the Texas in me. I believe in patriotism, principles, and tradition. I'm not talking about the grandstanding, "My flag lapel pin is bigger than yours" kind of patriotism, but the kind that means you give of yourself and make a sacrifice for something bigger.

I wanted to serve. I chose to compete on behalf of the United States of America, even if it meant never being an Olympic athlete. International federation rules state that once you slide for a particular country in a sanctioned event, even if just once, you can never slide in a sanctioned event for another nation. In committing to the U.S. team as a World Cup slider, I was letting go of American Samoa."

I was now committed to the United States, even with the realization I likely would not still be on the team three years later in Salt Lake City. Boyd was now out of skeleton and onto bobsled so the American Samoa skeleton connection was moot. Neither Boyd nor I would be racing skeleton for the small territory. Ken Tupua was most graceful and supportive of my decision—those are some good people out there in American Samoa.

Boyd now had bobsled, and I was about to be up to my eyeballs in sporting politics, charged with a goal even more ambitious and maybe even unattainable—to hatch a grand plan to turn American skeleton into an Olympic-medal-worthy program, with or without the assistance or cooperation of the USBSF. By comparison, sliding down St. Moritz at nearly eighty miles per hour was a kid's game.

Just a few weeks after the last post-trial champagne bottle had been emptied, Fallon and I became the first spouses to slide as national team members in a World Cup event, which took place at Park City in December 1998. One challenge had been met, but for me at least, the fun was only beginning. I was now ice-spike deep in U.S. skeleton, giving me a vantage point that provided a better view of how U.S. skeleton worked and didn't work.

I was about to find a whole lot of red tape to go with all that white ice. I soon realized that my most demanding work in the world of skeleton was only just beginning, and the off-track obstacles I would encounter far outnumbered the neck-numbing curves from all the sliding tracks around the world, combined.

Skeleton can be a cold, cold world.

CHAPTER EIGHT
A Slippery Slope

*Be a yardstick of quality. Some people aren't used to an
environment where excellence is expected.*
—Steve Jobs

It was one of the greatest achievements in U.S. bobsled history: the
unforgettable 1956 Olympic medal-winning moment still talked about over the
water cooler at United States Bobsled and Skeleton Federation headquarters in
Lake Placid. Mention the medal to a devoted American bobsledder, then take
another step forward and count the goose bumps.

The American Olympic hero was a Kodak engineer named Art Tyler, who
piloted a four-man sled he himself had designed and built to win a spot on the
medal stand. With his slick contraption on ice, Tyler won a bronze medal at
Cortina, Italy. It was a proud moment in U.S. Olympic bobsled history, rightfully
so, an accomplishment that continues to grow in significance in terms of defining
the legacy, good and bad, of the USBSF. In retrospect, Tyler's feat marked a
momentous first as well as a last for the sport of bobsled: his was the first sled
ever to use an articulated front and back, and it would be the last bobsled medal
won by an American for more than forty years.

Tyler won his bronze medal in 1956, and until 2002, no American bobsledder
had since won an Olympic medal. Nearly fifty years went by between bobsled
medals, and a lot happened in the interim. Sputnik. Color TV. Vietnam. Disco.
Star Wars. Star wars. The Me Decade. Saddam. Dot-com. Saddam. The birth,
life, and death of JFK, Jr. At the same time Tyler was racing to Olympic bronze,
I was a Dallas tyke, a month old and more than four decades away from realizing
one of my biggest challenges in life. It would not be scaling a twenty-four-

thousand-foot peak in China, drilling for oil in Alaska, or freely swinging a four-iron 195 yard shot—over the chasm protecting Carmel Bay—to the eighth green at Pebble Beach. It would be trying to talk some dollars and sense into the USBSF, a good-ole-boy network at that time.

My first serious foray into the sport of skeleton would play out like a microcosm of ABC's *Wide World of Sports'* unforgettable refrain: for me, the thrill of victory came in qualifying for the U.S. national team in 1998; the agony of defeat was, early on, trying to get U.S. skeleton fully funded and in a credible position to make a run at some medals once the International Olympic Committee bestowed its blessings on skeleton.

For that to happen, all ice trails would lead through the offices on Old Military Road, in Lake Placid, New York, home to the USBSF. The Iron Curtain, having long disappeared from Europe, had found a new home in Lake Placid. Some of the apparent weaknesses of the USBSF were lack of financial wherewithal and independence; lack of a definitive and disciplined business plan; poor communication among officers, staff, athletes, and members; no marketing personnel; no personnel devoted to skeleton; no brand ownership; weak administrative and coaching management; little competitive depth; a low level of trust among the athletes, staff, and coaching; and a lack of Olympic performance, with no medals since 1956. Frankly, the USBSF was not fulfilling some of its obligations and responsibilities as designated by the United States Olympic Committee's by-laws. Most troubling was the obvious cultural and communications dislocation among the officers, directors, and staff, and that of the athletes and the membership as a whole.

Viewed from the outside, there's a lot about skeleton that can have a strong, alluring pull on an outdoor sportsman. Its intriguing appeal involves speed, a sense of danger, intense competition measured in hundredths of a second, a chance to see the world, and a bonding camaraderie that transcends culture, creed, and socioeconomic status. Once inside the bubble, though, a skeleton slider discovers that he or she is part of a sport with little infrastructure, minimal outside assistance, no financial safety nets, and the unspoken requirement to keep personal credit cards handy. That was the scenario that I slid into when I upgraded my skeleton involvement from recreational curiosity to competitive preoccupation.

Other veteran sliders shared their war stories with me. Left stranded in the lobby of a European hotel, unable to pay the bill when a USBSF-promised allotment of funds suddenly vanished. The sliders were standing around between runs, their extremities freezing, listening to the usual drivel about how skeleton would be making it into the Olympics next time around, catching glimpses of the USBSF logo, letterhead, business cards, signage, etc., with references to skeleton nowhere to be found. Skeleton was part of the USBSF's name, but skeleton wasn't really in the game. How can you expect to gain Olympic status when your own national governing body hasn't gone to bat for you? It took awhile, but eventually the USBSF would slowly begin making cultural changes, such as changing the name of its newsletter from *The Bobserver* to *The Icebreaker*.

The USBSF offices in Lake Placid had just a "Bobsled" sign beside the entry door for years. This was pretty typical. Details matter, especially to the psyche of the athlete. Lou Gerstner, IBM chief executive officer, wrote a book that could just as well have been relevant to the USBSF. In *Elephants Can't Dance: Inside IBM's Historic Turnaround*, Gerstner embraces the notion that nothing in business is more valuable than a powerful corporate culture, one in which all managers are in sync in how they approach change. A voracious reader of such works, I knew that if the USBSF was to be united as one organization, cultural differences would have to be addressed and bridged, which would take effective leadership and vision.

The trick for skeleton would become one of laying a separate foundation for skeleton, and I already had a mechanism in place. Even before winning a spot on the U.S. national team, I had worked with Taylor Boyd and Clay Roark, the slider and coach from Calgary, to incorporate a new not-for-profit organization that would become known as the Texas Sliding Society. By-laws and articles of incorporation were drafted in the late winter of 1998 and submitted on March 2 to the Texas secretary of state. The timing wasn't entirely coincidental: March 2 is also celebrated in the Lone Star State as Texas Independence Day. The Texas Sliding Society would give us our own island of sovereignty from which to build and operate the sport, with contributions from friends and sponsors. Not that we were trying to be totally autonomous—much of the wording used in drafting the sliding society's legal papers was drawn from similar documents of the USBSF—just refined, updated, and streamlined.

The following Texas Sliding Society mission statement was drafted:

"TSS is organized, for the purpose of, and shall be operated to promote the sport of bobsled and/or skeleton sliding locally, nationally, and internationally; to introduce, develop, train, advise, and promote male and female athletes from

Texas to the sport of bobsled and/or skeleton sliding; to introduce, develop, train, advise, and promote junior or youth bobsled and/or skeleton programs for boys and girls; to participate in the sports of bobsled and/or skeleton sliding at the highest competitive levels possible; to develop recreational bobsled and/or skeleton sliding as well as competitive racing teams; to assist in the procurement of equipment and gear for training and competition and to insure that said equipment is maintained in the best possible condition; and to promote sportsmanship and camaraderie on and off the track."

The Texas Sliding Society wasted no time making an impact. It held its first meeting and a separate fundraiser in the fall of 1998, raising more than $10,400 to cover an annual budget earmarked to fund marketing costs, the two skeleton schools directed by Roark, and skeleton athlete sponsorships. With actual revenues exceeding budgeted expenditures, TSS was able to allocate $2,350 in additional funding that went for travel expense reimbursement to coaches Peter Viaciulis and Dave Graham, and to veteran slider Juleigh Walker. The following March, the society was able to reimburse Viaciulis another $2,266 that he had spent to cover slider and future Olympian Lea Ann Parsley's European training. In just twelve months of existence, the Texas Sliding Society was filling a piece of the financial void in the skeleton program.

"It seems like so small an amount of funding," Parsley said, "but it makes all the difference in the world to someone who is young, inexperienced, and spending anywhere from forty to eighty hours a week training and conditioning—which doesn't pay any wages. I couldn't have done half as well as I ended up doing without that experience I gained in Europe, and I'll forever owe the Texas Sliding Society. They built the foundations of a medal-winning team."

While TSS was showing the money, not everyone was showing love. During the USBSF annual meeting in August 1999, I had proposed a pledge, on behalf of the Texas Sliding Society, of a six-figure investment that would ambitiously finance the entire U.S. national team's skeleton budget for an entire year. The president of the USBSF at the time was taken aback and mentioned that this was the largest contribution in the history of the USBSF. During the discussion phase of this skeleton funding proposal, several bobsled athletes made it clear to the (USBSF) board that they were not happy about the lack of financial support for the bobsled programs as "their" budget always seemed to be shrinking. Now with skeleton sufficiently funded for the year (1999–2000), they wanted the same—and no one could blame them. Inherent cultural differences between the bobsled administrators and coaches, and the skeleton sliders, were surfacing under the pressure, like fault lines in continental shelves. The athletes were coming to recognize that the USBSF had not served bobsled well nor skeleton at all. Now the bobsled athletes were beginning to realize they had been boiling to a slow death under the management of the USBSF since 1956. At one point, a frustrated and confused athlete was heard to angrily mumble with paranoia, "Who is this Texas *Secret* Society?"

In order to make all this work, giving skeleton the financial backing and administrative clout it needed and deserved, I had to walk the tightrope of ensuring funding of skeleton to the point where the sport could operate somewhat autonomously and yet still be sanctioned by the USBSF. TSS was donation-driven. Anyone contributing funds to TSS doing business as USA Skeleton, would do so only if they had assurance that their contributions would not end up in the treasury of the USBSF, which could disburse those skeleton-earmarked funds as it saw fit. It was generally felt that the money would float away from skeleton and into administrative or other uses. USA Skeleton was wary of USBSF's past financial challenges and its bias in favoring an underfunded bobsled program.

The foundation of the USA Skeleton challenges structure was the Skeleton Program Committee (SPC). It included USBSF executive director Matt Roy; me as skeleton program director; Davenport as coach; Viaciulis, as an assistant coach; and two athlete-elected representatives from amongst their ranks, with said elections to be held annually. Sliders, who just a few years earlier had been racing without funding and without a say, now had both. I asked the USBSF board to approve the SPC as an official committee of the federation, and they did. The SPC—not bobsled coaches, USBSF administrators, the president, or the board, as they did for bobsled—made operational and management decisions for the skeleton program. We operated as an outsourced contractee in today's business terminology, which meant that the USBSF did very little for skeleton but would get all the credit. And that was okay with us because we now had something new and different in terms of the ability to grow and be productive. And more importantly, we—the athletes included—knew we could be successful through this structure. There was complete buy-in.

The story of how a forty-something oil-company executive departed the board room long enough to enter a phone booth and jump out a world-class skeleton slider might have been even more compelling had I gone on to compete in the Olympics. But it became clear as the 1998–99 World Cup sliding season unfolded that my best shot at making it into the Winter Olympics would be as a champion for the athletes or a facilitator, but not as a slider. I had earned my way onto the U.S. national team. Competing under the flag with the five interlocking rings was a whole different story.

No harm in trying, though. As a World Cup rookie, I notched top-thirty finishes in two of the four World Cup races, finishing twenty-eighth at Park City on December 5 and then twenty-seventh, thirty-six hundredths of a second ahead of teammate and future Olympian Lincoln DeWitt—a rookie as well—a week later in Calgary. My worst World Cup finish that first season was thirty-ninth at Koenigssee, Germany, although a day later I posted a surprising sixteenth-place finish in the Stubai Cup held in Igls, Austria. Both of these races were affected by heavy snowfall, working to my disadvantage in the first race but to my advantage in the second. At the season-ending 1999 American Championships in Park City, I placed third. Fallon, who had been the U.S. women's first alternate in World Cup competition, took third place in the women's race, behind winner Juleigh Walker and runner-up Tricia Stumpf. In retrospect, Fallon's consolation was besting the likes of future Olympian Tristan Gale and the U.S. women's number two World Cup slider that season, Babs Isak.

It's no surprise that my best World Cup finish had been at Calgary. I considered that my home track, where I was most comfortable and confident. My strong showing at the Stubai Cup at Igls boded well for me with the upcoming World Championships in Altenberg coming up in two weeks and with the benefit of an off week in between for some rest. At the invitation of Canadian coach Markus Kottmann, a native of Switzerland, I altered my off-week plans and agreed to meet Kottman the following weekend at St. Moritz. This would be a rare chance to slide at skeleton's venerable birthplace and to do so without the pressure of World Cup competition. The St. Moritz invite was skeleton's equivalent to a member's invitation to play a round of golf at Augusta National Golf Club in Georgia, or at the Cypress Point Club in California—the best of the best for many reasons, including the people, the quality, and the traditions and history.

I was familiar with the St. Moritz track, having visited there exactly a year earlier as a spectator to the World Championships. This time I would go there as a seasoned slider, accompanied by Kottmann as well as a pair of fellow World Cup rookies, Canadians Deanna Panting and Turc Harmesynn. I made the long drive from Munich, Germany, to St. Moritz, arriving the night before we would take our scenic runs.

I recalled from the World Championships the year before that the toughest section of the track was a tight, 180-degree left turn called "Horseshoe" nearly halfway down the track. We began our first run about a third of the way down so we could gain enough confidence and get a feel for the technique so that we could be ready to try going from the top on our next run with less risk of seriously injuring ourselves.

Markus, who in the past had competed for Switzerland and knew the track, suggested entering Horseshoe on the left, a technique also referred to in sliding as "late." Normally, one would enter a left turn in the middle-to-right side, or "early." However, Horseshoe was a very tight turn and required aggressive "driving" in order to exit without losing time (or worse). Markus assured us that by entering the turn late, it would be easier to negotiate it smoothly and safely. The first run was as exciting and awesome as I had anticipated. I had no problems negotiating Horseshoe at the lower speed, and the track was smooth, beautiful, and fast. Very fast.

Our second run began from the top of the track, at the bobsled start. I had memorized and visualized the run and was relaxed. But I was also anxious, as this was my first full run on a track new to me. My name was called first, and so I toed the line and pushed off. The run was going well as my speed compounded, and I was entering and exiting turns just as I had planned. The trees of the surrounding forest were flying by me, but everything was smooth. As I approached Horseshoe, I lined up my sled just left of center and hit my entrance perfectly. Horseshoe, however, had been redesigned in the years since Markus had last slid there, with the turn, unbeknownst to me at full speed, now requiring an early entrance so that the centrifugal force would not push the slider too far up the wall of the turn. I entered late, though, and tried to correct by keeping the sled low. I kept it too low. Upon exiting the turn, the laws of physics forced my sled up and into the overhanging roof of the exit portion of the turn. The next thing I remembered was waking up, sliding on my back in the track about a hundred feet below the Horseshoe exit.

I was able to get up and walk off the track with the assistance of two track workers. Breathing was difficult and painful, as was any attempt to lift my left arm. Taylor, Fallon, and I all got our lumps in this sport, and this was my turn—in a serious way. X-rays at the time were negative, although two years later a routine x-ray would reveal several calcified hairline fractures in my left rib cage. Needless to say, I was done at St. Moritz and in no shape to race in the World

Championships the following week.

It wasn't Markus's fault. I had just learned another valuable lesson in skeleton sliding: never assume you are good enough to slide a new track prior to watching others slide through the difficult sections and walking the track each day before sliding. Whenever risks are to be taken, proper due diligence is required in order to expect productive results. I was continuing to pay my dues. With interest. And taxes.

Other sliders injured to the extent I was might have opted to take the next flight home so they could nurse their wounds back in the United States, but I soldiered on to Altenberg. If I couldn't race in the World Championships, I could at least be there to offer encouragement to my teammates. At the very least, I could chauffeur folks around Altenberg, nestled in northeastern Germany between the restored city of Dresden and the Czechoslovakian border.

Unlike St. Moritz, Altenberg—cold and remote—didn't resound with Old European charm. It had been built by the East Germans in secrecy during the height of the Cold War. For many years, like most training venues utilized by Eastern bloc nations, it had been kept hidden from public view. It was a remote and treacherous track, specially engineered to incorporate the toughest sections of all known tracks around the world. It was yet another of Doc Frankenstein's hidden sports laboratories, where stone-faced, tight-lipped scientists, tethered to the Communist ideal of political advancement through athletic achievement, aspired to develop new formulas that would further advance the limits of human performance.

Altenberg is a brutal track—long, fast, and technically challenging. Unforgiving. Intimidating. Cotton-mouth scary. Foreboding. Long after Ronald Reagan beseeched Mikhail Gorbachev to "tear down that wall," Altenberg remained surrounded by barbed wire and a tank positioned at the entrance gate, leftover reminders of the Cold War. At times, on especially frigid days when the overcast sky looms a dark gray, Altenberg can feel like some sort of Gulag California, where it briefly dawns on a visitor that while it's possible to check in, there's also a chance you won't be allowed to check out.

Sliders have come close to checking out, for good, at Altenberg. Pity the Canadian slider, who, at the 1999 World Championships, came out of a turn late and smashed into the track wall, knocking him unconscious. Footage of the crash shot by Eurosport shows the slider's unconscious, seemingly lifeless body skidding limply down the track until his inertia finally ran out of steam.

It's a horrific scene that makes the crashing ski jumper in the "agony of defeat" sequence from ABC's *Wide World of Sports* opener look like a mild spill. The injured Canadian slider was evacuated via ambulance, as were two other sliders that same day. Lake Placid's old wood-splintering track and Altenberg's Death Spiral were in a class to themselves.

You could say that danger was slider Jimmy Shea's middle name. Shea, then rising as one of the top sliders in the world, had an affinity for Altenberg. The tougher the track, the better Shea performed on ice, and this week would be no exception. He had won a 1997–98 World Cup race at Altenberg, and here he was back again, this time with a world championship on the line. Shea's father, Jim Shea, Sr., a member of the 1964 U.S. Olympic Nordic combined team, had made the trip to Germany to cheer on his son.

By weekend's end, the Sheas and I had gotten to know each other a lot better. My injury was a long-term blessing in disguise. It forced me off the track and into a position of getting to know my fellow Americans from a different perspective—a leadership perspective. Unable to race but itching to be a part of the U.S. cause, I became a de facto coach in Altenberg, stepping in to assist Coach Peter Viaciulis and assistant Dave Graham, driving athletes around and helping to ensure that they would stay on schedule. Instead of being one of Shea's sliding rivals, I became a confidante that weekend, forging a bond that would be key over the next three years during our march to the 2002 Salt Lake City Olympic Games. Viaciulis also fell sick for a few days from some kind of virus he caught in Prague, and I helped pick up some of the coaching duties that week.

I drove the Sheas, Snorre Pederson, and his Norwegian teammate to the track and back each day for training and racing. I took video coverage of our athletes as well as their most threatening competitors, throughout the Kriesel (a 360-degree turn), and other critical sections of the track. It snowed hard much of the week, which is why it was a good thing that I had rented a Range Rover. The heavy vehicle allowed us to drive each day to the top of the track, ignoring the track officials at the upper-road section of the track and thus eliminating the need to lug eighty-plus-pound sleds and clothing bags from the parking area to the top of the track, a stretch of about a hundred yards or so uphill. Jimmy really got a kick out of us waving at the track officials as we drove past them up the hill, while they were frantically trying to wave us into the lower parking area.

One afternoon, with a few hours of free time on our hands, Shea and I drove to Dresden, the nearby city that had been virtually demolished by Allied bombing during World War II. We walked and toured the fabulous architecture of the palace grounds, with me being the voice of calming reason, talking with Shea to help give the topnotch slider a reprieve from the mounting pressure that went with being one of the favorites in the upcoming race on a treacherous track. I was unaware of it at the time, but I was filling a role that Viaciulis had performed for years, often rising early on the day of races to take long walks with Shea, using those times of solitude to mentally prepare Shea for that day's runs. I was trying to provide him a bit of relief. We were indeed establishing a bond, and a genuine friendship.

This was Shea's week, and it would turn out to be a pivotal week for U.S. skeleton, and, as the dominoes fell, for the movement to get skeleton into the Olympics. Shea turned in a first run of 59.91 seconds, giving him the early lead and a .04-second edge over Canadian Ryan Davenport the 1996 and 1997 world champion.

Shea led from wire to wire for the two-day event over the four runs, eventually winning the championship with a total time of 4:00.22, giving him a comfortable edge of more than a half second over runner-up Andy Bohme of Germany, and making him the first American to win a skeleton World Championship. He won a bronze medal as well for finishing third overall in the final World Cup standings.

After finishing his fourth run as the victor, Shea was escorted by Viaciulis to drug testing, where he would have to wait in a back room until he was able to urinate. He hadn't been drinking much in the way of fluids that day and was dehydrated. He would need some help.

"This was before they had many rules," Viaciulis said. "There was a case of beer sitting in there, and Jimmy asked if he could have one. Someone went out and found some cigars for us, so there we were a little later, drinking some beers and enjoying our cigars."

It was a great moment for Shea and U.S. skeleton in general. Things were starting to click, and we knew this would help broaden the awareness of skeleton in the United States. More significantly than that, it would add momentum to get skeleton into the Olympics.

I was also seeing something that I would use later, something I might have missed had I not been injured that weekend. Driven by a passion for the sport and a desire to do something, anything, positive as I convalesced, I was beginning to recognize and categorize what it takes to motivate a team of athletes and provide them the support—logistical and otherwise—that they needed in order to be champions. Still, if skeleton was going to make it onto the Salt Lake City program for 2002, a lot would have to happen in a short period of time. And it wasn't going to happen without vision, action, and manpower provided by the national governing body, the USBSF.

Help was needed for the heavy lifting, and it would take an outsider with the kind of clout that gets people elected governor of a state. The man with the muscle would be Mitt Romney, who would step forward to rescue the Salt Lake City Games from what could have been a devastating bribery scandal involving two key members of the Salt Lake Organizing Committee. Less than eight months after the 2002 Games, Romney would parlay his Olympic organizing experience and leadership into winning the Massachusetts gubernatorial race. In all likelihood, that made Romney the first skeleton-sliding governor in American history.

Shea had introduced Romney to the sport soon after Shea had returned to the United States following his World Championship victory at Altenberg. Romney's enchantment with skeleton was almost immediate, and he would become the cleanup hitter skeleton needed to get into the Olympics for 2002. First, though, there was plenty of housework to be done in the here and now for strengthening the U.S. skeleton program, and it would take much more than just a broom and dust rag.

With the 1998–99 sliding season complete, I was ready and willing to resume doing the dirty work. In the afterglow of Shea's golden victory at Altenberg, the USBSF kept its celebration to a dull snore. There would be no additional administrative staff, budgeting, or management plan for skeleton. Less than three years to go, presumably, to the 2002 Winter Olympics, and U.S. skeleton was still without an officially sanctioned supporter.

There would be no skeleton off-season for me. On April 30, 1999, I sent USBSF executive director Matt Roy a sixty-five-word memorandum proposing that a skeleton program director be designated so that a program to fund skeleton could be initiated. On May 21, a Friday, the USBSF held a meeting in which it authorized the creation of a skeleton program director's position, and I was picked to fill the slot. Two days later, armed with extensive notes I had compiled for months, I fired off to Roy an e-mail that went into much more detail as to what needed to be done. It was an opening salvo. It read like a business executive summary, an abbreviated action plan that challenged the USBSF's status quo on skeleton and other matters. This mission statement touched on a number of steps that I planned to take. Among them were:

* Coordinating accounting/budgeting and administrative matters.

* Contracting with world-renowned, athletic-marketing agency International Management Group (IMG) to assist USA Skeleton in securing long-term funding from sources such as corporate and individual sponsors.

* A desire to revisit and change the selection criteria for the U.S. national team, which would in effect mean a departure from the USBSF's long-standing use of a physical testing system used for bobsled athletes.

* A statement that Viaciulis; FIBT official Kevin McCarthy, a Utah resident; and I would be attending the annual FIBT Congress in June.

* Notification that I was in the process of soliciting candidates for an additional position that would entail day-to-day management and coordination of details for USA Skeleton. My e-mail took it a step further, soliciting the USBSF to feel free to refer the names of any qualified candidates whom they might know.

You didn't have to be too canny to read between the lines. I was trying to reinforce the fact that skeleton would build and control its own program. It would be funded for the upcoming (1999–2000) season, and I made it clear that we were working diligently toward separating the needs of the skeleton program and skeleton athletes from those of the bobsled administrators.

One of the topics of contention between the administrators and the skeleton athletes that would linger into the 1999–2000 season and beyond involved the bobsled coaches' sacred six-item test. This summertime test, part of dry-land assessment for all sliders, was designed by bobsled coaches to evaluate the push ability and potential of bobsled athletes. Curiously, skeleton athletes were required to take the same test and were ranked relative to bobsledders according to how they performed in thirty-, sixty-, and hundred-meter sprints, the vertical jump, the five-hop long jump, and the shot put. Hundred-meter sprint?? Shot put?? If ever there was any reason to consider that skeleton athletes might have a reason to try steroids, this was it.

Clearly, it would be necessary to alter the system and tailor design a dry-land fitness test better suited for skeleton athletes, yet with the understanding that test results wouldn't play a role in determining World Cup team qualification.

You would have thought we were asking the USBSF to cut off its own right arm, the way they fought us on this point. USA Skeleton gamely debated the issue and eventually won a skirmish in getting the test abbreviated by one item with the decision to drop the shot-put requirement. USA Skeleton eventually shaved it down to a four-item test that dumped the hundred-meter dash, an event irrelevant in a sport that requires fewer than twenty sprint steps to load onto his or her sled. Once on the sled, there is no further need to run, except maybe to jump into somebody's arms after crossing the finish line with an Olympic medal—after the sled has coasted to a stop, of course.

For the skeleton team to succeed, it would need its own support system, built from the ground up. The USBSF had always operated as a pyramid—with the officers and directors at the top, staff members in the middle, and the athletes on the bottom in the Atlas-like position of supporting the whole thing on their shoulders. Successful organizations understand that success is first and foremost about excellence, and excellence is usually expensive. They plan on ways to work around barriers by doing what is right and what is needed, and budgeting accordingly. That takes quality leadership as well as professional staff persons who know that the best way to overcome obstacles is by facing them immediately, and then by building a supportive environment where excellence is valued and, therefore, success is achieved. A key component of such a success philosophy is the familiar precept of servant-leadership, an alien concept to an inherent entrenchment atop that pyramid. I envisioned an inverted pyramid, one in which the USBSF's officers, directors, and staffers would be doing Atlas's heavy lifting. Done right, with the right prioritization, they would then be able to ensure that athletes need not concern themselves with a single thing but focusing on training and competing to the best of their abilities.

There was precedent for skeleton to go it somewhat alone, although the real goal was to be prepared to compete in the 2002 Olympics. Luge, a third sliding sport, had split off. It had developed its own structure and had been autonomous since 1979, when the United States Luge Association was chartered as a direct result of the Congressional Amateur Sports Act of 1978. Then again, it also helps that luge also has its own globally sanctioned governing body, the International Luge Federation.

With such connective clout, USA Luge enjoys dual status of Olympic class member organization of the United States Olympic Committee and national governing body for the sport of luge in the United States. As a non-Olympic sport still, skeleton, on the other hand, would have little choice but to remain under the auspices of the USBSF if it had any hope of Olympic certification. That's the power of politics. The best thing I could do to give skeleton a fighting chance was to figure out a way to fund the skeleton program and the sliders in a way that fit the USBSF by-laws yet did not give the Federation hands-on control of dispensing the funds—the contributors to TSS required this.

Enter USA Skeleton. TSS was the main driving force behind the formation of USA Skeleton, which, as we discussed, was simply a "doing business as" name on behalf of the Texas Sliding Society, a 501(c)(3) not-for-profit organization. This gave skeleton and skeleton sliders an umbrella organization separate from the USBSF, thus allowing skeleton to raise funds and control its budget while also still being anointed by the USBSF, necessary for the national and international sanctioning required to be able to race worldwide. The name "USA Skeleton" had not been reserved by the USBSF for lack of budget, so TSS believed it was necessary to protect the name while Olympic status was pending; therefore, it took the time and expense to acquire the name. The skeleton athletes themselves designed a logo, and eventually sliders on the U.S. national team would get their own apparel with skeleton identification.

The impetus for USA Skeleton would be twofold: one, the athletes and coaches desperately needed a credible program with structure, leadership, and its own identity; and two, the program needed to be able to operate on its own financially, without risking intervention relative to the USBSF's particular capabilities, needs, or preferences.

The goal of USA Skeleton was to provide an environment in which athletes could maximize their abilities and achievements. We wanted the athletes to be able to focus completely on doing what they do best—training, competing, and achieving. If each athlete did his or her job, then the team would reach its goals. We did not want the sliders to continue worrying about the shortcomings of the USBSF and other associated matters. USA Skeleton was set up by athletes for athletes. I committed to the athletes and they committed to me and to the program goals.

To pull all this off, to properly structure and fund the skeleton program to have it Olympic-worthy in time for the sport's anticipated return to the games in

2002, I would need more than just great athletes. I also would have to surround myself with savvy and experienced administrators willing to share the yoke and the vision. Veteran sliders and coaches such as Viaciulis, Terry Holland, and Clay Roark would time and again prove instrumental in helping me navigate through a minefield fettered with explosive devices with labels such as Politics, Apathy, and Selfishness.

Among the others who would step into the breach was Kevin McCarthy, a veteran Delta airline captain living in Park City, Utah. At the age of forty-eight, McCarthy had been introduced to skeleton on Super Bowl Sunday in 1997, the same day the new Park City track for the 2002 Games was officially opened. McCarthy was friendly with a member of the commission that had built the Park City track. When he heard there was going to be a ceremonial series of bobsled runs to christen the track, McCarthy asked if there were any spots left.

"I called my friend and he said to come on out, that there was one seat left in one of the four-man bobsleds," McCarthy recalled. "I was in the sixth bobsled to go down the track. The fellow driving it was Randy Will, who was going to be the USBSF's director for the Park City track."

McCarthy has since retired from Delta and is now working as an aviation security consultant. At the time, he had been training to become a ski-jumping judge. But the subjectivity of the sport and what he saw as biased judging convinced him that he needed a different sport to latch onto. He found it soon after meeting Will.

"I asked Randy how bobsled worked," McCarthy added, "and he said, 'You get a rule book and the fastest one down the track wins. No subjectivity. To get involved, you first need to learn how to slide, and the best way to do that is to start with skeleton before you make a go at bobsled.' He had been a three-time Olympian bobsledder as well as a skeleton slider. He assured me that by starting out with skeleton, I would get to know the ice better."

Getting track time would be no cinch, however, especially with skeleton still being on the Olympic-agenda outs. Told that the USBSF would only allow members of a sanctioned sliding club to use the track, McCarthy went out and recruited several friends to help him form the Bear Hollow Skeleton Club. One of those recruits was a local ski instructor who was taking computer programming classes at night while working a day job with flexible hours. Lincoln DeWitt had always been fascinated by things that pushed the edge, such as skiing moguls and racing mountain bikes, but nothing of the truly daredevilish variety inherent in skeleton.

"I was hooked after the first run," said DeWitt, who a year and a half later would make the U.S. national team. "But my intention was not to compete, only to have fun. They had built this $25 million or whatever facility in our backyard. We took the attitude, 'It's there. Why not take advantage of it and use it?'"

During that summer of 1997, McCarthy and DeWitt bought skeleton sleds of their own and began taking part in club races during the 1997–98 season. They weren't able to find any available rule books, so they settled for photocopies an acquaintance had made for them. Randy Will helped these neophytes learn some basic sliding techniques, breaking them in the old-fashioned way, by advancing them up the track in increments until they were ready to go from the top.

Even though most new sliders were emboldened Baby Boomers already well on the high side of thirty, McCarthy still stuck out as the older man of the mountain, nearly twenty years older than DeWitt. And it showed. After one trip down the Park City track from the top, McCarthy's neck hurt so badly he couldn't hold his chin up. That didn't bode well for future runs down the track. With his chin guard dragging the ice all the way down, McCarthy was pelted with ice crystals that sprayed his face and went into his goggles. In essence, he was being sandblasted by ice crystals that really sting when you're hitting sixty miles an hour.

"By the time I got to the bottom of the track the second time," McCarthy said, "the blood from my face had gone up and behind my ears and was running down the back of my neck. I got home around midnight—we usually slid at night under the lights—and I sat on the couch eating M&Ms and drinking Guinness. I'm wired. I finally get calmed down and get to bed. When I got up the next morning, my wife, Dee, saw me heading for the shower and exclaimed, 'Oh my God, what happened to you? You look like you just went a few rounds in the Texas Chainsaw Massacre.'

"I was a sight to behold. Next day, I was right back out at the track, working as a volunteer at an America's Cup race. My nose was one big, swollen red thing. I still get razzed about it to this day."

On the brink of fifty, McCarthy, Rudolph nose and all, had to be telling himself, "I'm too old for this [stuff]." Too old to race, perhaps, but not too old to jump into the sport and find a way to get fully involved. At the time, Will and Viaciulis were the only two Americans certified as skeleton judges by the FIBT. Sensing McCarthy's enthusiasm to get involved, Will asked if he were interested in becoming a skeleton judge.

"As a pilot, you can fly all over the world for nothing, so why don't you take it on?" Will asked. "I'll write a letter of recommendation and you take the test."

Within a year, McCarthy had passed the FIBT test and had indeed been around the world, working as an official at skeleton races, implementing a rule book several inches thick and written in three languages. Running races. Measuring spikes on the bottom of sliders' cleats. Interacting with national and international federations. Checking sled designs and runners' temperatures. Making sure who owned the rights to put a sponsor's name on the racing bibs. Who gets how much money out of what, and what do you do with the television people? If and when to put the track shades up or take them down. McCarthy's welcome to skeleton officialdom was a whirlwind, but it beat getting beat up on the ice just months away from being of AARP age.

Eventually, McCarthy would add bobsled judging to the duties listed on his expanding, not-a-paid-job description. More bobsled officials were needed because there was a movement afoot to open Olympic bobsledding to women, a crusade engineered in large part by International Olympic Committee executive board member Anita DeFrantz of the United States. DeFrantz, a two-time Olympian who had won a bronze rowing medal in 1976, had made it clear that she wanted to see women's bobsled added onto the 2002 Salt Lake City Games docket. Only problem was, skeleton supporters had similar aspirations. There was lingering concern that there wouldn't be room enough for everyone, especially with the two sports being close cousins of one another. The politics of sport, once again, were at work. Skeleton sliders were again beginning to think they would be the odd sled out, and it would be October 1999 before they would get the final verdict regarding which sports were in and which would be left out of the cold.

"It was a full boat," McCarthy said of the pushed growth of women's bobsled alongside his expanding skeleton duties. "At first there wasn't even a rule book for women's bobsled—we were writing it as we went along. The women couldn't use the men's bobsleds. Those things are really heavy, and the women could barely move them. So we had to change stuff on the run, make up things. At the same time we were feverishly going out and recruiting women, trying to build teams. The United States wasn't alone in all this: with the IOC it was the same thing as it had been with skeleton—we had to have something like seven, eight, or nine nations fully engaged in the sport before they would even consider it for inclusion."

In the middle of all this, the USBSF came to McCarthy, asking him to wear another hat, that of USBSF club development director, a front man for any sliding club that came looking for certification and a little bit of administrative guidance. A club just like, well, the Texas Secret Society. Uh, make that the Texas Sliding Society, represented by the likes of Taylor Boyd, Clay Roark, and Fallon and me. Between his newfound USBSF role and hopping around the globe judging races, McCarthy found himself bumping into me with increased frequency. We hit it off as friends with a shared determination—to pump some credibility into USA Skeleton and get it into the Olympics.

USA Skeleton's relationship with the USBSF would be a wild ride down a bumpy track, at any given moment on the verge of going out of control. You could draw the analogy of a skeleton slider chasing a bobsled team down the track, getting a late push at the start but quickly making up ground, accelerating through the turns and trying to pass the bigger, more-cumbersome bobsled blocking the way. It would take some bold and cunning maneuvering to get around the bob, but just maybe it could be accomplished with some compromise and without both participants crashing into a wall.

Or not.

At times, drastic action was called for, and that required ample planning. One time, McCarthy and I met others at Viaciulis's Westport, New York, home to enjoy some camaraderie and barbecue while hunkering down to map out a strategy to take before the annual meeting of the USBSF in 1999. If we were going to get anywhere with the USBSF, we were going to have to be a squeaky wheel.

"That's when Robie really committed to this, determined to make it work," McCarthy said. "We went to the meeting with a united front—all of the athletes, too, and with Robie as director. Robie finally gets the floor and said, 'I propose to do this and this and this,' and they're all just looking at him like, 'Yeahhhh, rrrright.' They just stare at him and giggle under their breath. 'You've got to be kidding,' they said. 'Where do you think you're going to get the money?'

"Robie said, 'We're going to raise the money ourselves to support this budget.'

"They said, 'Yeah, sure; you want us to let you spend it and you haven't even raised it yet.'

"He said, 'I will personally guarantee it. I will cover it right now, and then

I will pay myself back from whatever we raise.' That is when somebody wanted to know who 'the Texas *Secret* Society' was. There was much skepticism." More so than not, it seemed to be, in my opinion, an attitude of scarcity rather than one of abundance. This was not a zero-sum game.

By the spring of 1999, however, it had become common knowledge that the International Olympic Committee was considering men's and women's skeleton for the 2002 Salt Lake City Games, even though skeleton veterans had heard this kind of thing for years and had considerable doubt it would go in their favor this time around as well. Most didn't want to get their hopes up too high. Shea had just won America's first skeleton world championship, but it registered a 0.0 on the USBSF's Richter scale. Still, they had no plans to add administrative staff or budget, and it did not appear they were about to devise a plan that would have them formalizing and managing an actual skeleton program. Not only that, there also was the specter lingering from earlier in the 1990s, when the USBSF experienced some financial issues with leaders within the organization. This, in an organization that hadn't won an Olympic medal since 1956.

To address the USBSF's legal and management problems, the United States Olympic Committee intervened and appointed Jim Morris interim president of the USBSF, apparently until he could get the Federation's wrinkles ironed out. Morris, a White Plains, New York, attorney, until then had been the USOC's legal representative investigating the USBSF's case. Morris's title would turn out to be more than interim, though; four years later, in 1998, he was duly elected, by fewer than ten votes, to a full four-year term as president, making him and Matt Roy the point men when it came time for USA Skeleton and me to make its case for full-fledged USBSF support.

My May 1999 memo to Roy would be the beginning of what I described as an ongoing determination to overcome "bureaucratic inertia." The memo spelled out a bold and ambitious program whereby USA Skeleton would take the initiative to raise funds for the skeleton budget. In June 1999, I proposed a budget of $395,953 in expenses that would be covered by a planned $398,600 in revenues, with $300,000 of the latter provided via a loan from Fallon and me. No response. More inquiries . . . still no response. I would retain the services of International Management Group's Denver office, a worldwide leader in the sports industry, with the kind of clout that comes when you have a clientele led by Tiger Woods and the ability to produce and package its own network sports programming.

It would be late summer before the USBSF finally relented and approved the budget, empowering USA Skeleton to put together a salaried coaching staff, with "salaried" being the buzzword. Until now, pay for skeleton coaches, such as Viaciulis, had been minimal and scattershot at best. I consulted with Taylor Boyd and Terry Holland on the issue of picking a coach. It was unanimous: two-time world champion Ryan Davenport, now retired and building sleds, would be head coach, and Viaciulis his assistant, with Davenport getting a three-year deal with an annual salary of $50,000 a year. His task: to get the Americans in shape to win medals at the 2002 Games, assuming, of course, skeleton would be on the Salt Lake City docket.

Getting Davenport to come aboard was not a slam dunk. I flew to Calgary more than once to make my pitch to the multitalented, brainy Davenport, who by now had left his competitive days behind to focus on his love of building sleds. Holland also tried to plant the coaching seed with Davenport, who kept repeating to Holland that he wasn't interested. So, new tactics. When I flew to Calgary in August 1999 to cajole Davenport a second time, I played on Davenport's growing bond with the Japanese, who by now were getting into the sport.

"I like the Japanese. I get along with them very well," Davenport said. "Part of what interested me was the cultural difference. When Robie flew up the second time, he suggested that if I were to take the U.S. coaching position, it would look really good on my resume when I went to work for the Japanese. I figured he was probably right. Besides, by then, everyone was pretty much suspecting that skeleton would be announced as an Olympic sport in the next month or two, and this would be a good opportunity to coach the home team on the home track."

Convincing Davenport, as it turned out, was the easy part. The hard part was getting the USBSF to go along with it. Agreeing to let me and USA Skeleton fund the skeleton program was acceptable, albeit reluctantly, to the USBSF, but picking a coach? Federation officials suggested that I consider several candidates. Those included a retired bobsled athlete and a couple of assistant bobsled coaches. And they weren't joking. It would also mean that Viaciulis, the most experienced American skeleton coach in history and the one willing to work for beans, would be out of a job, if you want to call it that, considering he was not getting paid.

I simply wasn't going to tolerate this continuance of good-ole-boy administration. It was going to be an uphill battle, because we wanted to change everything in skeleton from the ground up. I was having great difficulty understanding how a bobsled athlete or coach could know how to teach skeleton driving and, ultimately, inspire world-class results in international competition.

Additionally, the USBSF's first reaction to the hiring of Davenport was one of suspicion. They believed he was using the coaching opportunity in order to prepare (as an athlete) for the Olympics on the Olympic track. We wanted Ryan as coach because he was the best-qualified person in the world. The USBSF's approach was based more on who's "local" or "available." One USBSF official recommended a specific bobsled coach for the position, and when I asked why, the official stated: "Because he deserves to go to the Olympics." That's the kind of mindset we were up against.

Maybe the decision had already been made. The way I saw it, the head coach of men's bobsled was apparently positioning himself as the coach over all USBSF coaches. I had cause for my suspicions. The fall 1999 edition of what was called *The Bobserver* quoted one coach as saying, "I am very proud to receive this award. I could not have done it without the support of my fellow coaches and the guidance of the U.S. bobsled and skeleton head coach, Steve Maiorca."

The same newsletter in a separate location identified Maiorca as "head coach," and someone else as "skeleton coach," but we knew nothing of an appointment to coach skeleton. Also, using grant money provided by the USOC for sending a skeleton development athlete to Europe for training and racing, the USBSF snubbed up-and-coming skeleton specialists Tristan Gale and Lea Ann Parsley in favor of a former bobsled woman turned skeleton slider. For whatever reason, that athlete didn't return to sliding the following year.

It was almost like the USBSF was doing whatever it could to restrict the skeleton program's evolution and improvement. After the skeleton national team trials in 1999, a bobsled athlete who failed in trying out for the team filed a protest. I investigated and after some effort, finally located the athlete, who suggested he had been put up to the protest by a coach. This coach later denied it when I confronted him. Then there still was the matter of Davenport, who ended up coaching the entire 1999–2000 season without a signed contract, which by the rules officially had to be tendered by the USBSF. Minor changes in the legal wording as well as apparent indecision delayed execution of the contract until after the Goodwill Games at Lake Placid in February 2000, the last event of the sliding season. For about six months, Davenport had coached without a contract, although I made sure he was paid his salary along the way. We proceeded without the paperwork, and the Texas Sliding Society, d/b/a USA Skeleton, paid Ryan on the come. This was the best thing for the athletes, it was the right thing to do, and it paid off for the program.

As the 1999–2000 sliding season approached, I remained determined to keep competing, even faced with what was becoming a heavy administrative load.

I still hadn't given up on sliding as an athlete. I continued to train hard during the summer of 1999. I believed I could improve my push time and therefore my competitiveness. Fallon and I persuaded Coach John Turek, the track and field coach at St. Mark's School of Texas in Dallas, to train us in speed and conditioning. John is a great coach and very well respected. He got us in shape. We spent our summer mornings at St. Mark's pushing our muscles to the limits. We were both trying to transform a lifetime's worth of long distance slow-twitch muscle fiber training into sprint fast-twitch muscle fibers. We'd go home at night aching, exhausted, but loving it.

During a break at the track one day, John and I were discussing the program's need for a manager with accounting and athletic experience. He said he knew the perfect person for the job: Kevin Ellis. Kevin, a young man from Killeen, Texas, was a two-time Division I All-American high hurdler, and a 1996 track and field Olympic Trials qualifier and participant. John introduced us, and Kevin and I hit it off immediately, even though he was hesitant about the idea of getting involved in a low-profile sport in a position that didn't seem like it would be long term. But I prevailed on him, with John's help. He came on as USA Skeleton's manager in August 1999, and not a moment too soon.

Ellis averred, as had I in 1995, that he didn't want to actually try sliding. So I let him know that as part of his overall training for USA Skeleton manager, he would be required to attend a skeleton school, and the next one was scheduled for October 1999. Ellis forgot to put on his gloves on his first slide and scraped up his knuckles badly, but he quickly grew to enjoy the sport and continued sliding.

At the time, he was probably the closest thing the skeleton program had to a genuine world-class athlete, that is, someone with his overall conditioning and range of fitness. Don't get me wrong—all sliders are athletes. Few, if any, at the time could come close to Ellis's level of push skill and ability. In no time, it was apparent that he probably was the fastest pusher we'd ever seen. Kevin qualified the following week for the U.S. national team—just one week after his first skeleton slide.

Fallon Vaughn loading
onto her Davenport
sled, 2000.

Early U.S. women skeleton sliders (l to r): Colleen Rush, Marta Schultz,
Lea Ann Parsley, Janet Ivers, Tristan Gale, Coach Ryan Davenport, Fallon
Vaughn, Babs Isak, Juleigh Walker, and Katie Koczynski, 1999.

Author loading at Utah Olympic Park, 2000.

The 1999–2000 United States National Skeleton Team
Men: 2nd; Women: 3rd in World Cup Team rankings.

Chris Soule, silver medalist; author; and Jim
Shea, Jr., gold medalist, following Goodwill
Games competition at Mt. Van Hoevenberg
outside of Lake Placid, New York, 2000.

Lincoln DeWitt, World Cup
Champion 2000–2001, signing auto-
graphs following winning the World
Cup test event for the Olympics
at Utah Olympic Park, 2001.

Kevin Ellis, one of the fastest skeleton push athletes in the world, 2003.

Kevin Ellis, sliding at over 80 mph through the field of view, 2003.

Coach Ryan Davenport, gold medalist Chris Soule, and silver medalist Lea Ann Parsley, following the final 2001–2002 World Cup competition at St. Moritz, Switzerland, 2002.

U.S. World Cup team following competition, with Swiss Gregor Stähli, overall skeleton World Cup champion and Olympic bronze medalist, 2002.

Nino Bibbia—with his 1948 Olympic Cresta gold medal— and author, 2002.

Courtesy of USOC

United States 2002 Olympic Skeleton Team. Bottom (l to r): Lea Ann Parsley, Chris Soule, Lincoln DeWitt, Jim Shea, Jr., and Tristan Gale. Top (l to r): Ryan Davenport, Kevin Ellis, Terry Holland, Debbie Gaither, author, and Peter Viaciulis.

Author and Taylor Boyd on Main Street in Park City, Utah, during the Olympic Winter Games, 2002.

Kevin Ellis, author, Tristan Gale, and Peter Viaciulis,
following Tristan's run with the Olympic Flame, 2002.

Olympians Chris Soule,
Jim Shea, Jr., and
Lincoln DeWitt, 2002.

Jim Shea, Jr., "holding court" during the Olympic Skeleton press conference, 2002.

U.S. delegation housing in the Olympic village—University of Utah, 2002.

Mike Holrock, Olympic bobsled race director; with David Kurtz; and Fallon Vaughn, forerunners for the Olympic skeleton competition, 2002.

The U.S. delegation entering the Olympic stadium during the opening ceremony, 2002.

Clockwise (l to r): Taylor Boyd, Kirsten Pederson, Debbie Gaither, Kevin Ellis, Babs Isak, and Fallon Vaughn at the 2002 Olympic Winter Games' opening ceremony, 2002.

A snowstorm enveloped the Utah Olympic Park during
Olympic skeleton competition on February 20, 2002.

Author monitoring a U.S.
slider's progress during
Olympic competition, 2002.

Chris Soule pushing during snowstorm in the first heat of Olympic competition, 2002.

Author and Chris Soule "high-fiving" following his final run (and second fastest time of the second heat) of Olympic competition, 2002.

Jim Shea, Jr., beginning his Olympic gold medal run, 2002.

Jim Shea, Jr., wins
Olympic gold, 2002.

Jim Shea, Jr., celebrates with
15,000 exuberant fans, 2002.

Lea Ann Parsley slides to Olympic silver through curve twelve at the Utah Olympic Park, 2002.

Author, with Olympic bronze medalist Alex Coomber, congratulates medalist Lea Ann Parsley in the finish area, 2002.

Author and Lea Ann Parsley await Tristan Gale's final running, 2002.

Lea Ann Parsley, Tristan Gale, and USA Skeleton sweep silver and gold in women's Olympic Skeleton competitions, 2002.

Gregor Stähli, Jim Shea, Jr., and Martin Rettl show off
their Olympic bronze, gold, and silver medals, 2002.

Lea Ann Parsley, Tristan Gale, and Alex Coomber celebrate their
Olympic accomplishments at the awards ceremony the evening of
February 20, 2002, in downtown Salt Lake City, Utah, 2002.

Silver, gold, and bronze, 2002.

Browning Vaughn, Tristan Gale, and Robert Vaughn, Jr., (holding Tristan's Olympic gold medal), 2002.

CHAPTER NINE

Olympic Ideals...
and Back Room Deals

Man needs to seek a higher cause,
rather than the self.
—President George W. Bush

There is an Olympic ideal, and it exists in our collective imagination. It falls somewhere in between our own fantasy of reaching the pinnacle of athletic success and a dream of self-actualization. We attain that dream by living vicariously through the medal-winning achievements of those to whom we pledge our allegiance.

Many of us who have grown up in America, especially post-World War II Baby Boomers, were brought up believing that the Olympic Games, summer as well as winter, offer a once-every-four-years global sporting experience unique for its purity of drama, fair play, and amateur ideals. The TV-commentating likes of Jim McKay and Bob Beattie have drilled this into us over the years.

By its nature, the Olympics—its melting-pot existence displayed in the multitudes of multi-colored flags from participating nations and territories—epitomizes virtues held dear to the hearts of Americans bound by blood to the red, white, and blue: virtues such as sportsmanship, perseverance, loyalty, and honor. There's something inherently American about the Olympics, as it is a showcase of what can be achieved through sacrifice, excellence, ambition, and courage. All we ask for a few brief and shining moments every four years is to indulge ourselves, to wrap ourselves in the flag—other countries are welcome to join in—as we continue to embrace the Olympic Games as a reflection of who we are, or at least want to be. As Jim McKay once said, "It's not about the statistics, but about the human stories." The Olympics are spectacle like no other, and often a spectacular one at that.

We don't own the games, but we revel in them as much as anybody from anywhere else in the world does. For many of us who grew up in the 1960s and 1970s, hearing the familiar ABC's *Wide World of Sports* refrain about "the thrill of victory and the agony of defeat" will forever be synonymous with what the Olympics has meant to us for decades. Excuse us for being provincial when it comes to the Olympics—but there is much about it we prefer to call our own. The thrill of victories: Billy Mills running bravely at the 1964 Games in Tokyo; the U.S. men's hockey team spinning gold in 1980 at Lake Placid; gymnast Mary Lou Retton somersaulting and twisting her way to gold in 1984 in Los Angeles. The agony of defeats: the U.S. men's basketball team in 1972 at Munich; Mary Decker Slaney crashing to the track in 1984; and speed skater Dan Jansen twice losing his edge and falling to the ice after the death of his sister, although he did pick himself back up and return four years later to capture gold.

There is nothing quite like the drama of the Olympics, winter or summer, when it comes to stirring the most primitive of spectating emotions for American audiences. Until the autumn of 1999, skeleton was like any other popular sport or discipline grounded in so-called amateur idealism; it aspired to be sanctioned by the International Olympic Committee for inclusion in the games. For a sport to officially bear Olympic status is to carry a stamp of credibility for the rest of the world to see—that there is something at the end of the road worth competing for above and beyond a prize as pedestrian as a national championship. In an Olympic sport or discipline, it's all about going for the gold once every four years. Ownership of such a medal is testament to the fact that you truly are the best in the world, at least on that day, and it is a title that lasts for four years, provided there is no failed drug test, rules violation, or unscrupulous judge(s) to spoil the party.

For at least fifteen years leading up to 1999, skeleton sliders had been hearing the same old song and dance: that their particular discipline presumably was next in line for addition to the Olympics. In hindsight, though, it seems they were probably hearing these rumors because they were the ones starting them. Wishful thinking, perhaps. Wistful yearnings, in reality. America's pioneering generation of sliders of the early 1980s figured they had a shot for Sarajevo in 1984 or, at the latest anyway, Calgary in 1988. When neither of those panned out, their thoughts turned to Albertville in 1992, then Lillehammer in 1994. On and on it went, and where it would stop, nobody knew.

"In light of all this Olympic talk, we were really naive about what it takes to become an Olympic sport," Peter Viaciulis said, in retrospect. "People were going around saying that it would be no problem getting in for Albertville and then it would be a shoo-in for Norway, and it just went on and on. One thing that became crystal clear was that if the United States had been the only nation to say, 'Let's include it,' it would not have happened.

"There needed to be a building up of a critical mass coming from enough different directions to make it work. We didn't even know that short-track speed skating existed, and when it got in [for the 1992 Albertville Games], we were like, 'Where in the heck did that come from?' But they were probably saying the same thing about skeleton when we finally got in. You have your blinders on; you don't see what's going on with other sports."

As much as the Americans were hoping for skeleton to get into the Olympics, there was little to indicate that the United States was even close to being prepared to compete in the Olympics. World Cup medals were as rare as sandy beaches for the American sliders, and the athletes were dependent on a national governing body lacking the resources to properly fund and train them. So what right did the U.S. sliders have to even speculate, beyond the scuttlebutt, about getting their discipline into the Olympics? Even as the end of the 1990s approached, it was still clear that the United States was setting itself up for a home-track disappointment, maybe even embarrassment, if skeleton were to make it into the 2002 Games only for the Americans to fail to win a single medal.

By the spring of 1999, it was common knowledge the IOC was considering men's and women's skeleton for the 2002 Olympic Winter Games, even if there was considerable doubt among the skeleton veterans that the decision would go in their favor. I think most didn't want to get their hopes up too high. Even though Jimmy Shea had just become the first American to win a skeleton World Championship, the United States Bobsled and Skeleton Federation had no plan to formalize and manage an actual skeleton program.

Without any apparent anticipation, the USBSF was completely unprepared to afford and handle an increase in management activities related to a skeleton program headed to the Olympics in less than three years. The skeleton community, as small as it was at the time (approximately eighteen active and several interested and retired sliders), would have to organize and build their own program—sooner, rather than later.

Skeleton, technically, is not its own sport. It is a discipline that falls under the auspices of bobsled: at the national level that means the USBSF, and in the international scheme of things that brings us to the Federation Internationale de Bobsleigh et de Tobaganning (FIBT), better known in English as the International Bobsled and Skeleton Federation.

For a sport or discipline such as skeleton to be considered for ratification by the IOC, it must first be submitted for consideration by that sport's/discipline's international governing body, in this case the FIBT. It is not a formal application process per se, but it is one that must follow a chain of authority upwards. Getting a proposal before the IOC to consider skeleton was not something the United States could do on its own, even though it was in the position of being host country for the 2002 Winter Games. In years past, host nations had been given some say in adding a sport or discipline of its choosing for its games, but that allowance no longer existed.

Generally, there are two schools of thought as to how and why skeleton finally was able to make it out of its limbo status and onto the Olympic docket. The first says that the emergence of world-class U.S. athletes able to win international medals, leading with Jim Shea, combined with Mitt Romney's newfound fascination for the sport and by his enhanced influence with the Salt Lake City Organizing Committee, was the push that skeleton needed. The other school of thought says it was not a U.S.-led campaign that got skeleton into the Olympics at all, but an international effort that had been informally yet aggressively launched in the early 1990s—before Jim Shea had even been introduced to a sled.

Shea has his own version, which, while intriguing as a story line, skews the account heavily toward the role played by his success and his association with Romney, who has since become the governor of Massachusetts.

"There were something like seven sports trying to get in at the time," Shea recently said, looking back on events that transpired in 1999. "One day Mitt Romney showed up at the track in Park City. He was the financial guy. He looks at me and says, 'Why do you think skeleton should be in the Olympics?' Instead of being like everyone else and saying something like, 'Well, we deserve it because there's this many countries participating' and all that, I appealed to his interests.

"I said, 'I'm not sure about this, but my guess is that SLOC is a bit short in trying to raise money here.' And he said, 'Yeah, we're short about $250 million.' So I said, 'I wonder how much money NBC would give you if you added three sports [women's bobsled, men's skeleton, women's skeleton] into an existing venue [the Park City track]. How much did you pay for this thing here—$24 million and then $500,000 for the shading? Well, why don't you utilize it? I wonder how much NBC would pay you for three more sports. You already have the volunteers and everything else in place.'

"He came back the next week and told me, 'You know, Jimmy, I looked into those numbers, and I'd like for you to tell me a little more about skeleton.' Then it took off. It was all about money. That's how skeleton got into the Olympics."

Shea's account might be part of the underlying equation, but skeleton's journey to Mount Olympic likely was an amalgamation of the two schools of thought. While it was important to skeleton's cause to have American muscle behind its campaign to get included, it involved a process over which the United States and the U.S. skeleton program had minimal hands-on control, at least when going by the book.

"A lot of people were involved, and it was a decision ultimately made by the IOC executive committee," said Bob Storey, who as of 2005 was in his tenth year and third term as president of the FIBT. "The decision rested solely with the IOC executive committee and was not a decision that could be made by the USOC or the FIBT. In order to get a new discipline admitted into the games, the international governing body over that discipline has to apply for Olympic status. The fact is, we had applied five or six years before skeleton finally got in.

"It's not a formal application process. How it works is that there is an informal organization called the Association of International Winter Olympic Sports Federations, which consists of the presidents of the governing bodies for the seven Winter Olympic sports. Yes, there are more than seven Winter Olympic events, but all of them fall into one of the seven [umbrella] sports, like skeleton is a discipline under the auspices of the FIBT and snowboarding is a discipline within skiing. The process in getting skeleton to the IOC executive committee for consideration is not so much that you need a 'yes' vote from each of the other six Winter Olympic sports, you just don't want any 'nos.' You have to be diplomatic about it."

Diplomacy on behalf of skeleton was something that Storey and fellow skeleton advocates such as David Kurtz and Paul Varadian had been exercising for years. They had been doing it quietly but effectively, writing letters starting in 1990–91 and gingerly pigeonholing officials from other Winter Olympic sports every chance they got, whether it be at a congress in Calgary or an airport lobby somewhere in Germany. Kurtz and Varadian were the key players in the early 1990s. They shared an affinity for skeleton, having both slid themselves, and they had the kind of international connections that would give them the clout needed to start spreading the word.

Whatever they did in those early years, though, they had to do it without the FIBT's blessings. Until 1994, the FIBT was led by Klaus Kotter, a diehard bobsled man. Kurtz's encounter with Kotter outside his hotel room at a 1994 FIBT congress said it all. Although cousins in sliding, bobsled and skeleton were polar opposites in the world of international sporting politics, with bobsled's embedded power structure not about to go out of its way to give a hand up to skeleton.

"A lot of the people," Varadian said, "who gravitate to these administrative roles are former athletes or locals in communities where bobsled is big, and they have risen through the ranks. Then these people get to travel all around the world while having someone else pay for it, and they become very territorial. They fight back when threatened.

"We had petitioned the FIBT to pursue having skeleton admitted to the International Olympic Committee program for the 1992 Games in Albertville, but the FIBT did not support that. We asked again for Lillehammer in 1994, but were denied again. They felt that skeleton was not only a threat to bobsled but that it wasn't well-developed enough across the world. Our argument was a catch-22, the chicken and the egg thing, in that the development wasn't going to start steamrolling until the Olympic status was given."

Even without the FIBT's support, Storey, Kurtz, and Varadian continued to work behind the scenes on skeleton's behalf throughout the 1990s. They sent letters to members of the IOC executive committee extolling the virtues of skeleton. At FIBT congresses, held yearly, they talked up the sport to anyone who would listen. Their pitch to the IOC quickly evolved into one of fiscal considerations, pointing out to the committee that the costs for Olympic bobsled venues were exorbitant and that putting more disciplines on the tracks would help pay for the amortized costs. Skeleton, in itself a cost-efficient discipline, had great potential to do just that. The best new skeleton sled and runners cost about $3,000, while bobsleds and runners cost about $30,000. Besides, as Varadian points out, by the late 1990s, there were more skeleton descents being made on tracks than bobsled descents.

A major breakthrough came in 1994, when Storey was elected to replace

Kotter as FIBT president. Suddenly, the FIBT went from being skeleton's biggest Olympic obstacle to being its most credible supporter. From there on, it was a matter of nurturing relationships. This was a people business, after all. Varadian figures that by the late 1990s, he was friends with about three-quarters of the IOC's Executive Committee, including president Jacques Rogge. Making friends was a Varadian specialty. Sometimes he would send an e-mail, on other days a letter. If he didn't see who he wanted to see at the water fountain outside a meeting hall, he would arrange to sit close during the meetings. It was political lobbying at its best.

"We tried to develop a master plan for going at these people from multiple directions," Varadian said.

Storey, Kurtz, and Varadian weren't just effective letter writers and people persons—they also understood marketing and the value of making the right political connections. They had their work cut out for them. By the mid-1990s, new sports wanting to get into the Olympics no longer had the availability of an interim step, "demonstration" status. This was a chance to show off their wares in a given Olympiad in an unofficial manner that packed a potent public-relations punch not otherwise available. If skeleton was going to get in, it would have to be the result of extraordinarily effective salesmanship out of the public eye, as well as heavy doses of innovative marketing and the occasional "serendipitous" meeting with another country's key sports official. To be in the right place at the right time took the right kind of detailed planning.

"Bob Storey really took it to heart," Kurtz said. "It was starting to get very competitive to get a new sport into the Olympics, and on top of that he had to develop an international women's bobsled program. He knew where to go. The IOC took good care of Bob because he was always doing something to help somebody out. He was well-acquainted with Gilbert Felli, who at the time was the IOC's Olympic Programme director. When Felli's son came over as a foreign-exchange student, Bob's family not only housed him, I'm sure they really welcomed him as part of the family. That's just the kind of people they are.

"Bob also is very savvy in communications. We started our own TV production company by putting in charge veteran media guy John Morgan, a Lake Placid insider and bobsled and skeleton proponent, and we started to seriously lobby the IOC with a thirty-minute video. However, we decided not to use ESPN's telecast from the 1992 World Cup at Lake Placid because it was too brutal, and there were no women involved at the time. What we did was piece together excerpts from various World Cup events and then send the video to key members in places like Africa and Korea—all the key people.

"We lobbied heavily. We also put together the petition for both women's bobsled and men's and women's skeleton, although we always made it a point to mention skeleton first."

For a sport to get onto the Olympic program, biding its time and paying its dues is not part of the selection criteria. Large-scale, worldwide participation and spectator excitement is. That explains why snowboarding, with its Generation X appeal, took less than ten years to get admitted to the Olympic program from the time it was taken on as a discipline by the International Ski Federation. Snowboarding is eye candy for viewers and tailor-made for television, and its core demographic is comprised of the same younger, goods-buying generation that in this day and age drives television ratings.

Consider this: in an article posted on the IOC's Web site referencing its Olympic Programme Commission and the Commission's selection criteria, the following statement is prominently posted:

The attractiveness and popularity of the Olympic Games depends to a large extent on the quality of the sports programme. It must be varied and of high quality, and must produce competitions that are exciting, attractive, action-packed, and athlete-focused. The Olympic Programme must also reflect the constant evolution of public expectations. Consequently, it was felt that the regular review of the programme was needed to ensure that its composition continues to be relevant and meet new expectations.

As a side note, it is my observation and belief that golf and lacrosse fit the IOC's selection criteria and should be viewed as appropriate and productive additions to the summer games in the future. There is no question of golf's worldwide appeal and lacrosse's being the fastest-growing sport in the United States.

Although a much newer kid on the block than skeleton, snowboarding had a lot going for it when the IOC was considering new disciplines during the 1990s. Snowboarding's growth between the early 1980s and the late 1990s can only be described as explosive. According to the Web site www.abc-of-snowboarding. com, in 1983, fewer than 10 percent of U.S. ski areas were inclined and/or equipped to accommodate snowboarding, but by 1997, a vast majority of ski areas had thrown their gates open to snowboarders. Money talks. Going into the

1998 Nagano Games, snowboarding's popularity and fan base had taken a big bite out of the skiing industry, with the number of U.S. skiers having declined by 25 percent while snowboarding's numbers had increased 77 percent. Not only that, the number of people who snowboard is predicted to overtake skiing's numbers by 2015.

It's no wonder the International Ski Federation (FIS) embraced snowboarding. If you can't beat 'em, let them join you—before you have to join them.

"The driving force behind snowboarding getting into the Olympics was the International Ski Federation," said Tom Kelly, vice president of communications for the United States Skiing and Snowboard Association. "While the U.S. Ski and Snowboard Association was very engaged in the sport, it can't really play a meaningful role at the IOC level. FIS president Marc Hodler, one of the most powerful members of the IOC, pretty much made it happen.

"The process was twofold. The first step was getting it on the formal Olympic program. That was done around 1994 or so, although at the time it was considered too late to put it formally onto the program for Nagano. But it was not too late to get the Nagano organizers to opt, on their own, to include it. I think it was in late 1995 that Marc Hodler convinced the Nagano organizers to handle it, and in return the FIS helped Nagano out with some things like additional athlete housing and other costs.

"Snowboarding's rapid growth, youth, and cultural opportunities were key parts in Hodler's being able to successfully pitch the IOC."

There is an old adage in the salesman's manual that says the best time to make a sale of your product is right after you've closed a deal. This might be what the International Ski Federation had in mind when it got snowboarding into the Olympic agenda. Just a few years earlier, the FIS had been successful in getting freestyle skiing, a hybrid of alpine skiing and acrobatics, admitted as a demonstration sport at the 1988 Calgary Games. Four years later, in 1992 at Albertville, moguls were made an official discipline of the Olympics and was followed two years later in Lillehammer by aerials. All this was accomplished in less than two decades: the International Ski Federation had recognized freestyle as an official sport beginning in 1979. The sport's first World Cup series was initiated just a year later, and the first World Championships took place in 1986 in France.

The big difference between freestyle skiing/snowboarding and skeleton was in how much love each received from its respective international governing body. The FIS embraced and nurtured its two newest disciplines, while skeleton well into the 1990s, was practically scorned by controlling elements of the FIBT, and the latter was not a problem limited to the United States. In 2005, the FIBT Web site address still reflected a traditional mindset: www.bobsleigh.com.

By the time the 1998 Nagano Games rolled around, skeleton was languishing well behind snowboarding in terms of numbers. Where snowboarders numbered in the millions, skeleton sliders numbered, at best, in the thousands, with the hundreds probably being more accurate. There's no mystery to that disparity of participation. Snowboards are less expensive than skeleton sleds, and access to venues is on opposite ends of the spectrum. As of 1998, there were only three skeleton-worthy tracks in North America, compared to the hundreds of ski areas that could easily host snowboarders, and that doesn't count the snow-covered backyard slopes and neighborhood hills easily accessible to snowboarders.

Compared to snowboarding, skeleton remained one of the sporting world's best-kept secrets, although there were factors working in skeleton's favor, beyond the established political ties of advocates such as Storey, Kurtz, and Varadian. Like snowboarding, skeleton had an adrenaline quality characteristic of Xtreme sports. Skeleton's blazing speed combined with the inherent danger posed to individuals constantly exposed to mishap would give the Olympics some new blood (in more ways than one). Another more subtle aspect playing in skeleton's favor, according to Storey, was a developmental aspect that helped win over some bobsled diehards within the FIBT. Skeleton has the potential to be a breeding ground for future bobsled drivers. Certainly, solo driving a sled headfirst down a track at eighty miles an hour has to translate well to negotiating a big bobsled down the same tracks.

As soon as Storey assumed the presidency of the FIBT in 1994, skeleton's prospects for five-ring status improved significantly. Favorable knowledge of skeleton already existed throughout the FIBT's ranks. Storey, Kurtz, and Varadian had already laid the groundwork with the other six winter sports federations and most members of the IOC's executive committee, which in turn had a lot of sway with the IOC's Programme Commission. The pieces were falling into place on the international level. Ironically, however, the biggest behind-the-scenes Olympic obstacle facing skeleton as the 1990s slipped by was an American one. Although the IOC by 1998–99 was ready to sanction skeleton, it was not going to force it down the throats of the United States Olympic Committee or the Salt Lake Organizing Committee. And therein lay the rub.

As far as IOC executive committee member Anita DeFrantz was concerned, skeleton was not at the front of the line. Women's bobsled was. DeFrantz, a two-time U.S. Olympian who won a rowing (women's eight) bronze medal in Montreal in 1976, had never been shy in pushing for gender equity. After all, she had been a beneficiary of it herself. When DeFrantz won her bronze, it was the first time women's rowing had been contested at the Olympic level. Men's bobsled had been around for decades, but as of 1998—now that women's hockey had been admitted into the Olympics—bobsled was one of only two remaining winter disciplines without a women's division. The other was ski jumping.

The docket was getting crowded. Women's bobsled and men's and women's skeleton were all disciplines under the auspices of the same sport of bobsled. It wasn't out of the question for three new sports to get added for a single Olympics, but for three disciplines under the same umbrella to all get in at the same time was asking a lot. A possible impasse was in the works. DeFrantz, and in turn USOC and SLOC, were doing a full-court press on behalf of women's bobsled, while much of the rest of the winter sports world, most notably the European nations, were heavily in favor of skeleton over women's bobsled. It seemed inevitable that the only acceptable solution might be to either add all three disciplines for the 2002 Games or none at all.

"We made the case to the American contingent," Storey said, "that men's and women's skeleton was a more dynamic sport than women's bobsled, and was certainly better developed internationally. We said we would be happy to go along with women's bobsled, but that our top priority would be skeleton. Basically, we told Anita that if she continued trying to get women's bobsled in at the exclusion of skeleton, then my membership would not be interested in putting women's bobsled in. I wouldn't call it an ultimatum on our part, but something that was worked out over a period of time."

According to Storey, also a member of the IOC's Programme Commission, the IOC would not have forced skeleton on SLOC if the committee had remained steadfast against skeleton. Eventually, a compromise was reached in which all three disciplines would be added for the 2002 Games, although that would mean maxing out track time at the Park City track. Each of the three disciplines would need practice time as well as race slots, meaning there would be no room for error should the weather not cooperate. That likely was a factor in the decision to go ahead and run the skeleton races on schedule during the 2002 Olympics despite a heavy snowfall that perhaps placed a higher premium on a slider's start-order seed than his or her push or driving skill.

As soon as Salt Lake City was awarded the 2002 Games, which the IOC did in 1995, skeleton supporters began petitioning the Salt Lake Organizing Committee to keep an open mind about skeleton. Kurtz took the lead, having been selected as an attaché by Storey to serve as a liaison between the FIBT and SLOC. Kurtz's mission, which he chose to accept, was getting skeleton into the games, which would mean removing any opposition that might emanate out of the United States.

"Actually, we had thought years earlier that we had a shot at 1998 in Nagano," Kurtz said. "I thought we had the support of the Japanese, but then the IOC jammed snowboarding down their throat, even though it would mean having to pay about $3 million for a whole new venue that Japan didn't have in its budget. However, there were untold thousands of people snowboarding by then, and it was obvious that having snowboarding in the Olympics would be a great boon for snowboard manufacturers. Draw your own conclusions."

Kurtz made his first skeleton pitch to SLOC at a July 1998 meeting of their board of trustees. His oral presentation went over like a lead balloon.

"I was absolutely shocked," Kurtz added. "They were thinking of their budget. Before this, Bob Storey and I had vowed to each other that we would demand inclusion of both sports (women's bobsled and skeleton) or neither— we would keep them linked. There was another meeting in August, and that's when SLOC asked us to make a choice, and we knew they were predisposed to women's bobsled. Jimmy Shea was there, too, but they wouldn't let him in because they knew he was too radical an advocate of skeleton. Anita was there. I refused to make a choice, though, and that's how I left the meeting."

That wasn't the end of things, however. Soon after returning home to Pennsylvania, Kurtz received a telephone call from Bonnie Warner, a veteran Olympic luger and future NBC correspondent who was at the August meeting. Warner wasn't calling for a friendly chat, either. Kurtz said that Warner told him she was going to go to the media to blame Kurtz as the man responsible for keeping women's bobsled out of the Olympics. Instead of hanging up on Warner, as he might have pondered, Kurtz reminded her that it was the FIBT's position that both sports go in and that she also needed to realize that Europe heavily favored skeleton over women's bobsled.

Sometime later, Bonnie became a very competitive bobsledder, fifth overall in World Cup points in 2001–2002, narrowly missing the Olympic Team. She is quite an athlete. Eventually she became a proponent of USA Skeleton and a friendly supporter.

Undaunted, Kurtz knew that while it was not within SLOC's power to pick, on its own, a new sport or sports for its games, it could resist any additions recommended by the IOC. For him to succeed, it would take perseverance and finding new ways to polish his pitch. That meant being ready for any unforeseen contingency that might come his way, such as an Olympic-sized scandal that might come along and disrupt the lobbying process. Which is exactly what happened next.

In late 1998, the roof caved in on the Salt Lake Organizing Committee, and the problems carried over into 1999. In what became known as the Great Olympic Bribery Scandal, it was revealed that some SLOC officials had doled out millions in gifts, travel, scholarships, medical care, jobs, and other luxuries to IOC officials (as well as their relatives and companions) to see to it that Salt Lake City would indeed be picked to host the 2002 Winter Games.

Certainly, greasing the skids to enhance one's chances of landing an Olympiad is a sport as old as the ancient marathon, but the gall with which IOC members with hands out were compensated was mind-boggling. IOC representative Jean-Claude Ganga of the Congo Republic reportedly admitted receiving $70,000 in direct payments as well as free medical care and a favorable stake in a Utah real estate deal allegedly netting him $60,000. Ganga would later state that such arrangements are "normal." Other accusations reportedly made said that SLOC had also supplied visiting IOC members with prostitutes, made campaign contributions to an IOC member running for mayor of Santiago, Chile, and provided college tuition for the children of IOC members from Ecuador and Libya.

Four separate investigations into the bribery scandal were initiated involving SLOC, USOC, IOC, and even the U.S. Justice Department, the latter to see if there had been any violations of federal anti-bribery statutes. Many of the IOC representatives who allegedly received payoffs also happened to be officials from foreign governments. As shocking as all this was, revelations would show this to be close to business as usual. Similar charges would eventually be made and documented implicating Atlanta (1996 Summer Games), Nagano (1998 Winter Games), and Sydney (2000 Summer Games) for bribery violations on a similar scale.

The short of it was that, for the 2002 Games, three high-ranking SLOC officials, in addition to a number of other committee members, either resigned or were fired. Committee president Frank Joklik resigned after admitting that IOC members had been bribed to bias the 1995 vote that awarded the 2002 Games to Salt Lake City. Dave Johnson, SLOC's vice president, also stepped down, and furthermore, the committee severed a $10,000-a-month consulting agreement with former SLOC president Tom Welch, who had been the leader of the bidding committee responsible for hosting visiting IOC members during the "recruiting" process.

So much for the concept of an Olympic ideal, if ever there was one. Historical scrutiny suggests it may never have existed. Longtime IOC president Avery Brundage's white-knuckle grip on organizational power rivaled that of J. Edgar Hoover's at the FBI. Brundage uttered the classic line, "The amateur code, coming to us from antiquity, embraces the highest moral laws. No philosophy, no religion, preaches loftier sentiments."

Contrary to myth, athletes in the ancient Olympics were professionals who competed for prize money, a revelation brought forth in David Young's 1984 book *The Olympic Myth of Greek Amateur Athletics*. In fact, the very concept of amateurism reportedly didn't even exist in classical Greek culture. Although the Salt Lake City scandal was a matter entirely separate from the ideal of amateur athletes, it involves unethical behavior that shouldn't have been a shock to Olympic followers. They had long been subjected to such misdeed as women swimmers buffing up on steroids, basketball officials blatantly determining the outcome of a gold-medal game, and full-time-employed Soviet Union hockey players passing themselves off as amateurs. The legendary Jim Thorpe lost all his Olympic medals when it was discovered that he had previously played semipro baseball for twenty-five bucks a week.

The Olympic ideal? How about the ancient games, which featured a four-horse chariot race that sometimes ended up in gory pileups? Or a ferociously violent sport known as pankration, which was nothing more than anything-goes brawling? It's no wonder that ancient depictions of competitors showed facial gashes, cauliflower ears, and noses that had been broken numerous times. Married women were forbidden at games sites, and is it any wonder? Most of the tens of thousands of spectators who journeyed to these ancient games were men who would carouse with prostitutes of both sexes at nightly, luxurious feasts. These were different times, for sure.

The International Olympic Committee is the supreme authority of the Olympic Movement and was founded in 1894 by French educator Baron Pierre de Coubertin, who was inspired to revive the Olympic Games of Green antiquity. The IOC is an international non-governmental, nonprofit organization, and it exists to serve as an umbrella organization of the Olympic Movement. It owns all the rights to the Olympic symbols, flag, motto, anthem, and Olympic Games. Its primary responsibility is to supervise the organization of the Olympic Summer and Winter Games.

One of the most powerful responsibilities of the IOC is to select the host city for the Olympic Games. These days, national governments and local organizing committees combined spend many billions of dollars on each Olympiad. Most cities and governments use the Olympics as a way to facilitate infrastructure and facility development and to provide a tremendous economic boost to the region. The costs have skyrocketed in recent years because of additional security requirements to keep the games safe from potential terrorist attacks.

The IOC's membership is very political. Individual members yield substantial influence, reflecting the organization's autonomy in terms of how it remains independent from any governmental influence and thus lacks a degree of accountability to its constituencies and the public. The briberies accepted by IOC members during the Salt Lake City bidding process reinforced this perception and ultimately tested the structure and fabric of the "old way" of doing business.

In hiring Mitt Romney following the bribery scandal, SLOC gained an energetic, intelligent, and personable man with a can-do attitude. He very quickly righted the ship in 1999, recreating sponsorship demand and producing what would turn out to be the most successful Olympic Winter Games ever, producing a profit in excess of $100 million.

With the 2002 games just a little over three years away, the IOC elected nonetheless to keep the games in Utah. It probably was too late to attempt a change of venues. Hundreds of millions of dollars—including federal tax dollars—already had been pumped into Utah to help it prepare for the games. However, it still was a risky proposition from a financial standpoint. Some major corporate sponsors that had signed on for the Salt Lake City Games now threatened to pull out. It took a soft shoe, some fast talking, and tremendous leadership by Romney, a prominent Massachusetts businessman and member of the Utah-based Mormon Church, who had become the newly appointed SLOC chief executive.

"The Olympics is about sports, not business," Romney told a meeting of the organizing committee's board. "The Olympics is about athletes, not managers. The managers have messed up, but the athletes haven't."

Even then, there was concern that many athletes could be hurt by the scandal's ramifications, a possibility should SLOC be forced to scale back its games-hosting budget if ongoing fund-raising efforts were to falter. That came from an authority no less than Dick Schultz, executive director of the USOC.

"There are contingency plans in place already in case we could not meet our revenue goals that we would scale back the budget accordingly and keep these games on budget," Schultz said. "We would always take a look at renegotiation of certain contracts and arrangements between SLOC and the IOC if that became necessary to do to ensure the games are successful."

If any sport had reason to fear any such cutbacks, aware that it might end up designated as fiscal fat that needed to be trimmed, it was skeleton. Ditto for women's bobsled, for that matter. The saving grace for those disciplines was that their shared $25 million track venue had already been built, and any extra expenses related to creating additional housing space in the Olympic Village, conducting the races, and so on, were reasonable enough to be easily offset by added sponsorships and other financial gains over and above what had been earmarked for other Winter Olympic sports.

Then again, there still was the gender-equity factor being championed by DeFrantz. In a roundabout way, the Salt Lake City bribery scandal might have been the final piece to skeleton's Olympic puzzle. It also helped that Storey was able to get IOC president Juan Antonio Samaranch to write a letter supporting skeleton that was distributed to IOC members worldwide. The bribery irony was that the ouster of Joklik, Johnson, and Welch from SLOC power and influence opened the way for Romney to take charge of the committee around the same time that Jimmy Shea was becoming the first American to win a skeleton World Championship. It was serendipitous. Shea met Romney, the two hit it off, Romney got onto a skeleton sled and went through a skeleton school, and on October 2, 1999, the IOC made it official: men's and women's skeleton, as well as women's bobsled, were all being formally added to the Olympic agenda, starting with the 2002 Games.

At the time the announcement was made, Romney was preparing to board a plane to go to Lausanne, Switzerland, to make one last pitch on behalf of skeleton. Now, there was no reason to bother.

"My body was trembling when I heard the news, and I'm not normally a guy who cries easily," Kurtz said. "I had always thought that when they finally made the decision, it would be anticlimactic, but it wasn't. So much had been sacrificed by so many people in dealing with these petty fiefdoms. At least my life hadn't been for folly. Other than my first training run down the track at Lake Placid, this was my biggest thrill in skeleton."

The announcement that skeleton was now an Olympic sport did not shock or shake up USA Skeleton. We had been preparing for this momentous occasion for months, and now it was time to see how well the organizational foundation would hold up under the pressure of now not only having another World Cup season about to begin, but also a twenty-eight-month timetable to ramp up for the 2002 Games in Utah.

For starters, USA Skeleton had a salaried head coach in two-time world champion Ryan Davenport, a seasoned assistant coach in Peter Viaciulis, a competent and reliable accountant and manager in Kevin Ellis, and some leadership as program director in me. A budget and funding proposal was in place for the 1999–2000 season, while work continued on in developing a marketing program and a longer-term funding plan.

This was the shot heard 'round the world for skeleton sliders. After decades, the International Olympic Committee had ruled in favor of the inclusion of men's and women's skeleton for the 2002 Olympic Winter Games. Our whole world changed overnight. I was at the Park City track helping our athletes prepare for their initial days of on-ice training when we received the word that skeleton was in. We were pumped, and our training session was definitely more serious and focused than usual.

We went into the 1999–2000 season knowing that if we could succeed, if we could overcome, and if we could make the program we were building successful, we could succeed on the largest amateur athletic stage in the world—the Olympic Games. We subsequently learned that, based on the World Cup nations' rankings from the 1998–99 season as well as an expanded women's field due to this new Olympic status, the United States would be allocated four male and three female positions in the World Cup field for the 1999–2000 season—the maximum allowable allotments.

The drive for Olympic gold for the American skeleton sliders had finally begun.

CHAPTER TEN
American Sliders

High expectations are the key to everything.
—Sam Walton

Getting into the Winter Olympics was a major victory for skeleton, but it would be a major embarrassment for, in particular, the United States if the Americans were to ultimately fail to exploit our home-track advantage.

Well into the 1990s, U.S. sliders had been little more than cannon fodder at international events . . . spectators more than spoilers, save for the occasional medal-winning effort turned in by an Orvie Garrett, a Jim Shea, or a Chris Soule. The hardy Americans had made plenty of friends around the world, but that's to be expected when you're the life of the parties, making life easier for opponents by not consistently challenging for medals. In those days, competitors from other countries enjoyed, certainly, being around their gregarious American comrades, who were much more adept at drinking others under the table than they were in beating their opponents down the track. Those lovable Yanks brandished the best toasts and they could climb atop a bar table or stool and warble drinking songs with the best—other than maybe the British sliders—but shaving a second or two off their individual runs was a skill many hadn't yet mastered. They would need to in order to be ready for Salt Lake City in 2002.

Shea's breakthrough victory in 1999 at Altenberg in the World Championships was a watershed moment for the United States, a glimpse of what Americans were capable of accomplishing in a sport dominated by Europeans. That triumph was the source of a glimmer of hope for what might come three years later in Utah. That's "Might" with a capital M. Before Shea came along, there still were relatively few Americans sliding on skeletons. Those on sleds were many of the same thrill seekers who had jumped aboard out of curiosity during skeleton's rebirth in the 1980s. There was little new blood in American skeleton by the mid-'90s. Until the sport received an infusion of funds and focused leadership, there was no reason to expect that getting Olympic certification would mean anything to the nearly 300 million Americans who wouldn't know the difference between a lunch tray and a skeleton even if you spotted them the runners.

A new breed of American world-class slider had begun to emerge. Almost all these newcomers had something in common: a high skill level in at least one other sport but a noticeable lack of skeleton pedigree. At any given moment during much of the 1990s, the number of topnotch U.S. sliders capable of competing at the international level could be counted on one hand. The occasional national telecast or high-profile newspaper or magazine article featuring skeleton had brought out some curiosity seekers wanting to know more about the sport. But the mad dash to get into the sport wouldn't begin until well after the International Olympic Committee had sanctioned skeleton as a Winter Games sport.

If there was one thing that American skeleton needed, besides more medals from Shea, Soule, et al., it was the kind of fascinating human-interest story that could be grasped by millions of people who otherwise wouldn't give a whit about a sport that could be named after a Stephen King prop. And it would be really nice if that story featured a protagonist with Olympics-rich bloodlines as well as a personal tale of overcoming the odds to become a hero to generations. Skeleton was a sport that needed to be sold, and for that to happen, its story had to be told, in high drama if possible. Parts of it would have to be embellished and stereotypes demolished, but given the right circumstances and the right smiling countenance to put a face on it, USA Skeleton had the potential to be something really special. With or without the medals, but preferably with. And it could not rely on its national governing body for publicity, financial support, vision, or leadership. Those things had never been there for the skeleton athletes, there were no plans to change, and there was little time left to prepare for the Olympics.

Five-foot-eleven, weighing 180 pounds, and with short, bowed legs—he resembles more of a high school shortstop than a world-class Olympic athlete. He's dyslexic, which often creates someone who is quick on his feet and makes impulsive decisions. Acquaintances brag on Shea, saying he is at his best when the stakes are highest and the chips are down, and that he has an ingenious sixth sense for sniffing out on sight a person's true motives to go along with an uncanny ability to self-promote.

He is cocky enough with print media to take control of an interview by starting and stopping a reporter's cassette recorder to tape a few proclamations, before jumping up and walking away to do something else. There is no animosity involved and no offense taken by the reporter, except to wonder what in blue blazes is going on.

The Jim Shea Story, years removed from Salt Lake City, remains the best thing skeleton has going for it, and it is a doozy. It is an epic spanning three generations, beginning with his paternal grandfather Jack Shea, who won two speed skating gold medals at the 1932 Winter Games in Lake Placid. Jack's son and Jim's dad, Jim Shea, Sr., didn't win an Olympic medal, but he did compete in an Olympiad, skiing Nordic combined and cross-country at the 1964 Games in Innsbruck, Austria. Together, the Sheas accomplished a first in Olympic history—they became the first three-generation Olympians in which each competed in a discipline different from the other two. "I have to admit, I never saw this coming," Jim Sr. told Sports Illustrated in February 2000. "Jimmy played some good lacrosse and a little hockey while he was growing up, but he didn't get hooked on the skeleton thing until a few years ago."

A drunk driver killed Jack Shea, then ninety-one, in January 2002, less than a month before the 2002 Opening Ceremonies. It was a devastating loss for both Jims, although it would prove not to be a debilitating one for Jim Jr. He hadn't been sliding at a gold-medal level going into the Games—his best 2001–2002 World Cup finish before Salt Lake had been a second place at the comfy environs of Lake Placid with no other finish better than fourth. In his last race before the Winter Games, at St. Moritz, he was disqualified in the second and final heat for starting too soon.

To get a more complete picture of Jim Shea, Jr., we go back to when he first got involved in skeleton sliding, circa 1994. In those days, one was more likely to find him passed out in the back seat of a car than standing straight and tall on a skeleton medal podium. Shea says he sometimes slept in cars because he had to scrimp to get by. The Shea family's proud Olympic lineage—even mom Judy had been a supremely skilled alpine skier, narrowly missing making the U.S. Olympic team in 1964—appeared to be coming to an end by the time Jim Shea, Sr. moved his family from Connecticut to Lake Placid in 1988.

It's not as if young Jimmy suddenly became a winter sports phenom just because he now had a Lake Placid zip code. For kicks more than for sport, he and several newfound friends gravitated to activities such as "urban surfing," which was nothing more foolish than balancing on the hood of a car being driven thirty miles an hour by one of the other guys. Another favorite activity was heading out to a sixty-foot cliff overlooking Lake Placid, off which Shea and friends would launch themselves into the water, Jimmy often leaping in full monty mode. Even though he feared heights more than he did exposure, Shea enjoyed standing on top of the cliff just so he could confront his fears at the same time he was conquering any leftover vestiges of modesty.

"I would stay up there five minutes. I didn't want it to be over," Shea years later told *USA Today*. "As soon as I jumped, it'd be over. I'd have to climb back up to get that feeling again."

There's no doubt that Shea loves a good time about as much as he does being the center of attention. (Like the time he was in the back of a room at a news-media event and someone yelled out, "Hey, there goes Jimmy Shea!!" sending reporters scurrying over. Shea himself had been the one who yelled.) A dead ringer for his grandpa Jack—an old photo of a young Jack in his twenties bears an uncanny resemblance to present-day Jimmy, genuinely affable when out of competition mode, almost always looks like he's about to tell a joke or is just about to laugh at yours. Attribute that to the permanently furrowed forehead and upraised eyebrows, one slightly higher than the other. Another thing about Shea: he can't sit still for more than a few minutes at a time. Got something to say? He will listen, his eyes sparkling, but get it out of your mouth quickly. This guy is always on the move.

"Jimmy respected his grandfather tremendously," said Peter Viaciulis, the long-time coach who for years was Shea's closest thing to a skeleton mentor. "He never said anything about the Olympics being his destiny because of what his grandfather and father had done. It was when we finally became an Olympic sport that it became a part of what Jimmy was doing. When he won the World Championships, I told him, 'That's going to help the sport become Olympic,' and he said, 'Yeah, I know.' He had thought about it, obviously, but had never really voiced it."

Between the stints catching waves atop car hoods and doing cannonballs into Lake Placid, Shea also fiddled around racing motorcycles, speedboats, snowmobiles—anything that went fast enough to test his mettle without requiring a whole lot of exertion. To generate some income, he said he got into the restaurant business with some friends, which is a fancy way of saying he waited tables and tended bar. By now in his twenties, he decided to explore Lake Placid's wealthy offering of wintertime sports and its handy venues. He and his buddies ruled out ski jumping before deciding to give bobsled a go. It was a nice alternative to hood surfing and involved speeds at least twice as fast.

Shea was a quick study. He experienced some success in two-man bobsled at the national level, but it would not be a long-term proposition. Bartenders got nice tips, but it wasn't the kind of living needed to support participation in a sport whose primary piece of equipment had a going rate of well over $20,000 at that time. So, instead of going for broke by risking going broke in buying a bobsled, Shea took one look at skeleton, liked what he saw, and figured that a $500 investment for a sled was more like it. Suddenly, the Shea family Olympic connection showed a glimmer of hope for continuance, although it would be at least another few years for all the pieces to come together.

Shea took up skeleton racing on a dedicated basis and did well enough to be named 1995 U.S. rookie of the year by the United States Bobsled and Skeleton Federation. But that didn't mean as much to him as it might have meant to others, because he knew the best competition was in Europe. If he was going to have any chance of becoming one of the best, he would have to go live and train overseas, rubbing elbows with the fastest sliders in the world that included the likes of Austrian Christian Auer, Canadian Ryan Davenport, German Willi Schneider, and Swiss Gregor Stähli. Outside his family and a few friends, there was little to tether Jim Shea to Lake Placid, so he packed his sled, a suitcase, and a few other odds and ends and took his biggest leap yet off the high cliff, this precipice overlooking a future that held who-knew-what. He headed to Europe, his intent to stay for a while.

"Guys today are so spoiled," Shea said in January 2005, polishing off a sandwich at a local restaurant near the base of Mount Van Hoevenberg outside Lake Placid, a few hours after the end of the 2005 America's Cup races. "When I started out, I started off with guys like Orvie Garrett and Danny Bryant," he added. "We went to Europe and paid our own way. It's hard for guys like me who paid their own way for so long and then have to listen to these new kids coming along and complaining about not getting their per diem allowance quickly enough. You look at them not understanding where they're coming from.

"In those early days of sliding we were definitely a lot rowdier. We got into a lot more trouble, nothing serious. Now it's a little more serious and a little more structured. A lot of the fun has been taken out of it, unfortunately."

After paying his way over to Europe in the mid-1990s, Shea found himself strapped for cash, trying to get by while further learning the ropes of international skeleton competition. It was rare that he had enough money to even pay for a box disguised as a motel room, so when he couldn't bum some space from a fellow slider, he would sometimes sleep in the sled sheds at the bottom of a track.

"I froze my butt off," Shea recalled. "I used to cook for myself with one of those little camper stoves. I would cook my breakfast and lunch right out in front of the start house. I wanted them to see me there, freezing, hoping they would feel sorry for me and give me a couple of free training runs. Once in a while they would. I also used to help out with the track crews doing odds and ends. I made a lot of great friends and had a lot of great experiences, so it wasn't all bad by any stretch."

One friend he made in Europe was a Swiss girl named Mia, who invited Shea to go home with her for Christmas and to meet her family. No dummy, Shea accompanied Mia to St. Moritz. She showed him all around town. It was, he said, like he had died and gone to heaven. "It was a great, great Christmas that I'll never forget," he said. "Her boyfriend wasn't very excited about it, but I had a great time, man. That's what it's all about."

To some degree, there was the family legacy hanging over Jimmy, a shadow that no one mentioned in polite company, but which followed him in his early years. There was also the challenge with his dyslexia, which in some ways provided the passion and the drive to succeed in spite of any odds stacked against him. Jimmy was just not the sort of boy or man to refuse to play the hand life dealt him. But I also believe Jimmy would have pursued winter sports with the same zeal even if the Olympic museum at Lake Placid didn't boast those grainy yet beautiful black-and-white photos of his grandfather holding aloft his two gold medals, or pictures of his father competing in the 1964 Games.

From the day Jimmy first rode a bobsled, he didn't look back. He persevered to become a lead slider on the U.S. skeleton national team, competing internationally as he chased his dream of following in his father's and grandfather's footsteps. Following a World Cup tour in Europe, Jimmy insisted on learning more about sliding, which is why he decided to stay behind and not go home for a while.

Coach Viaciulis sat Jimmy down and told him, "You have to come home with me because you don't have any money, you don't have any transportation, you don't know the language, and you don't really know where you are." Jimmy just gazed back at Peter, and, with his all-American, eternally optimistic grin, said he was staying. This was the kind of challenge he had lived for, and something that had been missing in his life had been fulfilled.

With almost no money, Jimmy hitchhiked across Europe to train on various tracks. He slept in bobsleds and sheds, and he practically begged the European sliders to teach him the skills and art of the sport. They saw the sacrifices he was willing to make, and, impressed, more often than not they complied with his requests for guidance and expertise. As a result of that hard-won training and tutoring, in 1998, Jimmy became the first American to win a World Cup race. His family's Olympic legacy combined with his international success helped in bringing the sport of skeleton to the attention of the FIBT, the Salt Lake Organizing Committee, and the International Olympic Committee.

Shea's journey through Europe wasn't a total hardship case. On a good night, he might find a cozy place in a barn loft for cozying up, where he had the luxury of catching some of the heat emanating from the livestock below. All he needed now was a little bit of room service, and he would have had his own three-star hotel.

"Once in a while I'd get a hotel room and wash my clothes in the tub," Shea told *USA Today*. "I wouldn't shower for three weeks on end. I was a total grub, doing what I had to do. All that mattered to me was getting runs and learning about sliding."

While he was acclimating himself to the life of skeleton vagabond, Shea was beginning the long, slow climb up the international ladder. In 1994–95, his first World Cup season, he never finished better than twenty-fourth in any of the World Cup races, until he got to Lake Placid for the last event preceding the World Championships. The home cooking and familiar surroundings paid off. Shea finished second at Lake Placid behind Austria's Franz Plangger, picking up enough points to jump him up to twenty-first in the final World Cup overall standings.

A year later, Shea climbed all the way to eighth in the final World Cup standings on the strength of a fourth-place finish at Lake Placid, an eleventh at Altenberg, and a pair of top-fifteen placings at La Plagne (France) and Calgary. Yet as good a season as it was for Shea, he wasn't top dog among Americans. Enter relative newcomer Chris Soule, who finished seventh, one spot ahead of Shea in the final standings. Shea and Soule were both in their twenties, moving up the charts rapidly, and giving American skeleton its best one-two punch ever—the kind of nucleus that would go a long way toward establishing the credibility of USA Skeleton once we could get the program rolling.

Where Shea brought the winter-sport name recognition and the aw-shucks quality of Everyman to the table, Soule provided the leading-man looks and the Hollywood charisma, and it was no big surprise when he ended up getting part-time work as a movie stuntman. Driving a skeleton eighty miles an hour down a steeply banked, icy track must have been somewhere in his job description, which for stuntmen means doing whatever the director needs done to get the right shot.

Soule's first trip down the icy track had been a near-disaster. It was as a brakeman in a two-man bobsled, his driver the much-experienced Brian Vasser. Vasser gave Soule a few basic instructions before they were to push off, starting with a directive to count the curves so they could keep track of where they were on the track. Things were fine for the first four curves, when suddenly the G-forces caught up with the novice Soule, forcing his head down, so disorienting him that he lost count around the time they were being slingshot through curves six and seven.

"By now we're going like hell," Soule recalled. "I didn't know where we were. My head was being pushed toward the bottom of the sled, and now there was blood coming out of my nose. And we're still going faster and faster."

Going through one particularly big curve, they hit a wall and Soule, through the mental fog, figured they had four or five curves left to navigate. At some point he felt Vasser's helmet bumping down on his, and it was Vasser's desperate way of trying to tell Soule to start hitting the brakes. But before Soule could bring their speed under control, they were airborne about ten feet off the ground, headed, thankfully, straight into a pile of snow. The bobsled landed on top of the two sledders, although neither was seriously hurt and both were able to walk away.

"That was my introduction to sliding, and I don't know how close we came to killing ourselves," Soule said.

Although a newcomer to sliding, Soule, who had grown up in Connecticut, had had a good taste of extreme sports. Rock climbing and bridge jumping were among activities he had tried. His girlfriend at the time was a skiing aerialist. Everywhere Soule turned, it seems, he was meeting someone with Winter Olympic experience or ties that would soon be rubbing off on him. Living and working in Lake Placid, he even had a neighbor who had been an Olympic luger.

On top of that, Soule met Shea at a restaurant where they worked together, Shea as a waiter and Soule as a cook. He also would often run across speed skaters at a neighbor's house or at a party.

"I didn't know it was such a big deal at the time, but I would be at parties where there were something like twenty Olympians hanging out," said Soule, just nineteen at the time he was meeting all these athletes.

Intrigued by what he was hearing about sliding, Soule showed up for summer testing administered by the USBSF, although he remained skeptical about his sliding potential because he was lean and better equipped for endurance sports than he was for a sport that rewarded explosive power.

"I really wasn't shaped for the sport, and when I did the testing I scored poorly," he said. "I didn't have any form, knew no technique, and didn't know what I was getting into."

What he was getting into was a bobsled, and that's what he concentrated on for his first two years before shifting his focus onto skeleton. Soule's first full season of World Cup skeleton racing was 1995–96, and he proved a quick learner. His three best finishes were twelfth at Altenberg, fifth at La Plagne, and thirteenth at the World Championships—en route to a seventh-place ranking in the final World Cup points standings. Soule's results over the next two years would be remarkably similar—consistently in the top fifteen in World Cup races and both times in the top ten in the final overall standings. These results were quite unique, in that it usually takes the best potential athletes at least three to five years of World Cup experience before they start finishing in the top ten.

Soule, much like Shea, until now had been a self-made man, scraping together dollars to pay his own way to races and persevering through countless on-track bumps and bruises to refine his driving techniques. It was a bumpy ride, but a fun one, too. No pain, no gain and all that jazz. In addition to his work as a cook polishing his culinary skills, Soule also did some painting and landscaping. Over time, he gained a reputation as a so-so pusher with an uncanny ability to pick up tenths of seconds through his driving down the track. He could compound his speed like no other slider. Chris is an extremely talented driver of the sled, probably the most natural we had.

"Skeleton was instinctive for me," the easygoing, at times self-deprecating Soule said. "Unlike bobsled, I would be able to drive my own sled and make my own decisions. Besides, I wasn't able to afford a bobsled at the time. Skeleton just fit me. It just felt right to be going down the hill headfirst on top of a sled. I know that sounds kind of odd, but I realized I was excelling at it pretty quickly. I did well enough that first year that I won rookie-of-the-year honors from the USBSF.

"I was able to put myself in position to make the national team, you know, but I had to weather some bruises throughout the season. I knew it was going to take a lot of determination to get through it all, and that was one of the biggest draws for me. There wasn't a formal program at the time, meaning the only way I was going to learn was by going down the track, over and over. I must have gone down the track 130 to 150 times that first year.

"It was a tough track and I took a beating. Europeans stopped going to the old (Lake Placid) track because it was such an aggressive track. You run into a wall and you rip your speed suit. But I kept at it. I was learning that if you put a shoulder down, the sled would do this and if you pressed a knee down, it would do that. Lift your head up and you can feel the wind pushing into you, which tells you that's one way to slow yourself down if you have to."

Through skeleton, Soule would later get his first gig as a stuntman working for director Ridley Scott on the movie *G.I. Jane*, starring Demi Moore. Soule and Terry Holland helped Scott set up camera locations and stunt double work for skeleton scenes that were supposed to introduce Moore's character early in the film, only to end up on the cutting-room floor. The film's stunt coordinator, however, liked what he saw in Soule, inviting him to Jacksonville, Florida, where Soule spent another four months working with former Navy Seals to complete stunt shooting for the film.

"I ended up being a stunt double for five different actors in that four months, and I did falls," Soule said. "I even jumped out of a helicopter and into the ocean. If you've seen the film, I'm the guy who did the stunt where one of the characters falls down a hill and breaks his legs. I was kind of a rugged kid growing up, so I was used to pushing my body a little bit extra. I looked at it the same way I did in doing my sport. I planned as much as I could, went through the motions as much as I could, and then tried to pull it off."

Soule also has done some modeling work, and his TV and film work also includes *Sex and the City*, *The Siege*, *At First Sight*, *Stepmom*, and the soap opera *Days of Our Lives*.

Shea and Soule weren't best of friends, but they were friends. They were two of a kind, skeleton sliders who spent several years honing their craft with minimal hands-on instruction. Together they formed the nucleus for what was gradually becoming a national program that soon would be rivaling its European counterparts. Without the Olympic banner to show off and still with little money or support coming its ways from the USBSF, U.S. skeleton would need to find a new breed of world-class sliders without benefit of a high-profile image to help trumpet its existence.

A number of the American sliders who had competed during the eighties and well into the nineties, daring pioneers such as Bryant, Garrett, and Holland were now hitting their forties. In order for the United States to continue moving up in the sliding world, it would have to get quicker, and, inevitably, younger in the numbers games. More recruits would be needed to produce the kind of competitive depth that would translate in to more top-ten World Cup finishes. While the Europeans had a richer skeleton history, they still needed a strong U.S. team to gain full credibility and sanction in the eyes of the Federation Internationale de Bobsleigh et de Tobogganing and the IOC.

The closest thing USA Skeleton has to an authentic hero off the track as well as on is a woman, and her name is Lea Ann Parsley. The Ohio native is a registered nurse with three degrees, including a doctorate, and she has been a firefighter since she was a teenager. In 1999, she was honored as Ohio's Firefighter of the Year for crawling through a shattered window of a trailer home engulfed in flames to save the lives of a woman and the woman's disabled daughter.

Parsley, a five-foot-eight, raven-haired beauty who, if they were so inclined, could pair with the handsome Soule to give skeleton its own marquee cover-caliber couple, went to Marshall University on a basketball scholarship. She ended up throwing the javelin and doing the high jump as well. She's also a certified emergency medical technician whose other vocations have included fighting forest fires. She can play the drums and sing, having soloed on an Olympic-inspired CD titled *All I've Got.* Yet, the single Parsley is anything but egotistical. She's a devout Christian who does much more than pay lip service to values such as humility and selflessness—she lives them. Her teammates have referred to her as Eeyore, the lovable, self-deprecating character from Winnie-the-Pooh. One teammate has another description for her: "She's a fembot," Tristan Gale said. "Lea Ann can do anything."

"Athletes tend to think they're always the best, that they're always going to win," Parsley once told *USA Today.* "You have to have a little of that to be successful. But I try to tone that side down."

Unlike Shea, Parsley did not have an Olympic-caliber lineage, although she is a descendant of the McCoy family, as in the Hatfields and McCoys. And unlike Soule, she didn't happen to gravitate to Lake Placid as a teenager, performing menial odd jobs to piece together a living while being introduced to sliding and making the party rounds around Lake Placid. An accomplished handball player as well, Parsley one day sat down at her computer and started surfing the Internet, searching for some possible handball-sponsorship ideas. Somewhere in there, she stumbled across bobsled, then, upon further review, skeleton. She had loved roller coasters as a kid, and this sounded like a sport that would fit her bill. Thirty at the time, she was about to embark on a second athletic career.

It wasn't a smooth ride for the natural athlete. Just a month after she first got onto a skeleton sled, Parsley went to Germany and badly cut her chin on the front of her sled while crashing in a curve during a practice run. She got the injury bandaged, returned to the top of the track the next day, and again got banged up, splitting her chin open again when she messed up at the exit of a turn, going airborne and landing on her sled.

"You're trying to remain calm while at the same time you're making split-second decisions as you're entering these turns so quickly," Parsley said, comparing her work as a firefighter and nurse to skeleton racing. "My fire job and nursing job run parallel to what I do as an athlete. We spend so much time preparing for the moment. In sports, it's the race. In my other jobs, it's the crisis situation. Yes, both are very risky and can be a little scary, but all that preparation and training and practice brings that risk level way down. Going eighty miles per hour is pretty intense and running into a burning building is pretty intense, but after you've done it so many times, it becomes second nature."

Parsley qualified for her first U.S. national team in 1998–99 as a B Teamer, able to race in North American events but not yet on the World Cup circuit because the United States was restricted to two World Cup sports for women that year based on the previous year's nations' standings. Parsley would make it to the A team for the 1999–2000 World Cup season. She was a quick success, never finishing worse than sixth in any of the six World Cup races, while completing the season fourth in the overall points standings.

A year later, Parsley would be joined on the World Cup circuit by the spunky and diminutive Tristan Gale, the poster girl for the depth-building success of the first two skeleton schools held at Park City, Utah, in January and October 1998. Gale, then eighteen, was one of about fifteen to twenty sliders that participated in the second school. In Gale, a New Mexico native, American skeleton had gained a seasoned winter-sport athlete with ample experience in alpine ski racing. Her parents had moved the family to Salt Lake City, where Tristan raced alpine for eight years at Snowbird, Dick Bass's resort—just over the mountain from Park City—before changing to skeleton.

Actually, her switch to skeleton was more accidental than intentional, more impulsive than planned. In the summer of 1998, she tagged along with a friend of hers, Steve Holcomb, a fellow veteran ski racer who was trying out for the men's bobsled team. Gale accompanied Holcomb and became more than just a spectator, herself taking part in the series of tests measuring things like strength, speed, and agility. Like Holcomb, she scored well enough to merit serious consideration for bobsled. She was told she was too small (at five feet two and about 110 pounds), which was fine with her. She wasn't interested in competing at bobsled, only in adding morale support to Holcomb, who to this day is an excellent driver for USA Bobsled.

Others at the tests had taken notice of Gale's superior athletic skills, suggesting that she would be a natural for skeleton—if only she knew what it was. She would soon find out. The new acquaintance planting the skeleton seed in Gale's head was none other than bobsled veteran Pat Brown, the former coach of the Jamaican bobsled team.

"Pat said to me, 'You really ought to look into skeleton—I think you've got a shot,'" Gale said. "He pointed at Lincoln DeWitt and told me, 'There's a guy who already does it.' I was told that skeleton is sort of like luge on a bobsled track, except you go headfirst at eighty miles an hour with your chin going over choppy ice. I said, 'Nah. My parents love me, and I'm not suicidal. There is no way that you're going to get me on that sled.'

"I'm not a crazy person. I don't bungee jump. I don't have any of those 'need-for-speed' leanings. Sure, I like to do some things that make the adrenaline pump, but I don't want to risk myself doing it."

Gale didn't walk away, though. She later took part in a skeleton push competition. Despite her small stature, Gale's surprising speed and strength paid off. She won the push championship against women who had been sliding for five years or more. She then returned home to begin her senior year of high school, but was called back in the fall after the Park City track was iced with the skeleton school about to get underway.

"They told me, 'Give us one day. We'll send you down from the junior start.' So I decided to give it a shot."

With plenty of caution, though. Gale would go off starting out halfway up the track, but she would have every part of her body covered by some type of padding; hockey pads, football pads, soccer shin guards, and two mouth guards. She was going to make sure, despite any urgings to the contrary, that nothing was going to get hurt should she either come flying off the sled or crashing into a wall.

Gale's mom had come out to the track to watch her daughter make her first skeleton descent, standing by near the finish line, out of sight from where Tristan was up at the halfway point, but well within a mom's yelling range. Somehow, the order of sliders got mixed up. Gale was supposed to be the first girl down the track, but another ended up going ahead of her, only to crash right in front of Gale's mother and slide off down the track out of sight in limp unconsciousness.

"I could hear my mom screaming her head off," Gale said, "and I was yelling back at her down the mountain, telling her it wasn't me. She finally was able to see that this other girl was a lot bigger than me, and she put two and two together." Tristan was handed a walkie-talkie to try to calm her mom down. She finally got through by saying, "Mom, it's not me . . . I'm up next!" After they got the other girl off the track, the announcement was made; "Track is clear for Tristan Gale." "I can only imagine what my mom was thinking at that point. You know, she doesn't let me go near cliffs or anything like that. I'm sure there are still some fingernail marks embedded in the stands between turns eleven and twelve. She is so cute."

Like Parsley, likewise a natural athlete, Gale advanced quickly in the skeleton ranks. After acing skeleton school, she tried out for the national team, and made the B team for the 1998–99 season. She placed tenth at the North American championships, held at Calgary, and fifth at the U.S. championships at Park City. In 1999–2000, she was the top American at the North American championships, this time at Park City, and came in fourth at the U.S. championships, also at Park City. Her 2000–01 results in those two championships dropped to eleventh and fifth, respectively, but she won two of the three America's Cup races that season, at Park City and Lake Placid, and was fourth in the third race, at Calgary.

Like other American sliders around her, Gale was a product of minimalist instruction, picking up tips piecemeal from the likes of assistant coach Peter Viaciulis and veterans such as Danny Bryant, as well as watching more-seasoned competitors and gleaning bits of pushing and driving techniques from what she saw. One thing working in her favor was her ski-racing background. While skeleton tracks don't have flags or gates, they do have the kind of demanding curves that an experienced ski racer has dealt with before.

"It's the same kind of lines a ski racer will see in giant slalom [GS]," Gale said, "although the curves in skeleton are coming at you a lot faster than they do in GS—they come at you as fast as the turns in slalom, yet you are going the speed of downhill. If you're a good alpine ski racer, then skeleton is a sport that works out for you. I wasn't that good at the speed events [downhill and super GS] in ski racing because I was light and just didn't like going fast. All my ski-racing friends are so floored that I'm doing this sport because of my reputation for not liking to go fast. But it's different when you're on the sled, at least in my mind, and that's all that matters.

"When I first found out that the Olympics were coming to Salt Lake City—basically, my hometown—I was so excited, and I hadn't even heard of skeleton at that point. I couldn't wait because that meant all of the ski racers would be coming to town. That was still my mentality, and, you know, it worked out for the best. Once I got into skeleton, it became my life, completely. You sacrifice everything: our personal life, your friends. That's fine as long as you have a goal and don't mind working toward it. The people who remain in it are those who really want it."

The Olympics/Utah connection would light a spark for skeleton not just in Gale but in the life of another local resident. Lincoln DeWitt was a former college track athlete (running the 800 and 1,500 meters at the University of Pennsylvania) who had moved to Utah years earlier and was a ski instructor from 1990 through 1996. He was a computer geek by day, even though at six feet two and a rugged 190 pounds he didn't look the part of a dweeb. DeWitt became intrigued soon after the Salt Lake Organizing Committee started building the bobsled track in preparation for the 2002 Games.

Together with his friend Kevin McCarthy and two other pals, DeWitt signed up to try skeleton in the fall of 1997. It was public knowledge that about $25 million had been invested in the new track that was practically in DeWitt's backyard, prompting him to exercise the if-you-build-it-they-will-come rationale for trying anything at least once. DeWitt and his three pals pooled their resources to buy two sleds to be alternated among them. DeWitt was hooked after his first run.

"That whole first winter," DeWitt recalled, "one of my friends and I were up there pretty much for every sliding session that was made available. We missed only a couple. Most of the sessions were at night and on the weekends, so I could work around it. My work was flexible anyway. I'd work odd hours, which also helped me when it had come to skiing. On days where we had gotten some new powder overnight, I'd work seven to nine in the morning, go out and ski until noon, then go back to work."

For much of that initial sliding season in 1997–98, DeWitt and friends took dozens of runs down the Park City track, trying out different things to improve their times, as much as they could, anyway, without much in the way of available tutelage. They would occasionally run into a bobsledder and hit him up for some sliding tips, although little of what they heard proved useful—the two disciplines were so different in so many ways.

"We might ask some guy, 'How do you make a sled go left?' and we wouldn't get the same answer twice," DeWitt said. "Most of what I was able to figure out on my own had to do with dealing with the lines; how to get into and out of turns, just like in skiing.

"In the early days Terry Holland would help me out some. Half-jokingly, he would tell me, 'I'll gladly help you out until you get within a second of me on the track, and then you're on your own.'"

DeWitt's first year of sliding competition consisted mainly of local club races, in which a picnic table, if one was available, doubled as a medals podium. His early rivals in those small-time, low-key races included veteran slider Ralph Mirabelli, then in the midst of making the switch to two-man bobsled. Mirabelli would occasionally jump into the club races and more often than not win them, relegating the likes of DeWitt and DeWitt's friends such as Chris Haerter to battling for the silver and bronze medals.

DeWitt didn't stay hidden in the club circuit for long. He qualified for the U.S. national team for the 1998–99 season, joining the likes of Shea, Holland, and me, although Soule had taken a year's sabbatical to chase other pursuits for the time being. DeWitt's first year on the World Cup circuit was about everything a rookie could expect: no top-ten finishes, but at least a few encouraging signs such as a fifteenth at Park City, an eighteenth at Igls, and a seventeenth in the season-ending World Championships at Altenberg. He finished the 1998–99 season twenty-fourth in individual World Cup point standings. In 1999–2000, he would improve to thirteenth overall on the strength of top-ten finishes at Lillehammer and Igls. Lillehammer was his apex for the year: He finished sixth, just .63 behind winner Jeff Pain of Canada.

DeWitt was showing the kind of steady progress indicative of a skeleton program now getting a foothold financially with the credibility boost of Olympic certification and USOC support. Not that there weren't some red-faced moments along the way. Such as the time in December 1998, when DeWitt went north to Calgary to compete in his first World Cup event outside the United States. During one of his training runs early in the week, just seconds after he had pushed off and jumped onto his sled, DeWitt noticed coming out of the first turn that his sled sounded funny. It was veering all over the place. He had no directional ability, and it felt more like being on a flying saucer than a Flexible Flyer.

At first he thought that he had put too much "rock" in his sled, that he had gone too far in adjusting the bow of his runners, making them too rounded and therefore too unstable for the icy track. No, that wasn't it. Suddenly, it dawned on him: He had forgotten to remove his runner guards—strips of garden hose slit down the middle so they could be wrapped over his runners for protection between runs. His attempts to negotiate the turns were about as successful as trying to bust a three hundred-yard drive with the head cover still on his driver.

"I was only a hundred meters into the run, and I remember wondering if I should just bail right there," DeWitt said. "But we were only getting two training runs a day, and I didn't want to totally waste this one. What was funny was that I was actually going fairly fast considering I was running on rubber hose. My biggest fear that when I hit my first high-G turn, instead of going around, I would just fly up into the wooden roof. But I really didn't want to get off, either.

"So I just stuck out both feet farther to each side, not to slow down, but to help keep the sled more stable. I was fine, just kind of wiggling my way down the track. Still, I was ticked because I had blown a training run. I was going only forty or fifty miles per hour when I should have been going seventy. People were yelling and screaming at me over the fence, and I was going slow enough to wave back at them. As embarrassed as I was, I was glad to find out that someone else had done the same thing before me and my time was better than his. One of the Japanese sliders coming behind me almost did the same thing, but it bummed me that someone told him just before he went. You know, misery loves company."

By this time, Soule had returned to sliding after his one-year hiatus. He did even better than how he had left off at the end of the 1997–98 season. Soule's worst finish in 1999–2000 was ninth at Nagano, placing fourth or better in all other races. The strongest season of Soule's career so far vaulted him to second in the final overall World Cup standings, with Shea not far behind in seventh and DeWitt another six places arrears of Shea. Going into the 2000–01 season, America had its strongest men's team ever, which bode well for USA Skeleton's Olympic medal hopes, with the 2002 Winter Games being just over twelve months away. The American women were looking good as well.

The motivational processes were evolving and seemed to be working. The athletes convincingly believed in our USA Skeleton program and coaching abilities. Matt Roy, USBSF executive director, admirably expressed his surprise to me at the time that so many skeleton athletes were "buying into" the program. This "buy-in," in fact, was simply the result of structuring a fair and objective program as well as mutual respect between athletes and program leadership. Sliders such as Lincoln DeWitt, Lea Ann Parsley, and Chris Soule would actually apologize to me whenever they failed to medal in a World Cup event. But, this reflects the level of commitment and teamwork we sought in USA Skeleton.

The Olympic eligibility rules set forth by the FIBT required an athlete to participate for the same country in at least five FIBT-sanctioned races over the two seasons immediately preceding an Olympic Winter Games. This requirement in and of itself provided the athletes with a defined structure in which they could qualify for the games. The FIBT-sanctioned events included World Cup, America's Cup, Europa Cup, and World Championship participation.

Because of our outstanding individual performances, USA Skeleton now had adequate funding from the United States Olympic Committee through its PODIUM (Partnering Olympic Dreams into Utah Medals) program, which was developed to aid and assist Olympic hopefuls who have shown an ability to compete internationally and successfully. Parsley, Shea, Soule, and Tricia Stumpf earned the results we needed to fully fund USA Skeleton for the 2000–2001 season. This was a first for USA Skeleton, and it was well-deserved by athletes and coaches alike as a team.

PODIUM provided, among other things, a financial incentive to the athletes based on their World Cup and World Championship results. Typically, an athlete would have to finish the World Cup individual rankings and/or World Championships in the top five in order to qualify for PODIUM. That created pressure in these competitions. Some of the athletes who were not eligible for PODIUM, the "have-nots," as they referred to themselves, began to be somewhat divisive and to complain about the PODIUM athletes' financial advantage and perceived unfair status. Over time, almost all of the dissatisfaction came from athletes who missed the Olympic, World Cup, or national team by one or two positions. This is simply human nature and we dealt with it as best we could. But, as in all of life, it's about the achievers. Complaints are irrelevant unless possible solutions come with them.

A few sliders began to find illicit ways to attempt to improve their results by "juicing" their runners, which carries with it the same kind of ethical violations committed by baseball players using steroids or cyclists who use doping to gain an advantage. "Juicing," in the context of sliding, refers to the application of substances wiped onto runners prior to a run so there will be less friction between runners and the ice, thus increasing the speed of the sled. The program would have to have race juries wipe clean all runners with six hundred-grain sandpaper prior to a race and keep samples in baggies labeled with the slider's name. Some runners with unapproved metallic compositions and other irregularities were beginning to surface. Some athletes did not know any better; others did. There will always be individuals who are trying to take shortcuts, and the FIBT was required to stay a step ahead of them in order to ensure fair competition. USA Skeleton stood for fairness, and we intended to promote this attitude and police whenever necessary.

We had an organization, we had a team, and we had Olympic status. But could we compete as the pressure mounted?

CHAPTER ELEVEN

The Countdown to Salt Lake City

People don't plan to fail. They fail to plan.
—Mark McCormack

Now that the International Olympic Committee and the Salt Lake Organizing Committee had given their joint blessing to skeleton, it was up to USA Skeleton to turn the corner, to build on the foundation that had been laid over the last two years, and to field a team that would be medal-worthy by February 2002. We had the home-track advantage, money in our pockets, and a salaried head coach, Ryan Davenport, who had won two World Championships. The pieces were in place—but peace of mind in terms of high-level preparedness remained a bit more elusive.

Bringing in Davenport, a foreigner (he came all the way from Canada) was skeleton's way of emulating a tactic that women's gymnastics had used nearly two decades earlier in reaching across the Atlantic Ocean and bringing the legendary Romanian coach Bela Karolyi to the United States. Karolyi was the best in his profession when it came to turning pixie gymnasts into steely gold-medal winners. Davenport had at one time been the best there was in the world as a slider, getting down to the bottom of the track faster than anyone else. There was more to Davenport than just innate driving ability, though. He was a master technician with an incredible mind for detail, whether it be designing sleds and runners for maximal performance or being able to calculate track split times in his head. He was the perfect left-brain mentor needed to complement a bunch of Americans with right-brain creativity.

Ryan was our "mad scientist," using a laptop to keep interval times of all the sliders, but only as a backup. He kept the spreadsheets—and I'm not exaggerating—in his head. He knew to within a small fraction of a second the expected finish time of a slider on a given run based on their first two or three intervals and their past performances. He did this, he said, "just for fun," and to "keep his mind active."

For the USA Skeleton sliders, part of their motivation to move up in the World Cup rankings was the age old "us against the world mentality" in which they would prove themselves worthy, not only to the rest of the world but to the United States Bobsled and Skeleton Federation . . . with its inherent bobsled-first mentality.

We had something to prove to the USBSF, which for so long had ignored skeleton. We all wanted to achieve individual and team success without financial support, administrative assistance (or any help at all) from the USBSF. We had, effectively, for the first time, our freedom. We could operate independently, as well as efficiently and effectively. The athletes would be treated with fairness and objectivity. We were psyched, excited, and anticipatory of great things.

My goal was to create a working environment with no distractions. Davenport thrived in these circumstances. By taking over the coaching reins of the USA Skeleton team, the unassuming Davenport was willing to postpone an ambition to focus on his first love, sled building, through the 2002 Games. He had been around the world several times over and seen a number of nations that had tracks but little in the way of skeleton programs. France, for example; Norway, too. Those and other countries in a similar state had a few scattered athletes, but they didn't have the depth of talent beyond one or two good sliders to be able to compete well internationally. In a sense, Davenport was an ambassador for the sport of skeleton, but in a manner that was based more on technical knowledge than gregarious people skills. Yes, Davenport was liked by many, but he was not one to go in big for glad-handing activities.

It had taken a Herculean diplomatic effort on the part of Terry Holland and me to get the reluctant Davenport to commit to the coaching position, although the pledge of a three-year contract was an incentive hard to pass up. It also helped sway Davenport when I reminded Davenport how coaching an Olympic-bound team would look on his resume when he later tried to forge a working relationship with the Japanese, with whom Davenport longed to be associated. Besides that, Ryan was ready to purchase his own townhouse in Calgary, and the skeleton contract would provide him with financial security for this investment.

There was another factor pulling Davenport in the direction of coaching. The 2002 Olympic skeleton competition would be held at Park City, which in just two years had established a reputation as one of the most interesting tracks in the world. Davenport considered Park City an "easy" track to get down safely, which was good for beginners building up experience, and didn't require the most expert of driving skills. But the faster you go, the tougher the track becomes, which is where a slider's aerodynamics and driving skills would be especially crucial. It was just the kind of venue that would give Davenport the kind of ultimate challenge he adored, tinkering with sleds and tweaking sliding positions to get the most out of his sliders' runs. Where was the downside? There didn't seem to be one. Even with Jimmy Shea's 1999 World Championship, the United States was still an outsider to the world's elite skeleton countries, with nowhere still to go but up, yet the Americans had a full two-plus years to get accustomed to a home track and nurture that advantage.

Or was there a home-track advantage? Davenport had some doubts. Assuming the track had been designed and devised with an emphasis on bobsled, Davenport couldn't figure out why the track designers hadn't made the push area much longer so as to play to the American bobsledders' strongest suit—their push starts. Instead, the Park City push straightaway was relatively short. A longer push would have kept bobsledders pushing farther and longer, thus giving American sliders a longer stretch of track to better utilize their inherent advantage.

"I can only assume that there was no thought given by the track planners to construct a track to suit our strengths," Davenport said.

If there was anything the U.S. sliders could draw on with me, it was my ability to come a long way in a short time. That's what they needed to know considering that the Olympics were just twenty-eight months away. In just over two years leading up to the Olympic announcement in October 1999, I had practically come out of nowhere, making the World Cup team, sponsoring two skeleton schools, getting to know most of the individual strengths and weaknesses of U.S. sliders, surrounding myself with capable sliding coaches and experts, and learning the ropes in how to deal with the administrative and political realities incumbent when working with the USBSF. The athletes knew I was committed to the sport and was not just some opportunist. I was now juggling the dual role of competing slider and USA Skeleton program director.

"For the first time, we now believed that someone could take up our cause in dealing with the USBSF," U.S. slider Chris Soule said. "We believed that someone was actually interested in creating and building a fair, funded, and successful program, and that here was someone with the ability and wherewithal to accomplish it.

"The leadership team knew that the athletes are what it is all about. They also wanted to provide us the environment and opportunity to reach what it took to succeed. Robie respected us as individuals and our abilities as athletes. We respected him, his responsibilities, and his mutual commitment towards us. It became a 'One plus one equals three' formula."

What a difference a year had made I could personally attest to, just from the standpoint of sliding. The level of competition was intensifying. A year earlier, in the fall of 1998, I had placed fourth in the U.S. men's national team qualifying race, earning a spot on the 1998–99 World Cup team. This despite the fact that over that summer of 1998, I had not trained consistently in the push. Yet I had made it onto the national team. No such luck in 1999. Despite having spent almost the entire summer in intensive push workouts with Fallon and Kevin Ellis, I finished ninth in the selection races in the fall of 1999. I would not be returning to the World Cup circuit, at least not as a slider.

All athletes with sliding experience were allowed to enter the U.S. national team qualifying races, in which the two best of three races would count for each slider, with each race consisting of two heats. Ten men and eight women would be picked for the 1999–2000 national team, with the top four men and top three women designated for the World Cup circuit. Earning the men's World Cup team slots were Jimmy Shea, Lincoln DeWitt, Terry Holland, and Chris Soule, the latter returning after a year's sabbatical from skeleton racing. The three World Cup women: Tricia Stumpf, Lea Ann Parsley, and Babs Isak. The remaining eleven national-team sliders, total, would be able to compete on other circuits. Among those other eleven were Ellis, the quick-learning skeleton rookie; Tristan Gale; and Fallon Vaughn. The door was kicked open for non-national team sliders as well, given the option of continued training at Park City for the season, the idea being to get as many runs and gain as much experience as possible. I was trying to create a community of competent athletes as well as interested supporters. My motto was, "Inclusion versus exclusion, and objectivity versus subjectivity." The athletes loved it.

With the team picked, now it was time to figure out how high to set the bar for the upcoming sliding season. With that in mind, in late October I convened a meeting of coaches at the Hampton Inn in Kimball Junction, Utah, just below the Utah Olympic Park, which kind of became the skeleton headquarters from 1999–2002. Davenport, Viaciulis, and I pored over strategies, assessed the potentials of all the athletes, and did our best to calculate which sliders from what countries would be the toughest competitors on the World Cup circuit. The way we figured it, if team members finished according to expectations, both the U.S. men and women could expect to improve from fifth and sixth to fourth in the World Cup nations' rankings.

Even though our most critical goal was to move up in the World Cup standings, we also had the need to increase our team's depth and our athletes' experience level. We were making progress: in 1998–99, we had had a total of eighteen sliders ranked, whereas in the fall of 1999, that number now was twenty-five. The Olympics were only two years and four months away, and we had to expand our pool of potential athletes. That's where our policy of maximizing inclusion of participation rather than exclusion of all but the deemed elite made a difference. In the 1999–2000 season, USA Skeleton financed its portion of World Cup tour expenses, the World Championships, and all of the allocated positions for the United States in the North American Championships. This level of funding was unprecedented for U.S. skeleton athletes. This was critical for success.

Although skeleton is an individual sport, the focus of the coaches and my efforts were aimed at motivating positive team results. With each individual doing his or her very best in each competition, our team would climb in the World Cup standings. A team-building attitude was the key. Our international ranking, which dictated the number of allocated competition slots for World Cup, World Championships, and the Olympic Games, was the result of combined individual results. This was a real tightrope walk, because these athletes compete against each other in domestic, as well as international, competition. We were building a team spirit in an individual sport.

The U.S. team exceeded its goals, thanks in large part to the one-two punch of Shea and Soule. They combined for seven of the nine World Cup medals won by Americans in 1999–2000. Shea and Soule won gold and silver, respectively, at the 2000 Goodwill Games held at Lake Placid, while Soule won silver in the World Cup overall standings. On the women's side, Parsley won silver at the World Cup race held at Lillehammer, the first American to medal in women's World Cup competition, and Stumpf took bronze at Igls. In the final World Cup team standings, the U.S. men finished second overall and the women third. This was huge, an unprecedented move up in the standings. Shea placed seventh overall in the final World Cup individual points standings, while Parsley was the fourth woman overall and Stumpf tenth (despite missing one of the four World Cup races because of illness).

One area in which Americans had been especially strong in was the push. In finishing third in the women's 2000 World Championships, Stumpf, a World Cup rookie, had the fastest push in two of the four heats. Among the men, DeWitt had a breakthrough season, improving from twenty-third on the World Cup rankings list to thirteenth. He had the second-fastest average push for the season and posted the fastest push in three of the four heats at the World Championships, where he finished eighth. DeWitt also won the North American Championships held in late February at Park City. The Americans were building depth as well as familiarity with the medal podium.

"Having Ryan there made such a difference," DeWitt said. "It was all trial and error before that, and instead of having to take a bunch of runs to figure out one simple thing, Ryan's being there allowed us to pick up things in a lot less time."

The 1999–2000 season was our watershed. No other nation in history had ever moved from fifth (men) and sixth (women) to second and third respectively in one year. The new world skeleton order included Americans! Our sliders were focused, confident, and gaining what the coaches and I believed to be a competitive advantage. Our dry-land training was more intelligent. We were breaking new ground in improvements in sled and runner equipment. We were earning international respect and having a blast doing it.

Above all, in bringing the lessons of servant leadership and professional management to amateur sports, we were showing that the entrepreneurial model was besting the old, tired way of doing things. We were becoming Olympic medal threats, something some other U.S. Olympic sports hadn't been in years, if not decades. Everything was going right, and on time. I should have known—that didn't bode well. There still was the paranoia of certain persons representing USBSF to contend with.

Despite its newfound Olympic status and a 1999–2000 sliding season that had exceeded preseason goals, USA Skeleton still was not out of the woods in terms of its relationship with the "leaders" of the USBSF.

Accusatory letters, curt e-mails, angry messages, and even threats of lawsuits began to find their way to me. In working to get a skeleton team capable of going on the offensive in World Cup competition, I was having to go into defensive mode myself. I was the buffer between our athletes and the threatened "good ol' boys." One of my battles would be in getting the six-item test used for bobsled modified into a four-item version for skeleton athletes, a test more attuned to their particular skills and needs. There was more to this ongoing skirmish, though.

The USBSF and USA Skeleton were in the midst of their own cold war, and it wasn't about to thaw out any time soon. My commitment to fund the skeleton program through USA Skeleton meant that an aggressive marketing program would have to be launched to find the sponsorship dollars to pay back what essentially was a loan from other contributors and Fallon and me to initially fund skeleton. Ordinarily, marketing efforts are the domain of the national governing body, but in this case, I could not see any marketing effort or sponsorship money en route to skeleton. If the USBSF indeed had a marketing initiative for skeleton, no one in USA Skeleton knew about it. As a matter of fact, the USBSF had no professional marketing personnel or plan in place at that time. It was used to living off USOC funding and basically unaware of how to market itself.

Now was the time to go out and find sponsors who would likely be attracted to this "new" and exciting sport. All the factors were right for USA Skeleton to begin heavy pursuit of major sponsorship dollars with favorable economic conditions spurred in large part in the late 1990s by the dot-com boom. It was a unique and perhaps a one-time shot to establish a long-term relationship with one or more major sponsors.

Through fellow Dallas businessman and sports aficionado Ross Perot, Jr., Taylor Boyd and I were introduced to officials in the Denver winter-sports office of International Management Group (IMG), generally considered the largest sports marketing agency in the world, with a clientele that includes Tiger Woods, Pete Sampras, and Arnold Palmer. Sue McCarthy, IMG's director of sales in the Denver office, became the primary professional marketing contact for USA Skeleton. Working on a retainer basis, McCarthy would scour the United States for likely corporate sponsors. Closer to home, I hired Dallas' Debbie Tolson, an acquaintance of mine who had worked with me on fundraising projects for my alma mater, Culver Military Academy, to help chase down potential sponsors. It would be an aggressive campaign on USA Skeleton's part, one reflective of their ambition to give sliders all the backing they needed to successfully compete on a global scale, now and in the future.

At Sue McCarthy's recommendation, the skeleton program produced letterhead, business cards and apparel bearing the athletes' new USA Skeleton logo to expand visibility. Service mark protection for the name was applied for. A Web site address name was reserved as well. The Texas Sliding Society and USA Skeleton pins were not only very popular, they became an honor to wear.

I kept the USBSF informed of these necessary marketing activities, received no feedback, and was not told that I should do otherwise. We were responsible for building up this sport in the United States, and that's why we needed to reserve these important identity symbols before the International Olympic Committee announced skeleton as an Olympic Winter Games event. We had seen how the intellectual property industry was already getting burdened by cases in which companies were having their names "scalped" for Web site usage, and it was getting worse. We didn't want to be similarly held up by some opportunist exploiting our name for monetary gain before we could establish legal claim to it.

Sometime later, the topic of the USA Skeleton Web site would become an issue with the USBSF, although an entirely different problem had arisen. In the course of its campaign to find corporate sponsors for skeleton, IMG had visited with Adidas, only to find out that there already was a deal in place linking Adidas and skeleton. Well, sort of. The USBSF had entered into a sponsorship agreement with Adidas prior to my being named skeleton program director. Neither I nor anyone else in skeleton had any knowledge of the Adidas contract, and we certainly weren't getting any endorsement dollars or apparel out of the deal at that time. Earlier in its campaign, IMG had found another sporting-apparel company, Columbia Sportswear, interested in striking a deal with skeleton. Adidas and Columbia were, basically, competitors. Signing up Columbia would have conflicted with the pre-existing Adidas deal, even though Columbia's endorsement dollars would have been earmarked for skeleton.

Not only did skeleton lose out on a possible dollar deal with Columbia, but the USBSF had been losing out on dollars by having a "value-in-kind" contract with Adidas. Instead of providing dollars for use by the USBSF, the Adidas contract called for incentive dollars to be paid to the athletes for their World Cup and World Championships results. And even then, there were differences of opinion between Adidas and the USBSF.

This deal was a bad deal for the USBSF and its athletes. I don't blame Adidas—they were doing their job and doing it well. Of even greater concern was that, through this contract, the USBSF had pawned off skeleton's rights as part of a package deal with bobsled, leaving skeleton stuck in a deal with nothing to gain. It was only after IMG had queried Adidas that skeleton was provided apparel and included in the incentive dollars through the USBSF. All previous benefits had inured to bobsled.

USA Skeleton was paying IMG a monthly retainer of $3,500, in addition to success fees. In turn, the marketing company was achieving results through its major sponsorship drive. Sponsorship and revenue-sharing deals were reached with Cheering Bells, SDI apparel manufacturers, and various individuals.

Soon, though, IMG's ambitious search would run into another roadblock. After IMG contacted Visa with an initial proposal, Visa's marketing staff turned around and called the United States Olympic Committee to find out what was going on. Visa, it turned out, already had an endorsement deal with USOC, which in turn had a joint-marketing agreement with many national governing bodies, including the USBSF and, therefore, with skeleton on the trickle-down. Left hand, meet right hand. USOC, suddenly concerned that the USBSF was skirting the terms of the joint-marketing agreement and possibly in its responsibilities in accordance with its assigned national-governing-body status, fired off a letter to the USBSF inquiring as to its relationship with USA Skeleton and me.

The USBSF, now on the defensive, turned around and fired off a missive written by USBSF president Jim Morris and directed at me. Naturally, it wasn't a conciliatory letter opening the door to a polite discussion; in my opinion it was a rude and threatening letter that was copied to USOC. This was yet another example of the vertical and horizontal disconnection and lack of communication between USBSF leadership, staff, and a program director. In fact, it was difficult to communicate with and keep Morris informed of anything going on because he wasn't set up to receive e-mail, according to Matt Roy at that time.

Apparently, Morris also wasn't set up to know who the top skeleton racers were within his domain. During a fall 2001 trip to Utah for an annual meeting of the USBSF, Morris went out to the Park City track to watch some of the skeleton team trials. Kevin Ellis, about to begin his third season as a World Cup team member for the United States, had already set push-time records at the Utah track and on other tracks around the world, and was getting ready to go off on one of the trial's heats. Standing next to Morris at the start, I mentioned Ellis's record-setting performances to Morris, who in turn asked me, "Who is this guy? Where did he come from?" I was astounded. DeWitt always said that Morris had never recognized him.

Here I was, offering my time on a volunteer basis to do a national governing body's job for it, organizing a new program almost from scratch, advancing it hundreds of thousands of dollars (the advances and financial float had accumulated to more than $400,000 by 2000–2001), leading and motivating the athletes to achieve international success in hopes that the program could afford to repay the advances, and the "leader" of the USBSF was threatening legal action and to relieve me from the position for which I had volunteered with board approval.

The skeleton athletes, coaches, and I were building what was quickly becoming the most successful skeleton program in the world, giving it to the USBSF on a silver platter, and some could not see the forest for the trees. As a sidenote, Matt Roy, executive director of the USBSF, and I were working well together and developing a healthy respect for each other while the skeleton program was achieving a level of success unprecedented in history. All some could see was a threat, provoking a knee-jerk reaction. It was almost predictable, leading an organization with which the president was narrowly elected and so disconnected with the athletes.

Thanks to Roy and the measured, productive letter he wrote to the USOC, helpful sponsorship communication among the USOC, the USBSF, and me was initiated. It would allow for productive discussions on how best to market individual sports such as skeleton to some of the larger USOC sponsors. Eventually, the USBSF appointed me to its marketing committee, and IMG went on to represent the USOC.

All's well that ends well . . . except this wasn't the end of the trials and tribulations putting the USBSF and USA Skeleton at odds. Another issue would be the USA Skeleton Web site, which was launched during the 1999–2000 sliding season at a cost of $15,000 for the design and operation—all paid for by USA Skeleton. The USBSF's own Web site was seriously lacking, by comparison, carrying outdated and incorrect information. At the time, there was little evidence on the Internet of skeleton's mere existence. The USBSF Web site was stagnant, non-dynamic, or seldom up to date, nor was it being improved or expanded over time. Member feedback was virtually ignored.

After Shea won a bronze medal at the 1999–2000 World Cup race in Nagano, I arranged to have him introduced between periods at a Dallas Stars National Hockey League game at Reunion Arena in Dallas. Shea's brief on-ice appearance was accompanied by an overhead video presentation about skeleton and Shea that ended showing the Web site's URL of www.usaskeleton.com. The next day, the Web site registered more than five hundred hits.

Not too long afterwards, another hit came the way of USA Skeleton, and it was not the kind I was expecting. It was a letter from a New York resident named Guy Leo, threatening legal action if USA Skeleton didn't immediately pull the plug on its Web site. Leo explained that he had a webcasting contract with the USBSF, and that by launching its own Web site, USA Skeleton was trespassing on his property. I was being threatened with legal action from a person I had never met. And, once again, neither USA Skeleton nor I had any idea there existed a contract between the USBSF and the webcaster.

I couldn't understand why Leo hadn't picked up the phone to at least discuss his concern. So I called Morris to discuss this, and he immediately exploded. He obviously was emotionally upset over the USA Skeleton Web site. He demanded that operations cease because I had "no right" to the Web site. I knew, though, that TSS did have the legal ownership and rights to do as it deemed. Nevertheless, I let Morris know we would cease operations if Leo called me to discuss the situation.

Leo did call me, and we had a constructive discussion. I ended that conversation believing that Leo would work on the USA Skeleton Web site, updating and augmenting it to provide accurate, appropriate, timely, and useful information about the skeleton program and its athletes for purposes such as recruitment and marketing sponsorship. Upon request from Leo, I provided the URL codes to the site. Much of the content of the USA Skeleton Web site was incorporated into the USBSF Web site. Our content and design elements instantly gave the USBSF Web site a better look. Leo eventually admitted to me that he felt like he may have lost a court battle on this issue.

My intent was to do whatever benefited the athletes and expanded the skeleton community; exposure was part of the formula. My leadership and the skeleton staff were more important than the Web site, so I let it go in order to persevere with the program for the athletes' sake. I did not have the time for a court battle, nor was it that important in the overall strategic picture leading up to the Olympics. Leo has continued to upgrade the Web site at www.usbsf.com.

Getting the USBSF to expand its marketing effort would be an uphill battle every bit as treacherous and slippery as a downhill battle for a slider at Altenberg. Pleas to hire a marketing manager or professional sports marketer continued unanswered. Each time I was met with the familiar refrain of, "We can't afford it," relying on the traditional attitude of scarcity as opposed to an abundance mentality. Something finally did sink in, however, and in 2000, the USBSF hired Russian native Dmitry Feld as its marketing manager, hoping to tap into some of the same marketing expertise Feld had shown in raising funds at USA Luge. One of Feld's major moves was to convince the USBSF to hire veteran Florida sports marketer Scott Becker to assist him. Becker was to build on his demonstrated track record of closing major sponsorships for his clients.

Feld and Becker had their work cut out for them. They had little time, with the Olympics less than two years away. Then faced a business economy shaken up by a dot-com boom gone bust. Becker eventually was able to attract Verizon Communications to align itself with the USBSF, as it had with USA Luge, although very little of those Verizon funds were earmarked for skeleton initially. The best I could do was to negotiate from that Verizon agreement an outlay of $60,000 for incentives to skeleton athletes, tied into the World Cup nations' standings and Olympic medals for 2001–2002. The USBSF hadn't hit the big time in terms of marketing appeal, but it had made some major progress.

For that brief moment, funding was no longer the one major issue putting the USBSF and USA Skeleton at odds. Because of its Olympic certification, skeleton was now eligible for support from the United States Olympic Committee via the USOC's PODIUM program. In 1999–2000, Parsley, Shea, Soule, and Stumpf together had earned the results needed to fully fund USA Skeleton for the 2000–2001 season. Our financial gamble was beginning to pay off.

PODIUM was the saving grace for the USA skeleton athletes and our program. PODIUM provided, among other things, a financial incentive to the athletes based on their World Cup and World Championship results. Much of our time in the spring and early summers of 2000 and 2001 were spent drafting PODIUM requests for the following seasons. Examples of program funding under PODIUM included salary reimbursement for coaching, travel, expenses for qualifying athletes, and special needs such as technology and equipment.

The PODIUM program also provided us the ability to provide the athletes with more specific financial assistance. With the Olympics a mere year and a half away, I began to focus on our weaknesses. We needed more assistance in areas such as push training, physical and massage therapy, and sports psychology. Some of our athletes trained for strength and conditioning consistently, and others did not. Fast sprint times on a track didn't necessarily translate into fast push times on the ice. Specificity of training and technique is essential to improving and maximizing one's push time. I solicited strength and conditioning coaches to join our team through to the Olympics.

Following a few personal interviews, USA Skeleton hired a relatively young college coach with a good resume and sufficient experience with college-age track and field athletes. As it turned out, the structure of his training regimens, as well as personality conflicts with the athletes, ultimately created a wedge between the coach and the athletes. I made a second mistake when, after interviewing candidates, we also hired a physical therapist and athletic trainer. Although the trainer proved valuable to the durability and health of the team during the 2000–2001 season, his personality and demands upon USA Skeleton the following season made the situation more of a distraction to than an asset for the athletes. In both of these cases, the athletes were solicited for their vote on whether or not to keep these people on. Both were asked to leave the program. It was an uncomfortable situation at first, but I believe it provided the athletes with comforting evidence that I was willing to do the tough jobs on their behalf, which unfortunately included letting people go.

It was important to bring in this assistance to keep our team healthy and competitive. Fortunately we were able to find a terrifically qualified and popular strength and conditioning coach from Dallas named Bob King. Bob bridged our athletes all the way to the Olympics. A program without these services encourages each athlete to seek out diverse and potentially unqualified therapists, thus increasing the risk of delayed recovery or further injury. The seasons were getting longer with more races, and the competition level was growing more intense all the time. From a strategic and program standpoint, we had to rely on varying athletes peaking at different times while maximizing team performance. Fortunately, we were developing depth and the "weapons" needed to respond to that challenge.

As successful as the U.S. men and women were when it came to surpassing the USA Skeleton team goals for 1999–2000, they would achieve even more team-wide success in 2000–2001, continuing on an upward curve that now positioned them as truly one of the elite sliding nations in the world. Four of the top American sliders were familiar: Shea and Soule for the men, Parsley and Stumpf for the women.

A fifth elite U.S. World Cup slider would emerge in 2000–2001, and he did it in a big way. Lincoln DeWitt had finished twenty-fourth two years earlier in the World Cup points standings, and thirteenth the year before. In 2000–2001, he would jump all the way to first in the final standings, never finishing out of the medals in the last five World Cup races of the season. After beginning the season with a twelfth at Winterberg, DeWitt finished second at Igls, third at La Plagne, second at Nagano, third at Calgary, and first at Park City (the test event for the Olympics). Shea also had a particularly strong season, finishing no worse than seventh in any of the six races, to include a victory at La Plagne, and a third place in the final ranking. Soule would end up eighth. Among the women, Stumpf placed fourth and Parsley sixth, overall. In the team standings, the U.S. men ended up number one and the American women number two. Both final placings were a spot higher than USA Skeleton had devised in its preseason goals.

The depth of the American program was also evident in the second-tier America's Cup races, which typically include many sliders from foreign nations. The number one America's Cup man was U.S. slider Trevor Christie, while Utah resident Tristan Gale took top honors among the women. In less than five years, the U.S. skeleton program had jumped from producing the occasional World Cup medal to one that had the potential, at least to sweep the medals at the 2002 Olympic Games, provided we could secure enough slots to get three men and two women into the Salt Lake City Games.

The competition grew fierce, even among members of the same national team. Conflicts in personalities and attitudes among the sliders were coming to the forefront. No one knew that better than Kevin Ellis, the former trackster. Ellis was moving up the charts as a competitive slider. I also had hired him to be the USA Skeleton team manager. Among his duties was making travel arrangements for all the sliders, including himself. It was not an exact science, and Ellis would sometimes find himself focusing more on other people's off-track logistical foibles than his own on-track tactics in trying to become a faster slider. But that is what he was paid to do.

"There were lots of times," Ellis said, "when Robie didn't necessarily know where the athletes were. It was my job. I'd be booking flights for these athletes from their hometowns to some connecting point. There might be someone in Texas, someone in California, and someone in New York, and they are all going to the same place in Europe. The connecting point might be, say, Cincinnati, and then they would fly over to Europe together so that they would all get there and pick up the rental cars at the same time. That took a lot of time to square away.

"Everyone seemed to appreciate having all this taken care of in the first season, but by the end of the second season some athletes weren't really appreciating it anymore. A lot of that stuff I would just chalk up to human nature and brush it off. Still, there were some who took it for granted. How quickly they had forgotten how things used to be, just a couple years earlier."

Thanks to the PODIUM program, World Cup sliders had more money to work with, and that made for better accommodations on the road. One of the biggest early beneficiaries of PODIUM was Shea, who was allocated $50,000 by virtue of his winning the 1999 World Championships at Altenberg. Certainly, the USOC was willing to invest in athletes like Shea who had demonstrated the mettle to win medals. This was unique because, at the time of the grant, skeleton was not officially Olympic. The USOC was betting on skeleton's chances of entering the Olympics, Jimmy's ability to compete, and our ability to make USA Skeleton a success.

Shea mostly made good use of the money. On one occasion, he had Ellis reserve a room for the entire month of November at the Hampton Inn near the Park City track, even though Shea knew he would not be spending thirty days and nights there. He just wanted to make sure he would have no problem getting a room once he showed up to get in some training runs. Shea had earned his ticket, and he was going to make sure he got it punched.

"If I'm there, I'm there; and if I'm not, I'm not," Shea explained to Ellis, referring to the reserved hotel room.

I accompanied the World Cup team to many of their events. Connectivity was important and it seemed to keep the petty bickering to a minimum while I was around. In 2000–2001, my itinerary included Igls, La Plagne, and Calgary. As much as I was all business with the athletes when it came to sliding, I also nurtured an appreciation for stopping and smelling the roses every now and then. In between the races at Igls, Austria, and La Plagne, France, the athletes and coaches got in some bonding time while making the drive that took them from Innsbruck, across northern Italy, and into southeastern France.

At one point, a group of us caravanned out of the Austrian Alps, through Italian wine country, and then back up into the Italian and French Alps. DeWitt and Stumpf, friends from Park City, teamed up in one car. Soule and Dr. Mike Noyes, a medical specialist accompanying the U.S. team that year, shared a second car. Shea and I teamed up in a third vehicle. This was a good way for team members to get to know each other, although there no longer was the "hell on wheels" mentality that had characterized the travel-related travails of American sliders a decade or two earlier. No shenanigans, no whipping through border checkpoints in the middle of the night. Just the occasional temper tantrum or other manifestations exhibited by high-strung athletes under a lot of pressure.

Truthfully, it wasn't all gravy, sunshine, and happy thoughts. I was spared a lot of what Ryan had to deal with while on the road. Aside from being a sliding coach, he had to deal with egos, and one has to have a healthy ego to be a world-class skeleton slider. Invariably, Ryan would have to play the role of surrogate parent, such as deciding who would room with whom, or who would ride with whom, or even who would get the front seat. If it says anything, after the 2002 Games, Ryan told me that although he loved the experience, he would not coach a skeleton team again unless he was paid an amount of money so large that he couldn't in good conscience work for the person insane enough to pay the fee in the first place.

Once they got to La Plagne, on that December 2000 World Cup trip, a week before Christmas, the American sliders performed exceptionally well. Shea, DeWitt, Parsley, and Stumpf won four of the six possible medals on a long and difficult track relatively unfamiliar to the U.S. team members. The strong performance only added to the festivity of the season. In the morning before the team's races that afternoon, I had skied fresh, thigh-deep powder under the blue skies above the team's hotel. That evening, I joined Shea and Soule at a French café for a small-time celebration that included massive amounts of fondue and red wine. For a nightcap, the three of us found ourselves engaged in a friendly (albeit fierce) snowball fight outside the café with members of several foreign skeleton teams.

At this point in USA Skeleton's development, I knew the combined forces of the athletes' positive self-image, control of our destiny, success, momentum, and enthusiastic support were creating a snowball effect on our athletes and the program. As David Starr Jordan once said, "Wisdom is knowing what to do next," (and that was my responsibility) "skill is in knowing how to do it," (that was the responsibility of the athletes), "and virtue is in doing it." (That was our team's responsibility—our combined efforts in supporting the athletes in all needed ways and their performing to the best of their abilities).

The 2000–2001 season would end up on an upswing for the Americans, but come the fall of 2001, it would be time to get really serious about skeleton. Next up, Salt Lake City and the 2002 Olympic Winter Games. Suddenly, the dream was in sight.

CHAPTER TWELVE
Sprint to the Olympics

Satisfaction lies in the effort, not in the attainment.
Full effort is full victory.
—Mahatma Gandhi

It was a Tuesday morning in September. Like any other work day, Tristan Gale awoke in her bed at home in Salt Lake City, presuming that what she was hearing on the radio was some kind of dumb joke. Just one of those silly drive-time DJs talking smack, trying to goose the listeners. Still half-asleep, Gale stumbled to the bathroom, brushed her teeth, and then plopped herself down in front of her computer to log on to AOL and see what's up in the world. The welcome page told and showed her all she needed to know—the radio report had been no joke.

What was up was that planes were down: two airliners had crashed into the World Trade Center towers in New York City, a third plane had flown into the Pentagon in Washington, D.C., and a fourth plane had gone down in a field in southwestern Pennsylvania. September 11 was starting off as a nightmare. The bad dream stayed with Gale well after she reported to work late that morning at Home Depot. She worked in the gardening department, where her main task that day was organizing a new load of plants that had just been received, mostly large palm-like plants, the kind people buy to stick into a corner of their den or living room.

Except for the employees, the store was practically empty. And it stayed that way for Gale's entire shift.

"The only shopper I can remember coming in was a girl I knew who worked for the Salt Lake Organizing Committee," Gale said. "The whole day was incredibly sad. When I got home that night, the first thing I did was check my e-mail. There were at least five messages for me from foreign sliders all asking to see if I was okay, making sure that nothing had happened to me. There really was a sentiment of sympathy for the United States, with people in other countries seeing this as an attack against all Americans. A lot of people were wondering if Jimmy [Shea] was okay, because they knew he lived in New York, although he actually lived in upstate New York, well away from Ground Zero."

The terrorist attacks of 9-11 would weigh heavily on all of the American sliders throughout the 2001–2002 sliding season, and for a while there was some concern that the 2002 Games in February would be postponed or canceled.

"I'm really proud of how the U.S. turned around and went on to put on such a wonderful Olympics," Gale said. "There was no trouble getting inspired for us that year, wearing our red, white, and blue uniforms, and representing America. There were times in the aftermath of 9-11 that I would sometimes ask myself, *How do I go on doing this?* It came down to the fact that this was one way, other than serving in the military, that I could represent my country, and I know there aren't a lot of ways to be able to do that."

There was no getting around the fact that the tragic events of 9-11 would be a time of extended mourning for Americans, although the athletes, like anyone else, would have to work through it and get back to their lives. In exactly a month, it would be time to embark on a sliding season that would take the athletes through to the Olympic Winter Games. That would entail a five-month ordeal pushing them to their limits in both speed and endurance. It would be a season more memorable than fun, as intense and as trying as any experience any of the sliders had ever been through.

The emotional scars from the horrors of 9-11 were still fresh on the American sliders' psyches in mid-October, when the first segment of qualifying races for the U.S. national team were to be held in Park City. There would be six races all together, each consisting of two heats. The first three races would be held in Park City on October 12–14, followed three weeks later by a second set of three races in Lake Placid. It was a test of survival and endurance as much a measure of sliding ability, with sliders allowed to drop only one of the six races for points tabulation and final ranking.

Slider Colleen Rush will never forget the race she dropped, even if she doesn't remember much about it: On the last day of the trials, Rush had a terrible crash, suffering a concussion that, while it would bother her for weeks to come, she kept quiet from coach Ryan Davenport. She had gone into turn ten late in Lake Placid, hit the roof, and was knocked unconscious. The friction of her speed suit on ice burned much of the suit from her body and she regained consciousness sliding in tatters down the track on her hands and knees. As if that wasn't enough, the friction had burned the rubber palm area of her gloves into her skin. Sports advocate Terry Allen remembers meeting Colleen and Jimmy at the track in Igls, Austria, a week or so later, and as they talked, Colleen idly picked at the pieces of melted rubber that still remained in her burnt palms. At least one teammate knew about Rush's lingering injury—she shared a room on the road with Gale, who says Rush would display symptoms of concussions, such as bouts with nausea and nightmares.

"Colleen would tell me, 'If I tell Ryan, I will be taken off the team, and I know I'm well enough to race,'" Gale said. In fact, due to the severity of her concussion, Rush would not be cleared to slide for some time, and even then there were lingering symptoms. It was too bad, because she was improving rapidly and knocking on the door of Olympic qualification.

In keeping with USA Skeleton's pledge of objectivity, there would be no playing favorites at the team trials. Everyone was starting from scratch, with no points carried over from the 2000–2001 World Cup or America's Cup series. Fastest ones down the hill would make the team. Jimmy Shea would be on equal footing with relative unknowns Mike Cline and Brian McDonald, while Lea Ann Parsley started at zero, right alongside up-and-comers such as Gale and Noelle Pikus. Competition would be extremely tight. By now, there were a total of sixty-eight American sliders sanctioned by U.S. rankings—forty-two men and twenty-six women, which was nearly four times as many ranked sliders as there had been just three years earlier. While skeleton still wasn't a big sport among the American masses, the pool of high-caliber American sliders was getting deeper all the time.

New contenders emerged at the U.S. qualifying races. Zach Lund, a former luger, swept the three men's races at Park City, only to fall off at Lake Placid and drop to sixth overall in the Swiss points system (based on finish positions in races), fewer than sixteen points behind the fourth-place Shea, who squeaked in under the wire in securing his eighth consecutive World Cup team slot. The top three among the men were Lincoln DeWitt, Chris Soule, and Brady Canfield. In the women's division, Parsley finished first, ahead of Rush in second, and Gale in third. Conspicuous by her absence among the top women was Tricia Stumpf.

She had been granted a medical waiver excusing her from the qualifying races after suffering a torn hamstring in late summer, and the injury had been slow to heal. Stumpf, at the time, clearly was one of the top three female American sliders, and granting her a medical waiver for World Cup status would turn out to be a critical move when it came down to crunch time in January with an Olympic women's slot at stake for America. With Stumpf out for the first two World Cup races, Gale moved up onto the World Cup team in Stumpf's place, giving Gale her first crack at the elite competition in five years of sliding.

"It was a matter of experience and patience for me," Gale said in April 2005, "considering the fact that even to this day I still have had more runs down the Park City track than any other female."

The U.S. qualifying races had been grueling and nerve-wracking, spread out over time as they were. But there would be no time for the top qualifiers to celebrate. Their work was all in front of them. Their first task: to win enough World Cup points to ensure that the United States would get its full allotment of Olympic slots in February, three for the men and two for the women. In order to secure all five of those spots, the men and women would each need to finish the pre-Olympic World Cup season ranked among the top three nations, which they had done in 2000–2001 with room to spare.

FIBT eligibility rules were designed to provide the most competitive and successful nations more allocated positions than the less-competitive nations in the Olympic competition. USA Skeleton had been founded, in part, on the concept of maximum exposure in all international competition, which helped build depth and community. It certainly was not our intent to field a smaller Olympic contingent than we were capable of, especially with our "home-court" advantage for the Olympics. As far as we were concerned, the United States had legitimate medal contenders that went four or five sliders deep in both the men's and women's events.

The intensity of six selection races, combined with the required training before, during, and after the races, prepared our athletes for what was sure to be extremely tough international competition in the coming months. The 2001–2002 program schedule would be demanding physically as well as psychologically. This was the final season leading into the Olympics and therefore critical as far as team ranking and individual health and preparation was concerned. America's Cup competitions would be held in Calgary and Lake Placid in November and December. Europa Cup competitions would be held in Winterberg, Igls, and

Altenberg in November and December as well. The World Cup events were to be held in Koenigssee and Igls in November, and in Calgary and Lake Placid in December. Out of respect for the roots of skeleton sliding, there would be a fifth and final World Cup event held in St. Moritz, one month before the Olympics.

One way to automatically qualify for an Olympic berth would be to come out of the first four World Cup races ranked among the top three in the FIBT individual points standings. Unfortunately, that ruled out Tricia Stumpf. In order to earn a top-three ranking, Tricia would have had to compete in all four of the initial World Cup events. But because of her lingering injury, this was not possible. As an added consequence, with Stumpf unavailable for the first two World Cup races, the U.S. women would fall out of the top three in the nations' rankings, imperiling their chances of securing two Olympic sliding positions. The U.S. men, meanwhile, were ranked first, the same spot in which they had finished the 2000–2001 season.

Until Chris Soule won the St. Moritz race in January, no American slider finished first in a World Cup event. The good news was that the U.S. athletes, especially the men, were piling up top-six finishes and compiling plenty of points. Through the first four World Cup events, Soule finished either second or third every time, while Shea finished as high as second and nothing worse than seventh in any of the other three November/December races. If there was a reason for pre-Olympic concerns, other than Stumpf's lingering hamstring injury, it was the Lincoln DeWitt mystery. Number one in the world in 2000–2001, DeWitt had finished twenty-second at Koenigssee, eleventh at Igls, fifth at Calgary, and thirteenth at Lake Placid.

The Lake Placid World Cup had been a major cutoff point for the sliders. Those who came out of that race ranked in the top three would clinch Olympic berths. Following the first heat, Soule was ranked second and Shea third in World Cup points. By this time, it was snowing heavily and the track workers were struggling to keep the track in fair racing condition. As the two of them waited anxiously for their second heat at Lake Placid, an announcement came over the loudspeaker that because of inclement weather, the race had been called, and the results of the first heat would stand as final. That meant Soule and Shea were a lock for the Olympics. Immediately, the two of them began to whoop it up in celebration.

I could hear them yelling, laughing, and celebrating over someone's open radio. Parsley just missed for the women, coming out of Lake Placid tied for fourth with Gale; our next highest-ranked woman was at tenth.

DeWitt and Stumpf, like Parsley and Gale, were still on the outside looking in. Parsley's close call and Stumpf's injury were self-explanatory, but what had happened to DeWitt? His health was fine—no serious injuries, and there didn't seem to be anything wrong with his equipment. Or was there?

"I had figured I was one of the favorites going into the 2001–2002 season," DeWitt said, "but I knew I still needed to keep on improving, because with everyone else getting better, I knew that repeating what I had done the year before would not be good enough."

So, like the upstart golfer who wins his first major championship and then decides to retool his swing to advance to "the next level," DeWitt went back to the drawing board during the off-season. One thing he did was arrange through one of his fiancée (and future wife) Linda's contacts at Ford Motor Company to do some wind-tunnel testing at a Ford Research Facility. DeWitt's testing seemed to confirm something that Ryan Davenport had been telling him, that the front edge of the sled should be an inch or two ahead of the slider's shoulders for aerodynamic reasons instead of the shoulders being flush with the front. DeWitt, however, had another strategic tweak in mind, and it would involve an equipment adjustment. He was about to violate the age-old rule of: "If it ain't broke, don't fix it."

"One of the big changes I made as a result of the wind-tunnel testing," DeWitt said, "was to take all of the sled's ballast weight, which had been evenly distributed, and move it all to the very front of the sled. That way, I could move back that inch or two on the sled and still have balance at the same point."

Everything seemed fine at the World Cup qualifying races at Park City and Lake Placid. DeWitt clearly was the class of the field, especially once they got to Lake Placid after Lund had swept at Park City. In New York, DeWitt rocketed up the points standings to finish first, ahead of the likes of Soule and Shea, in what essentially was a World Cup-caliber event. But those results didn't immediately translate to success in the actual World Cup series. There was that twenty-second-place finish to kick off the season, followed later by the eleventh at Igls and the thirteenth at Lake Placid.

DeWitt would manage to work his way back into the points standings' top ten, although his slow start would have a detrimental trickle-down effect on his seeding at the Olympics (assuming he would even qualify for the Games), with Shea and Soule already having secured two of the three available spots. Here was the seeding problem for DeWitt: Olympic sliders were to be grouped in seeds of ten, with random draws determining start order within each grouping. Even though DeWitt had finished in the top ten in FIBT points, Olympic rules stipulated that each nation could have no more than two of its sliders in the top-ten grouping. That meant if DeWitt made it to the Olympics, the best he could hope for would be a seeding in the second ten (draws eleven through twenty), which, as fate would have it, probably played a role when Park City was slammed with a heavy snowstorm on the day of the Olympic skeleton races.

Before there would even be a shot at the Olympics, though, DeWitt would need to figure out what was happening to him. Why was he finishing so low (by his high standards) when he felt fine and deemed his driving as good as it had ever been? Frustrated at the midpoint of the World Cup season, DeWitt put in a long-distance phone call to a trusted confidante, former world champion luger and all-around sliding expert Wendel Suckow.

"I was frustrated beyond belief," DeWitt said. "I couldn't figure anything out and neither could Ryan. My lines seemed fine and I was driving well. And the equipment was fine.

"Wendel and I talked about it, and he says, 'For one thing, you're trying too hard.'

"I said, 'Yeah, I probably am now, but I wasn't before.'

"He said, 'So, what is different from last year? Is it the same sled?'

"'Yeah; same sled, same runners.'

"'Well, have you changed anything with that sled?'

"So I told him about the change of the weights, and he goes, 'Well, duhhhh, that's it.'

"I was like, 'No, that can't be, because the balance point is the same as it was last year.'

"He said, 'I don't care; it's different. *That's* your problem.' So I changed the weight back to the way it was the year before." DeWitt made these changes prior to the Calgary World Cup, where he placed fifth and began his climb back up the World Cup rankings.

If the World Cup qualifying trials and subsequent World Cup series hadn't been cutthroat enough, up next, right after Christmas, were the U.S. Olympic Trials at Park City. The trials would consist of four races of two heats each, to be held December 28 and 30, and January 4 and 6. So much for an excess of holiday spirit.

This was the situation: the U.S. men had secured the maximum three spots allowed for the Olympic Games, and two had been filled by Soule and Shea. That left one vacant men's spot, and it would be up for grabs among a group that included DeWitt and about a half-dozen others capable of beating him on any given day. In the women's division, only one Olympic spot was guaranteed. There still was a chance of a second spot being added after the St. Moritz World Cup race, but for now the women could only approach the trials with the expectation of finishing number one or bust at Park City.

The Olympic trials were yet another mental and physical endurance test over ten days. The days were intense and the participating athletes even more so. Some of the women athletes were brought to tears during the anxious days. One of the more emotionally volatile male competitors surprised me early one Sunday morning before a race by yelling obscenities at me in front of my wife and some of the other athletes. I tried to comfort these individuals as best as I could, but ultimately, each one of them would have to face his or her own demons.

As usual, I took my position near the starting block and encouraged each athlete as he or she toed the line. Not surprisingly, it came down to the last heat of the last race for both the men and women. It was extremely close. DeWitt and Gale won the Olympic Trials men's and women's divisions, respectively, and thus a trip to the Olympics.

DeWitt's victory was the more dramatic in terms of winning margin, with the top contenders flip-flopping rankings from heat to heat. The total of DeWitt's four runs was just .07 seconds faster than Brady Canfield, with Brian McDonald another .03 behind. Going into the fourth and final race, DeWitt trailed Canfield by .12 and led McDonald by .02. In the first heat of the fourth race, Canfield increased his overall lead on DeWitt to .24 second as McDonald jumped ahead of DeWitt by .02 overall. DeWitt, now in third with one heat to go, turned in a final run of 49.06 seconds, matching his first heat's time that day. McDonald closed with a 49.18 and Canfield a 49.37, opening the door just enough for DeWitt to leapfrog over both into the number one slot, earning him a spot in the Olympics.

For women's Olympic trials runner-up Lea Ann Parsley, though, her Olympic verdict remained dependent on the last World Cup race at St. Moritz. It would be up to Parsley and teammates Stumpf and Gale to do well enough to move the U.S. women from their tie for fourth into the top three in order to secure that second Olympic women's spot coveted by Parsley.

Even though Stumpf, still recovering and not at full strength, had failed to qualify for the Olympic team—she finished fourth at the Olympic Trials—she, with nothing to gain for herself, traveled to St. Moritz and fought her way to a heroic sixth-place finish. In the process, Stumpf defeated all of the German women who needed to be passed to help elevate the U.S. women into a top-three spot. Parsley helped her cause as well, finishing in second just one one-hundredth of a second out of first. Gale finished well back at St. Moritz in thirteenth, leading some to speculate that she hadn't gone all out in the race. The conspiracy theory was that perhaps Gale was calculating that if not enough points were scored by the U.S. women, it would keep the Americans out of the top three teams and thus deny Parsley that second Olympic slot, and Parsley, of course, posed one of Gale's top threats for a medal—if not the gold—at Salt Lake City.

"Yeah, I've heard that said about me, that I was sandbagging at St. Moritz," Gale said. "No way. That just goes to show how out of control some of this stuff gets with people.

"My guess is that Tricia's main motivation for going to St. Moritz was that she was good friends with Lea Ann. I was glad to see Lea Ann go and am only sorry that we couldn't have had a third American female there—Colleen Rush, maybe (Rush had finished third at the Olympic Trials behind Gale and Parsley), because then I think we could have had the chance to sweep all three medals. But nations weren't allowed to have more than two female skeleton sliders in the games."

Because I was handling the sleds at the bottom of the track, I was the first to Parsley when she came to a stop following her second and final run at St. Moritz. Our team approach to everything over the years, the building of relationships, the hard-won experience, and the lessons—it all came down to this moment.

Parsley tore off her helmet; her eyes were pleading. She looked up at me from her sled and asked, "Did I do it!?" I checked, double-checked, and triple-checked the boards, and then nodded in the affirmative. She grabbed me, we hugged and both wept with happiness and relief. Lea Ann had now earned the right to be an Olympian—the hard way.

I will never forget the heart of these two women, Parsley and Stumpf, laying it all on the line for the United States and the Olympic spirit. Only by poor luck had Tricia lost a hold on her Olympic dream. She had nothing to gain by going to St. Moritz, and yet she took the time and committed herself to her teammate, her team, and the United States. Tricia Stumpf is an Olympic champion in my book. In many ways, her committed focus in January 2002 reflected the soul of USA Skeleton and our program, which was that teamwork was not just a sport or business cliché, but a way of life.

The icing on the cake came from Chris Soule winning the men's race at St. Moritz, beating Gregor Stähli of Switzerland, at the time the number one-ranked slider in the world—and on his home track at that! DeWitt finished an impressive sixth in his last tune-up for the Olympics. Unfortunately, Jimmy Shea's second run was not counted as he pushed off and began his run before the track's timing mechanism was set. He was in sixth place after the first heat and ranked third in the individual FIBT standings. His disqualification dropped him to fifth place overall, not the ideal way to end the World Cup season with the Olympics right around the corner.

Within a week, though, Shea's DQ at St. Moritz was all but forgotten. As I mentioned earlier, his grandfather and close pal Jack Shea, an Olympic legend who had won two golds in speed skating in 1932, died from injuries sustained in an automobile accident in Lake Placid. It was a tragic death felt by the entire community, but it would become a powerful source of inspiration for Shea when he got to Park City in February.

With skeleton about to make its first Olympic appearance in fifty-four years, the Americans were ready to challenge for several medals. They had come a long way in a short time, quickly rising up in the pecking order of sliding nations. Where just ten years earlier they had been nothing more than a pesky insect buzzing the ear of the bobsled community, now they were looking every bit the part of a world power with a good shot at two medals and possibly more. Athletes were no longer having to reach into their own pockets and pull out credit cards to pay for World Cup entry fees and their European hotel rooms, and veterans from other countries were no longer laughing behind the backs of "those silly Americans."

Like any up-and-coming sport with more and more successes begetting increased expectations, though, skeleton still had its growing pains. Intensified competition meant heightened ambition, and the staunch desire to get or stay ahead would constantly tempt sliders to take shortcuts difficult for some to resist. Football has steroids; baseball, too. Skeleton had its own kind of "juice" as well—illegal compounds added to runners to make them glide faster over the ice. A few sliders were using this illicit way to improve their times. With the problem of steroids in other sports, policing juiced runners was a cat-and-mouse game. The mice, with outside help, were always looking for a new substance that would be undetectable when applied surreptitiously. In addition, there were unapproved metallic compositions and other irregularities showing up in runners.

When Davenport or I had a question about the legality of equipment and its components, more often than not we would turn to Kevin McCarthy, the former Delta airline captain out of Park City, Utah, and his FIBT jury associates, who, together with Lincoln DeWitt, had taken up skeleton on a lark back in 1997. As we've seen, McCarthy had gone on to become a Kevin-of-all-trades in skeleton, becoming proficient in numerous areas of skeleton administration, including race juries, race direction, and equipment testing. Through Davenport's political assistance, McCarthy found a spot on the FIBT's Materiel Commission, giving him a bird's-eye view in terms of equipment oversight and conformity to the rule book, which he would help write.

Two years out from the Salt Lake City Games, McCarthy approached Wolfgang Hoppe, the FIBT's vice president for materiel, and asserted a need to upgrade their method of policing sliding equipment, such as runners' material and the compounds being applied. Said McCarthy: "I told him that, 'What you people are using is 1950s' technology. We're talking about 2002.' Wolfgang tasked me to go out on behalf of the FIBT and develop an electronic system to test the runners. I got involved with something called Rahman spectroscopy, which is light amplification that could measure if there was anything on the steel of the runner that didn't belong there."

McCarthy came from a family of scientists—his sister, Maureen, has a PhD in chemistry and physics, and runs the office of research and development for the Department of Homeland Security. A brother-in-law, who has a PhD in nuclear physics, even took McCarthy to Argon Laboratories in Chicago, where they saw technicians working with a bobsled, applying some sort of substance to the runners.

"Finally," McCarthy said, "one guy pulls out a piece of steel and says to me, 'You want to know what the Swiss have on their runners?'

"'What do you mean?'

"He goes, 'Oh, the Swiss came here a couple of years ago and asked us how to do this process. They paid us, and we told them what they needed to know. We didn't know what it was to be used for, only that it would reduce the friction. Here . . . here's a piece of what they did. Don't worry; we didn't sign any nondisclosures. You can take it.'

"I knew this was going to be a problem. I had discovered that the Swiss had figured out a way to put diamond coating on the runners. This kind of stuff with runner technology goes back to the Cold War. You can affect the friction between ice and a steel runner just like you can affect the friction of ice and water against the hull or propeller of a submarine. The Soviets were real in tune with this kind of thing. With this stuff, you get real close to national-security issues and classified information. What you have here is dual-use technology."

With this kind of knowledge, McCarthy was able to develop a detection system that would work on sleds' runners, examining them to determine if anything illegal was present. Using a spectrometer, a race official could now detect illegal runners, although it could only go to the first molecular level of the steel. Still, that told a lot—for one thing, it told the Swiss that they now had to get back on the straight and narrow. They knew it, too, and asked that they be given a year before the rules were fully enforced so they could change back, get back on the right side of the rules.

"There's probably a lot of people," McCarthy said, "not just the Swiss, who would have been busted that first year. I would have busted them on the spot, and I'm sure a lot of them would have been U.S. people, too. We would later develop other kinds of electronic testing that we would use at the games to tell us the alloy content of the runners, the hardness of the runners . . . that kind of thing."

Several days after the Olympics, slider Ralph Mirabelli, an athlete representative on the USBSF board of directors, sent out a message, via Davenport, to U.S. national team sliders, informing them that illegal runners had been used during the 2001–2002 season. Mirabelli pointed out that many U.S. athletes, as well as international athletes, had not been allowed to use certain runners because the steel being used allegedly did not conform to FIBT regulations. Two days after Mirabelli sent out his letter via e-mail, a manufacturer responded to Mirabelli, insisting that the subject runners were in fact legal, based on the 2001 FIBT rule book.

Chalk another one up to a sport's growing pains.

Following the Olympic races and equipment testing of the medalists, Ueli Geissbuhler, Technical Chairman of skeleton for the Olympics, called me aside and, in no uncertain terms, told me certain equipment was not acceptable and would not be allowed the next year. The equipment issues will continue to evolve and challenge athletes and race officials for years to come.

Regardless of any questions surrounding any of the sleds or runners being used by any of the athletes, when the last of the Olympic races had been completed, race director Heinz Thoma declared the results official, and that was that.

Now, what had months earlier resembled a tight, close-knit family, had evolved into something more akin to a big family reunion, complete with squabbling in-laws as well as distant cousins with diametrically opposed political and cultural views. USA Skeleton had become its own little melting pot of diversity and occasional divisiveness, which, translated, meant that the Americans were pumped, primped, and ready to take center stage in Park City for the 2002 Olympic Winter Games. My response: bring on the games, let's put an end to the bickering, and let's focus on our opportunities.

CHAPTER THIRTEEN

The Olympics

The greatest danger is not that we aim too high and miss it, but that we aim too low and we reach it.
—Michelangelo

It was the night of February 8, 2002, and darkness had settled in over Salt Lake City. This was every bit the middle of winter, with snow on the ground, and the evening air and blustery breezes chilling tens of thousands of spectators to the bone. It appeared that much of the world had descended upon this gorgeous city that lies among the Rockies, its night lights sparkling as the cold and anticipation touched those in attendance as well as those billions around the world who were watching at home.

The opening ceremonies for the 2002 Olympic Winter Games began with the procession of nations, and the United States Olympic team was just minutes away from entering Rice-Eccles Stadium. The American Olympians—decked out in their red, white, and blue U.S. team uniforms—were all gathered together under one roof in a staging area, awaiting one last pep talk from a VIP before they would begin the last leg of their march into the stadium.

In less than thirty months, USA Skeleton had come from being a relatively obscure sports organization without Olympic objectives, a novelty at best, to part of a full-fledged Olympic sport about to enjoy the worldwide audience it had never before commanded. For America, especially, skeleton was about to be revealed as something entirely new and special. But were we capable of winning Olympic medals and creating a whole new breed of heroic athletes? None of us knew.

In one sense, the opening ceremonies seemed to last an eternity, yet they were finished in the blink of an eye. It was all high drama in itself, but there also was a sobering aspect to the moment, the still-stunning realization of what had transpired less than six months earlier, with the 9-11 terrorist attacks on America. Now, we were delegates of a U.S. Olympic team, about to be introduced to spectators and a TV audience who, still grieving, were seeing this Olympics—on American soil, no less—as a catharsis. It represented a way to remember all that was and is great about our country, while at the same time getting the chance to celebrate, in anticipation, the many memorable athletic performances to come.

Here we were at the Olympics, a two-week event that is supposed to represent the best in mankind and in peaceful competition, yet reminders of the post-9-11 world we were now living in confronted us constantly. Security was as tight as that at a military base. Access to the Olympic Village and competition sites was controlled as tightly as access at a nuclear facility. The area was surrounded by counter-terrorist snipers and special-force operatives poised to protect and defend.

The air was electric, with the energy of the stadium crowd permeating all that was around it. For the members of the USA Skeleton team, it was a time of great pride. We had prepared, worked hard, fought, and achieved to get to this point, and we could never have been more ready than we were right then. Yet, I had that same terrifying anxiety inside of me that I had experienced on my first skeleton slide down a track, speeding headfirst just inches off the ice at more than seventy miles an hour. I could only describe my feelings as adrenaline, excitement, and a splash of naked fear. As Dick Bass once said, "Man can take bad news, but he cannot handle uncertainty."

Suddenly, from inside our staging area, there arose a commotion at the far end of the assembled athletes. There on the podium walking toward us, his full entourage surrounding him, was President George W. Bush accompanied by his wife, First Lady Laura Bush. President Bush was there to give our delegation one last pep talk before we were to march out to the stadium—hopefully to glory and into history.

Before he stepped to the microphone to speak, President Bush worked his way by the assembled contingent of U.S. athletes, exchanging greetings and shaking hands, occasionally giving the thumbs-up sign as he crossed the room. I had known Mr. Bush for many years through the oil and gas industry. At one point, he took a glance over toward where I was standing and, without missing a beat, pointed to me and called out, "Robie Vaughn!" Then another big thumbs-up as he made his way to the microphone.

That's the kind of thing that makes presidents, presidents—to recognize someone completely out of context, while mentally preparing for a speech, and to be able to call out one's name without hesitation! My team members were as stunned as I was, and we did our best to remain in the moment. Now we had the whole world watching, including the president of the United States—the leader of the free world, the most powerful person on the planet.

The president's speech ended with those last inspirational words from Todd Beamer on board the United Airlines plane that went down in Pennsylvania on 9-11: "Let's roll!" The athletes were awed by the president's grasp of the moment and let out a resounding cheer lasting throughout the Olympic Games.

After a speech Vince Lombardi would be proud of, we marched out into the twenty-degree night—into the Olympic stadium. The orchestra was playing the Olympic theme "Light the Fire Within," amplified louder than any number of rock concerts combined. I'm not too emotional, but I possess a sense of history and am passionate about my pursuits. It was hard to hold back my emotions. I'm not sure I've ever been prouder to be an American, and the opportunity to represent my country was overwhelming.

Members of the USA Skeleton family played key roles in the opening ceremonies. Slider Lea Ann Parsley, herself a firefighter, was chosen as one of eight athletes selected to carry the tattered World Trade Center flag into the stadium. Jimmy Shea, his father Jim Sr., and Tristan Gale had a hand in carrying the Olympic flame on its way to the lighting of the Olympic cauldron.

The procession of nations marching into the Olympic stadium was something that hit home with slider Lincoln DeWitt. For one thing, he was at home, his Park City residence just a few miles away. Then there was the sight of counter-terrorist snipers looking down from the rooftops on which they were positioned.

"As host nation, we were the last team to enter the stadium," DeWitt said, "and I'll never forget when the snipers saw us, they took a few seconds to flash their flashlights at us as a sign of their support. Walking into the stadium was unbelievable. There were a bunch of spectators behind a chain-link fence watching us, and they were just going nuts. There was this great buildup the closer and closer we got, and then when we finally broke through into the stadium out of the tunnel, there was just this explosion of support for us. I'd call it awesome, except that isn't a strong enough word to describe the experience."

All we could hear was deafening cheering; all we could see were faces, a solid mass of faces wherever we looked, and flashes from cameras.

Leading up to the Olympics, there had been a competitive lull for the sliders. The last World Cup race had been held in mid-January, creating a competitive gap of about five weeks between St. Moritz and the Olympic skeleton races in Park City. Such a long stretch of lying low allowed ample time to heal up whatever aches, pains, and equipment problems might have arisen, but the real trick was in how to keep the Olympic sliders from growing stale—how to maintain the edge and momentum. I instinctively believed the athletes needed to stay fairly busy during that time in order to keep the appropriate level of focus and training necessary.

One of the things I wanted to do was get the entire team to Salt Lake City as soon as possible so they would have time to get settled into their digs at the Olympic village and to give them time to get acclimated to one another in a more relaxed environment. As a result, the skeleton sliders were ahead of the curve. We were the first U.S. Olympic team to check in with the United States Olympic Committee for team processing. This would give team members a chance to spend time together without the stress of an ongoing race or gut-busting trials competition—a chance to dine together, to work out together, and to attend other Olympic events leading up to their own competition.

The coaches and I used our time wisely in and around the Olympic village, playing the roles of gofers, getting to know who did what around the village and to procure necessary amenities such as hand warmers, extra chairs, pillows, etc. Terry Holland, one of the assistant coaches, was point man when it came to acquiring team apparel from the United States Olympic Committee. At least, he was for a while. Always a good negotiator with a bent for persistence, the committee's apparel distributors finally forced the omnipresent Holland to leave the team-processing facility with a stern request not to return. While Holland can be gracious and humorous, he was also tenacious.

"I'd get up at six in the morning and go until midnight, doing everything I could possibly do to accommodate the athletes," Holland said. "That included monitoring my own behavior when around them. 'Do you want eye contact or not?' 'Do you want someone to urge you on or to leave you alone?' 'Quiet conversation?' 'No conversation?' 'When do you want to sharpen your spikes?'

"We tried to make everything so seamless to the athletes that all they had to do was appear and do their thing unencumbered by any distractions that could put a dent in their performances. And it worked."

Still, the squeaky wheel got the grease, and USA Skeleton did well when it came to securing vital things such as credentials, parking permits, vehicles for moving around town, and tickets to the competitions and the opening ceremonies. The skeleton competition wouldn't be until late in the games, starting midway through the second week, and I wanted the sliders to attend award ceremonies for other events to get a sense and feel for what it would be like to win a medal. Positive reinforcement and visualization have long been effective tactics for preparing athletes for competition, and this was a perfect opportunity. And it happened every evening at the Awards Ceremony Plaza in downtown Salt Lake City. Gale particularly enjoyed the ceremonies and went down to see them on several occasions; she had a blast down there.

Even then, five weeks was a long time to keep everyone together, and sliders were given the leeway to spend days and nights wherever they chose—up until a week before the start of the skeleton competition. Athletes were also given the option of going on a pre-Olympic training trip to Lake Placid. Keeping track of the athletes had its pros and cons. Tristan Gale opted out of the village to stay at her family's home in Salt Lake City, while DeWitt took a similar tact, holing up at his Park City condo. Shea, too, also bolted for life outside the village, accepting an offer from local businessman Phil Thompson, a USBSF board member, to stay at his house in the run-up to the games' second week.

Each athlete had his or her own personality in terms of how to prepare. DeWitt, Parsley, and Soule gravitated toward structure and were disciplined when it came to their workouts and eating schedules. Shea and Gale were a bit more free spirited, oftentimes elusive, and it was difficult for us to keep up with them. Gale, not yet twenty-two years old, was much younger than all of the other sliders. The average age of the other U.S. athletes was nearly thirty. This concerned the coaches from the standpoint that they believed she might be having problems feeling like she didn't fit in with the others. Shea was an even bigger concern. We couldn't tell how much the recent death of his grandfather, Jack Shea, was still affecting him. That wasn't all, either. Shea's poor finish at St. Moritz, dropping him from third to fifth in the final World Cup standings, didn't bode well for his chances at Park City. Neither did the lingering blood-flow problem he was having in a calf muscle.

Additionally, I was concerned because Jimmy seemed to be enjoying the media hype a little too much, and it seemed at times that he was unfocused on the ultimate goal. I asked myself, "Has he given into the pressure and opportunity to medal by simply relaxing and riding the Olympian status?"

About a week out from the skeleton races, I moved the entire team to a townhouse within minutes of the Park City track. The move accomplished several things: it brought the team together, provided increased focus and regime discipline, and it allowed the coaches to communicate to the team all in one place; it put the athletes into the high altitude, further helping them along with acclimatization; and removed one of the unknowns that would otherwise interfere with training and race days—security and traffic. Staying in a townhouse would mean fewer distractions and logistical surprises that could be found in the Olympic village.

The final countdown had begun. The skeleton races were just days away.

One of the more interesting stories to come out of the 2002 Olympic Winter Games involved a slider who wasn't a member of the U.S. team, and his is one of the best stories that has not been told.

Mike the Greek's real name is Mike Voudouris, a United States citizen whose father is a native of Greece who barely speaks English. At the time of the 2002 Games, Mike the Greek was in his early forties, a bit out of shape, and living in New York City, working as a sports photographer and emergency medical technician. He was a relative newcomer to sliding and had acquired a Greek passport, hoping to slide for Greece in the games.

It would mean a lot for Voudouris just to get to Salt Lake City. On 9-11, as an EMT in New York City, he had at one point worked forty-eight straight hours in triage at Ground Zero, inhaling all of the sickening crud floating through the air. People were dying all around him, including seventeen of his EMT pals.

Voudouris had met Kevin McCarthy at a race in Calgary, and the two had become fast friends. The only way for Mike the Greek to get into the Games would be to qualify at a Challenge Cup being held in Altenberg, Germany, just two or three weeks out from the Salt Lake City Games. A limited number of spots were held open for sliders from smaller nations, also-ran nations not in the mainstream of sliding sports. The Challenge Cup would be offered in the Olympic spirit of inclusion, a back-door opportunity of entry.

Importantly, if these small nations were not involved, the FIBT would have had an even more difficult case to push forward with the IOC for including skeleton in the Olympics. Quite possibly, this would have been the avenue through which a slider such as myself would have qualified for the Olympics, representing American Samoa. It was similar to the 1988 Calgary Games, when an obviously lesser-talented but media-savvy Eddie "the Eagle" Edwards of

Great Britain competed in ski jumping. He went up against elite jumpers who probably could have beaten Edwards had they gone off the jump backwards. Edwards had, after all, been ranked fifty-fifth in the world as the lone Brit bloke in ski jumping.

Still, getting past the Challenge Cup and into the Olympics would be no easy thing. In selecting Altenberg as host site, FIBT officials had played a cruel joke of sorts on these lesser sliders, putting them on one of the most—if not the most—dangerous tracks in the world.

McCarthy said, "It had been built by the East Germans who had gone out and found the most difficult elements of all the top tracks in the world and incorporated them all into this one track. They had built it in a pine forest and didn't tell the rest of the world it existed. Only after the wall came down did they admit to its existence.

"I knew all of these kids from all these other nations, and I was there helping to officiate the race. During the days of training before the Challenge Cup, they were hauling these kids out of the track, and the ambulance was coming and going. There were a couple of unconscious sliders going to the hospital. An official who had picked this track was going to show these kids what the Olympics was all about. It was brutal."

After a couple days of training and several days of racing, it all came down to tabulating the final points results and then posting them, so the sliders could gather around them, like college students crowding around their posted test scores, to see if they would be going to Salt Lake City. McCarthy went to the start house to pick up the final points tabulation, stepped back outside, and found himself face to face with Mike the Greek, who's got his camera in hand and is shooting in all directions, capturing scenes from one of the most memorable weeks of his life.

"Mike comes up to me and says, 'God, I tried my hardest,' and I had the privilege of telling him, 'Mike, you made it in . . . by one point. You're part of the Olympics,'" McCarthy added. "We hugged each other and cried a lot. Then Luis Carrasco from Mexico, the Xtreme sports producer whom Boyd and I had first met in Calgary, comes over and says, 'Kuh-VIN? How about me?' I said, 'Join the hug. You're going.' They both had gotten banged up, terribly, but now they were going to be in the biggest sporting event in the world."

When Mike the Greek got to the Olympic Games, he was told that he would not be allowed to display the photo of the Twin Towers that he had affixed to the bottom of his sled. Officials ruled it a political statement that wasn't allowed in the games. So Mike the Greek got creative in how he would commemorate those who had died at Ground Zero. Using a box full of small Greek flag stickers, he arranged them in the shape of the two towers on the bottom of the sled.

Now if only he could make it through the Olympic race in one piece. When it got to race day, Mike the Greek pulled McCarthy aside for a private chat, telling McCarthy that he had separated a shoulder during his last training run. "He's an EMT; he knew it was broken," McCarthy said. "There was no question in his mind, but he didn't want to tell anybody because he was afraid they wouldn't let him compete."

Knowing that McCarthy, officiating the race, would be at the bottom of the track, Mike the Greek asked McCarthy to help him move his sled out of the track at the end of his runs because he knew he wouldn't be able to do it himself. He knew he was going to be in agony by the time he got to the bottom.

"He competed and completed the games, and he didn't finish last," said McCarthy, his eyes filing with tears. "He beat Carrasco, and they both beat the Argentine [German Glessner]. But Mike lost about a year to rehab after that. He had suffered some nerve damage in an arm. He was screwed up. But as he told me, 'I didn't come here to quit.'"

After three days of official training at the Park City track, the sliders awoke early on the morning of Wednesday, February 20, and looked out their townhouse windows to see the one thing they didn't want to see in the middle of winter: snow was falling, lots of it. These weren't just your frozen-garden-variety snow flurries, either. Park City was getting dumped on, and it was the kind of snowfall that suggested it wouldn't be letting up for a while—at least not until well after that day's races had started.

Park City would offer home-track advantage for the Americans, as long as it didn't snow on race day. Lots of snow was the great equalizer in skeleton, the rationale being that accumulating snow slows the track down, and a slower track reduces the advantage of superior driving skills. In other words, the faster a track slides, the more "technical" it becomes, and the slower it slides, the easier it is for the "best of the rest" to compete. This was particularly true with the Park City track.

Fallon, who had been voted by the U.S. men and women skeleton athletes as one of eight forerunners for race day, was there and she pondered what this would mean to all the resources and hard work we had invested in skeleton over the previous four years. Taylor Boyd, my old pal Rusty Getter, and Mark McKinley had all made the trip.

"My heart sank," Boyd recalled. "I'm thinking about the dream in all this, and how now it appeared it was gone. Poor Robie, all this for nothing."

"Up until then, it had been sunny every day during the games," slider Tristan Gale added. "When we got up and opened the door, there was already about six new inches of snow on the ground and it was still coming down. Everybody looked at me, with me being the smallest member of the team, thinking that having to slide in the snow hurts sliders more the smaller they are. I tried to be in denial about the whole thing, convincing myself that it wouldn't be snowing over at the track, even though the track is practically across the street and up in the mountains, and if it's snowing here, it's got to be snowing in the mountains."

With the snow coming down heavily and relentlessly, starting-order positions, which had been drawn just days before, would become a key factor in determining sliders' fates. It didn't look good for the Americans. The best draw any of the U.S. sliders got was fourth, both for Shea in the men's race and Gale in the women's. DeWitt's starting spot was especially poor. Because of the rule limiting each nation to only two men's spots in the top ten, DeWitt had to settle for the men's second grouping of ten. His draw would have him going off thirteenth in the first heat. Even with track volunteers tasked to do what they could to sweep away snow between sliders, it was clear that the sliders going off early would have an advantage over later sliders.

All the training, planning, and cumulative human effort behind positioning our athletes to achieve success was seemingly neutralized by the falling snow and, to a further degree, by the poor draws. I felt anxious and disappointed after all we had been through. But the competition would go on despite the weather.

It was D-day. Everything we had worked for all came down to one shining moment. All the pain, the struggles, the near-misses and close hits, the efforts, the politicking, the behind-the-scenes struggles, and the personal sojourns—all the sweat and blood of building a team was about to be rendered a verdict. Jimmy's struggles with his own demons and doubts. Lea Ann's hard-won Olympic spot and Tricia's self-sacrifice for the good of the team and nation. Ryan's, Peter's, Terry's, and my battles with the disconnected powers that be. Overcoming bureaucratic inertia to build a new team on an entrepreneurial foundation. We had paid our dues. We had gotten better with every contest, building a new tradition of excellence in a sport lacking much in the way of an

American pedigree.

All was relatively quiet and serious at the team breakfast that morning. It had nothing to do with sadness, though; it was contemplation about the day ahead and what each slider needed to do to conquer the track as quickly and efficiently as possible. Each slider had his or her own routine, and the sliders knew the others' routines as well as their own. Parsley, for instance, normally conversant and outgoing, would shut it down on race day, retreating into her own private world, not talking to anyone.

"She'd put on her hooded sweatshirt and just sit and not talk to anybody," Gale remembered. "Chris Soule, on the other hand, gets really pumped up, yelling and screaming. He can actually get kind of scary, but he knew better than to get in anyone's face."

Finally, still early that morning, it was time for the sliders to make their way out of the townhouse complex and up to the track for the competition. It continued to snow heavily, the abrupt change in weather conditions testing each slider's ability to remain focused and positive. It would have been tempting to just throw in the towel and start rationalizing ways to explain no medal this time around. Gale found herself going down that trail of self-pity, wondering if it would be a waste of time even to warm up, when she started seeing familiar faces: members of her hometown's Girl Scout Troop, Home Depot co-workers, friends of co-workers, her parents, her grandparents, neighbors.

"It crossed my mind at one point that they're not going to understand why I'm not going to do well," Gale said. "I mean, how do you explain this stuff to people who don't fully understand skeleton?"

For Jimmy Shea, the falling blanket of snow and gray skies did little to add cheer to what had been an emotionally draining four weeks following the untimely death of his grandfather. Earlier, I had sat down and talked with Shea for a long time, consoling the slider as much as I was trying to inspire him. I told Shea of the death of my own father at a relatively young age and how it was imperative that Shea not let his grandfather's death adversely affect his performance, to instead draw on the bond he had forged with Jack Shea as a means to move forward and to provide a source of inspiration. He knew his grandfather would not only want him to give his personal best, but would expect it. Before heading out to the track, Shea placed a photo of his grandfather inside his helmet.

The men would go off first that day in what would be a one-day competition consisting of two heats, with both times combined to determine the final results. There would be no time for between-race team meetings, meals, or strategy sessions. It was, simply, go to the top of the track, slide down as fast as you can, pick up your sled at the bottom, ride the truck back up the hill and wait for your next sliding position, make one more run, and cross the finish line. Then it would be over, accumulating snow and all. Compared to the U.S. team trials or Olympic Trials, this would be a snap.

The good fortunes of Switzerland's Gregor Stähli, winner of four of the five World Cup races that season, would continue when he drew the No. 1 start position and would be the first slider down the hill. Stähli put together a solid run and crossed in 51.16 seconds, to be followed immediately by Austria's Martin Rettl in a time of 51.02. As the snow continued to fall, Canadian Duff Gibson came down the track as the third starter, punching in with a 51.40 and setting the stage for Shea coming next.

Shea pushed off strong at the top of the track and drove well through the blizzard, his two generations of Olympic legacy resting on his shoulders as he negotiated his way through the turns en route to a clocking of 50.89 seconds. Shea's time would hold up as the fastest first run among the twenty-six men, giving him a lead of thirteen hundredths of a second going into the second heat.

The two other Americans hadn't fared well in the first run. DeWitt, starting well back in the field and no doubt hampered by the snow, managed to drive his way to a clocking of 51.63 seconds, although that was only good for eighth best after the first run. It appeared to me he had had a perfect run, but he must have caught some accumulated snow somewhere on the track. Soule crossed in 51.89, putting him in thirteenth place, well out of medal contention. He had some minor problems in the top portion of the track, which cost him the ability to efficiently compound his speed throughout the remaining run. DeWitt's shot at a medal was a long one, but it was likely within reach if he could somehow break the 51-second barrier his second trip down the track. But then, there still was the matter of the snow still falling.

"I was confident going into the Olympics. I was healthy and had been pushing well," DeWitt said, looking back. "My first run wasn't a perfect run, but it was a good one. I had one of the best runs I'd ever had up there, only to get to the finish line and see where I was placed. I was ticked off because I knew what was going on. It was the kind of snow that makes a difference in whole tenths of a second instead of hundredths. It was all explainable. It just wasn't fair.

"When it makes up its mind to snow in Park City—it dumps. Somewhere in all this I was hoping that the race officials would cancel for the day and use one of the backup days for the race so that it would make an even playing field for everyone. When I got back to the top of the hill, I complained a bit to (race director) Heinz Thoma, but he just threw up his hands."

By the time DeWitt went down on his second run, the snow had let up. It was now dusting the track instead of dumping on it. "Still, there was nothing I could do, except maybe attach a jet pack," said DeWitt, who had an even better push and drive for the second run, finishing with a time of 51.20 seconds that was fourth fastest for the second heat. Soule did even better than DeWitt for the second run, his 51.09 time was the second fastest of the heat but only enough to jump him up into seventh place in the final results, just two places behind DeWitt in fifth. Clifton Wrottesley, Irish Lord and Cresta champion, was a Cinderella story, placing an incredible fourth after no better than a thirteenth place in any previous World Cup or World Championship race.

There would be only one American men's medal that day, and the suspense was in seeing if Shea could hang onto the top spot and grab the gold, or if he would fall back a bit and have to settle for silver or bronze.

I couldn't believe the focus Jimmy had brought to that first run. His run hadn't been perfect, but it put him on the inside track for first place. As he crossed the finish line, I fully saw the look in his eyes. The look of determination and focus was piercing. It was as if he were looking right through me, not seeing me at all (sometimes it takes the brain a few seconds to disconnect from the high speed experience and focus—it's a melding of survival instincts and athleticism).

"Jimmy, it's all down to this," I told him. "And you have a guardian angel looking over you."

It was then and there I was reminded of the idea I'd taken from Colonel Mullane's speech nearly a decade before—the part about the shortest distance between two points not always being a straight line. Here we were, so far from where we had started, so many zigs and zags. Jimmy brought the heart of a champion to the ice. He was aggressive, and he had something to prove to the world, his family, and ultimately, himself. That kind of thing could have been a liability, if not channeled properly. The entire team and group chemistry had helped provide him with the support and program he needed to channel all of that desire, fury, need, and insecurity into a drive that would allow him to succeed.

The shortest distance between two points.

Jimmy pushed off like never before, starting out with a .13 second lead over the Austrian Rettl. But as Jimmy worked his way down the track, it was evident from the split times that he was losing a bit here and there in the turns—mere fractions of seconds. For a while, it seemed that his only hope was to somehow make it to the finish line before any more of his margin was eaten away. At one point, the split showed that Jimmy had lost all of his margin and that he was in danger of losing the gold, only for him to pour it on through the last couple of turns, completing the run of his life with a margin of victory of .05 over Rettl. He turned in a time of 51:07, the fastest run of the second heat. Jimmy that day had found the shortest distance headfirst. He had won the gold medal.

At the end of his run, Shea looked up and saw his finish position "1" and his cumulative time of 1:41.96 on the digital timer, and knew that he had won the gold. I grabbed Shea's sled and we high-fived. With TV cameras rolling, he jumped off the sled and pulled the photo of his grandfather out of his helmet and held it up for the world to see. There no longer was a cloud over Jimmy Shea, and the family legacy lived on.

"My grandpa was with me the whole way," an ecstatic Shea said. "I just tried to concentrate on the basics. There's so much going on. There were fifteen thousand screaming people. I was just having a blast."

As a member of the race jury, McCarthy had a front row seat to Shea's celebration. He was positioned at the finish line, his job at this point was to keep Shea's feet on the ground long enough to get him into drug testing so that his gold-medal victory could be sanctioned.

"After Jimmy won the gold, he dived into my arms and put this big hug on me," McCarthy said, "although I had to remind him that I was there to make sure he got to drug testing. I told him, 'Jimmy, you have X number of minutes to do this and I've got a guy here to escort you. Go with him. Don't drink anything. Don't take a piss. Don't throw up. Don't do anything. If you lose this guy, you will be disqualified.'"

Olympic gold for men's skeleton was ours. Now, it would be the women's turn to make Olympic history. Likewise, the women's race would come down to a tenth of a second or less in the final results.

By the time Tristan Gale had reached the summit of the Park City track, there was no question as to where her loyalties were. She had streaked her hair red, white, and blue, and had painted "USA" on her face. Whatever doubts she might have been harboring about her ability to perform in the snowy weather were well hidden, covered by a bubbling countenance that at least resembled confidence if nothing else.

It was 2002, and Gale was already thinking ahead to 2006. In her case, though, it wasn't a case of her thinking she had this one in the bag and was already counting on another gold in Italy four years down the road. It was more a matter of tempered expectations.

"I told myself that my whole goal was really 2006 and this was my time to just enjoy and learn from the experience," Gale said in 2005, looking back on Salt Lake City. "I was hoping for a top-five finish, with the idea that would give me something to build on for Italy."

While the guys raced in their first heat, the women's first heat to soon follow, Gale took herself out of race mode for a while and went and joined with spectators, hanging with the crowd to help get her mind off her own upcoming race. It would turn out to be a good move to prep her for the race. She found herself having a good time, like enjoying watching the Olympic awards ceremonies. She even forgot about the falling snow smothering the track. Nothing like being part of a crowd cheering on Shea to his first-heat lead to give an attitude adjustment to someone like Gale, who had been down in the dumps feeling sorry for herself.

After the men's heat was over, Gale returned to the start house, put on her racing suit, and stepped outside ready to go as the fourth woman scheduled down the track. When her time came at the start, Gale took off running across the ice, her spikes digging in, her short legs a blur in full stride as she pushed her sled toward the point where she would launch herself onto the contraption and begin her wild descent down the track. It ended 52.26 seconds later, giving her the early first-run lead and leaving her wondering how well it would hold up.

"One of the girls in front of me was really pretty good, and when I beat her, I started thinking, *Okay, now I have a good shot at a top-ten,*" Gale said. "Girls kept coming down, including those expected to win, and they weren't beating my time. I was like, no way—this isn't supposed to happen. When Lea Ann came down a hundredth of a second behind me, I figured, this is insanity. Then all of a sudden the heat is over and I'm in the lead."

The first run in the books, Gale led Parsley by .01 second, with Great Britain's Alex Coomber in third with a time of 52.48 seconds, and Germany's Diana Sartour in fourth at 52.55. While the men raced their second heat, all the women could do was wait and contemplate what their next run of fifty-two seconds plus change would mean for them. Back up in the start house, Parsley and Gale bided their time preparing for their final run, Parsley practically a statue, lost in her own world with sweatshirt hood pulled back over her head. Gale, fidgety and excited, could barely sit still. There they were, two elite athletes, separated by the beat of a hummingbird's wing yet about as far apart on the pre-race personality scale as two human beings could get.

"When Jimmy won the gold," Gale said, "Lea Ann actually took her hood off and acknowledged that Jimmy had won, then she put her hood back on and went back into her world. The way I saw it, Jimmy's winning the gold took all the pressure off us. That meant no matter what happened now, skeleton had made a name for itself in the United States. Jimmy had plowed the ground." But USA Skeleton was only halfway to its goal of medaling in both the men's and women's Olympic events.

Soon, Gale would follow suit, and she would do it as last woman down the track. She would know at the start exactly how fast a time she needed in order to win.

"My mindset was just to have fun with my last run," she added. "Lea Ann went right before me, and I was more nervous for her than I was for myself. I couldn't control her run, and I wanted her to do really well.

"When it was my turn going down the track the second time, the one thing I remember more than anything else was how loud the crowd was. It was constant the whole way. Usually, I never hear anything but just the wind whooshing by, but this was way, way different. I couldn't see the spectators, only what I usually see, which is the track and a few trees. I was totally able to focus.

"As soon as I crossed the finish line, I was just so excited to be done that I wasn't worried about my time at first. I could see my dad, Jim Gale, at the finish line, but it was snowing so hard again that I couldn't see the timing. I was looking at everyone around me to see if they were gold-medal happy or fourth-place happy. I couldn't tell from my dad—he has the same face whether I win, lose, or crash. Okay, I thought, I need somebody with some expression here. Then I saw Lea Ann. She ran down the track to me and picked me up, lifting me off the ground and running around with me while telling me I had won the gold. It was incredible."

Gale had clocked a 52.85 for her second heat, which was the second-fastest time for the women in the second run. The good news for Gale was that the fastest second run had been turned in by Switzerland's Maya Pedersen, who had been a distant seventh in the first run. Gale's combined time of 1:45.11 gave her the gold by a tenth of a second over Parsley, while the Brit Coomber took the bronze. In Dallas, our strength and conditioning coach Bob King was glued to his television set. He teared up with pride and joy as he watched history unfold. So many others would later admit to me of feeling overwhelmed with those same emotions.

The final skeleton medal count was in, and the Americans had won half of the six available medals: Shea and Gale with their respective golds and Parsley with her silver.

The rest of the Olympic experience would be a whirlwind of medal ceremonies, parties, and more celebrations, all acknowledging that USA Skeleton had come a long way in less than three years—from a budgetless existence to a peerless status among sliding nations of the world.

Even in victory, when it usually is about "me, me, me," our athletes were talking about "we, we, we." We had forged not just a program for individual excellence, but a true team. Amidst all of the fanfare, cheering, and the waving of flags, I looked up and saw Fallon, Browning, Robert, and some family and close friends from Dallas all sharing in this experience. I knew we'd done it and done it right. That was the important thing.

As I said, I'm not too emotional. But when I think back to Jimmy Shea making that last perfect run that won gold, or little Tristan Gale and Lea Ann Parsley dancing and jumping around on the track when Tristan completed her run, knowing they'd earned the gold and silver, respectively—yeah, I get a lump in my throat. But it was more than a feeling of personal pride. All of us knew, collectively, that something had connected that was bigger than any one of us, bigger than the champions or the directors or the athletes or maybe even the Winter Games themselves. Although we crown individual performance, we are the result of teamwork—we are a part of the whole.

We'd set our goals, put in place the organization to achieve them, pushed aside the bureaucratic barriers, changed the way things were done against the will of incredible inertia to do otherwise. For those efforts, we had won two Olympic gold medals and one silver, headfirst, together.

Mission accomplished.

Afterword

*What excites me probably as much as winning is
being able to make a difference in people's lives.*
—Payne Stewart

USA Skeleton had come a long way in less than three years, winning three Olympic medals en route. It soon became evident, however, that it would have to continue with new leadership. Just two months after Salt Lake City's Olympic flame had been lit, I stepped down as skeleton program director. I timed my resignation to coincide with the end of Ryan Davenport's three-year contract as U.S. coach, leaving it to the United States Bobsled and Skeleton Federation to take it from there.

In my letter of resignation, effective March 31, 2002, I reiterated the responsibilities that had been set forth in May 1999 when the board accepted my proposal to volunteer as skeleton program director. My summary of responsibilities in the letter was mainly about how the program would be organized and budgeted. No promises were made about an expected number of World Cup medals to be won or a precise prediction of how U.S. sliders would perform in an Olympics (assuming skeleton would even make it into the Olympics). Just getting USA Skeleton organized, structured, staffed, and funded would be a victory in itself.

The stated expectations would come later in the form of preseason goals set before the start of the 1999–2000, 2000–2001, and 2001–2002 seasons. For the first of those three seasons, the ambitious goal was for both the men and women to improve from fifth and sixth to fourth in the final World Cup nations' standings, respectively. The men made it to second, the women to third. For 2000–2001, the goals were to improve both of those rankings from the year before. They did: the men jumped to first and the women to second. The goal for the Olympic season of 2001–2002 was to maintain a top-three ranking in both men's and women's nations' rankings to secure the maximum number of Olympic sliding spots available. Once again, the United States was successful on both counts, with the men repeating their number one finish and the women tying for second, thanks in large part to Tricia Stumpf's gutsy performance at St. Moritz. A second preseason goal had been to win at least one Olympic medal apiece in the men's and women's Olympic competitions, and that goal was surpassed as well, with Jimmy Shea's and Tristan Gale's golds, and Lea Ann Parsley's silver.

There were other signs of just how far USA Skeleton had come in those three years:

* At least one medal was won by an American in every World Cup, World Championship, and Olympic competition held during each of those three seasons.

* A total of thirty medals in those competitions were won over those three years, compared to a total of six in the three years preceding 1999–2000.

* In America's Cup competition, U.S. sliders won twelve of a possible eighteen medals in 2000–2001. That haul would improve to sixteen out of eighteen a year later.

* In three years, the total number of ranked U.S. skeleton athletes had jumped from thirteen to ninety-two. Another sign of the growing interest in the sport was that in the six weeks following the 2002 Games, the USBSF and USA Skeleton had received more than one thousand e-mails from persons ranging in age from eleven to forty, all asking for more information on how to get involved in the sport.

My letter also included the following excerpt that explained my decision to hand over the skeleton reins:

> The Skeleton Program Committee and [I] are satisfied the skeleton program has operated and performed beyond anyone's expectations of just a few years ago. The foundation for future growth and success of the sport has been established in America. Only with quality leadership, qualified professional staff members, nonpolitical bias, and commitment

to fulfilling a well-thought-out, written plan will the future of the skeleton program, and the USBSF, continue on its successful path.

It is with this background in mind that I now weigh my interest and commitment to the skeleton program and/or USBSF and to family and business opportunities before me. The relationships with persons in the bobsled and skeleton communities, the fun we've had together, and the challenges and opportunities have all been productive, meaningful, and rewarding. As most of you know, my wife Fallon and I have two teen-age children, and it won't be long before [the children] are off to board-ing school or college. Business-wise, Vaughn Petroleum is currently in the midst of significant acquisition activity. Additionally, I will be co-managing another oil and gas company when it becomes a publicly held entity (Dorchester Minerals, L.P., began trading on NASDAQ in 2003). These opportunities and others are exciting and rewarding. And then, as many skeleton athletes kid me, with a small interest in the Pebble Beach Company, there is the always present and inherent requirement of maintaining a respectable golf game. So I am excited to choose fam-ily, business, and golf to be my future in the near term.

As of April 1, 2002, Don Hass and Trevor Christie will begin serving as the acting/interim skeleton program director and head coach, respectively. Both of these gentlemen are qualified and appropriate to lead the design phase of the 2002–2006 skeleton program business plan and the hiring process for coaching. It will be important for these positions to receive well-earned compensation from the USBSF during this interim period for their time, energy, and efforts.

For most of the U.S. Olympic team, the 2002 Games had been their fifteen minutes of fame. Jimmy Shea, buoyed in the national media by his inspirational story, achieved a level of true celebrity-hood, at least if measured by endorsements. Out of his gold-medal-related haul, he was able to build for himself a new home in the Park City, Utah area. For most other sliders, stretching their USBSF-allotted dollars as far as they can remains a yearly exercise in prudence and frustration.

While resigning as skeleton program director, I and the rest of USA Skeleton, in essence, handed back to the USBSF on a silver platter a solid skeleton program that had just won three of a possible six Olympic medals. (Interestingly, Americans had won three of the six previous medals awarded in Olympic Cresta in 1928 and 1948.) In the spirit of true entrepreneurialism, in less than three years, we had built a "company" that had quickly earned out its investment and shown a healthy return.

The U.S. skeleton program, in many ways, has reverted back to its pre-Olympic designation days of athletes scrambling to raise money themselves to pay for equipment and travel, maxing out their credit cards to make it happen. During the 2003–2004 season, for instance, the U.S. World Cup sliders at one point had to forsake an airplane flight and instead take a two-day ferry across the cold, choppy waters of the Baltic Sea to get from one World Cup site in Germany to the next one in Latvia. Those who only had to battle uncomfortable conditions were the lucky ones; others spent most of the time nauseated. Once in Latvia, an Audi that was rented was stolen from outside the hotel because someone didn't take the warnings about crime in the area very seriously or the offer of another team to secure the vehicle behind a locked fence along with theirs.

"Those ferries sink all the time," Tristan Gale said. "I think there's one that had sunk with the Swedish bobsled team on board. Half of us were losing our stomachs the whole time, and it's kind of hard to race right after something like that. That can be brutal."

Such is the continued legacy of skeleton, which has yet to be embraced by the vast majority of those who comprise the American sporting public. It's a fun sport to watch once or twice a year, when there's a global competition that merits major television coverage. But it remains a sport lacking mass appeal. Its moderately high expense, coupled with a lack of access to tracks, will probably keep the sport from ever reaching the level of popularity enjoyed by snowboarding and even freestyle skiing. However, according to TV producer, John Morgan, viewership for bobsled and skeleton in 1995 was approximately 25 million, and in 2005 it was approximately 450 million—much of this in Europe, on Eurosport. But coverage continues to increase in the United States, particularly on the Speed Channel.

Since 2002, some of the faces in USA Skeleton circles have changed; others have remained the same. As the U.S. team stood poised for the XX Olympic Winter Games, scheduled for February 2006 in Torino, Italy, a number of Americans appeared to be top candidates for more medals. Among the men, there's Chris Soule, who had been a consistent top-five performer in World

Cup competition since the 2002 Games. In 2002–2003, he won races at Lake Placid and St. Moritz, finished second at Igls and in the World Championships at Nagano, and ended the season number one in the World Cup points standings. Among the women, Tristan Gale continued to slide well, finishing eighth or better in all but one World Cup race, ending the year third on the women's World Cup circuit. Among the World Cup no-shows in 2002–2003 were Shea and Parsley, who didn't compete in the World Cup series, with Shea battling injuries and Parsley taking the year off to work on her doctorate degree. DeWitt has since retired from skeleton racing and is in the real estate business in Park City. He married his fiancée Linda soon after the 2002 Games and they now have a daughter named . . . Fallon.

I'm proud of Fallon's skeleton career, and not just because she performed much better than I did in competitions. She was a four-year national team member and World Cup team member in 1998/99. She placed as high as fifth twice, and never fell below ninth place while sliding at the America's Cup events at Lake Placid, Park City, and Calgary. Competing at the U.S. Olympic trials—the Verizon Championship Series 1 through 4—she placed tenth through the four races. Not bad for a "flat-lander" from Texas! Interestingly, her cross training must have been valuable, because in 2000 she also won the Brook Hollow Golf Club's women's singles, doubles, and mixed doubles tennis championships . . . and the women's golf championship as well!!

The next two seasons, 2003–2004 and 2004–2005, saw a bit of a U.S. decline in the World Cup standings. In the first of those two seasons, the only medals for the U.S. men was a silver by Shea and two bronzes for Soule. Parsley won the only women's medal in 2003–2004, a silver at Lillehammer. Things improved in 2004–2005. Soule won gold at Altenberg and St. Moritz to go with two bronzes, while relative newcomer Eric Bernotas broke through with a victory at Lake Placid and a silver at St. Moritz to make a late-season climb into sixth in the final World Cup standings, behind Soule at number two and Zach Lund at number five.

The biggest breakthrough story going into the 2006 Torino Games has been American Noelle Pikus-Pace, who had first appeared on the World Cup stage briefly in 2002–2003, finishing eleventh at St. Moritz. In 2004–2005, Pikus-Pace won gold at Winterberg, Igls, and Sigulda (Latvia), bronze at Lake Placid, and silver at the World Championships in Calgary to finish the World Cup series as the number one woman in the world. Also sliding strong for the

American women was Katie Uhlaender, who won silver at Lake Placid and finished number six overall, helping to give the U.S. women their first World Cup nations' title. Shea and Gale continued to compete throughout 2004–2005 on the America's Cup circuit with the intent to try out for the 2006 U.S. Olympic team. Among other Americans lurking as possible U.S. team members were World Cup veteran Brady Canfield, who won the overall America's Cup men's title (Shea finished second), and the female triumvirate of Courtney Yamada, Jody Barton, and Jessica Palmer, who finished one-two-three in the America's Cup women's standings.

"The athletes are continuing to perform like Olympians and are the real heroes in all this," said Terry Allen, director of the Utah Skeleton Association, who has been helping to recruit and train skeleton sliders since 2000. "The secret of whatever success there has been in skeleton has been supporting the athletes and giving them plenty of room and encouragement to go after success. You can't cookie-cutter them."

The major post-games highlight for the 2002 American Olympians was attending a U.S. Olympic team celebration in Washington DC that April. The entire team got a chance to visit the White House. At a reception on the south lawn, President George W. Bush congratulated the Olympians with an inspiring speech on a beautiful day.

It has been more than three years since I stepped down as USA Skeleton program director. My Dallas office is less than a hundred feet from where my accountant Kevin Ellis works. As of August 2005, Ellis was still very much in the thick of things in terms of USA Skeleton. Ellis has raced World Cup each of the three seasons going into the 2005–2006 year, with top-ten finishes in the final World Cup standings in both 2002–2003 and 2003–2004.

Together, Taylor Boyd, Peter Viaciulis, Terry Holland, Ryan Davenport, and I made a difference. The proof is in the numbers. When I stopped by Lake Placid in 2004 to visit the national team trials, I couldn't help but think it looked more like a World Cup event than it did just a U.S. tryout. There was hardly room outside the warming hut for all the sleds. I counted thirty-five men and twenty-five women sliders, and apparently there were another forty sliders who didn't qualify to compete that day. This is the way it should be—inclusion is productive; exclusion is limiting; objectivity is fair; subjectivity can be problematic if abused.

During that 2004 visit to Lake Placid, a number of people suggested to me that I should consider getting back into the leadership of the USBSF. I was nominated in 2002 as vice president of the USBSF and contemplated such a commitment while discussing it with my family and Boyd. Ultimately, the position would leave me far removed from the sport and from daily interaction with the athletes while forcing me to focus on organizational and political issues. Those considerations, combined with family and emerging business opportunities, resulted in a no go. When Boyd finally put the question to me, asking me if this was something I really wanted to do, I quickly admitted that it was absolutely not.

I've mulled it over time and again—part of me wanted to answer that call. But the entrepreneurial stage of development was complete with the skeleton program, and that's what had piqued my interest the most. I became involved because of the screaming needs the skeleton athletes had in 1999, my passion for the sport of skeleton, and the desire to lead the athletes and USA Skeleton by example.

When I look back and remember the smiles and overwhelming happiness that Lea Ann, Tristan, and Jimmy showed the world in 2002, I believe one may begin to understand the "why" of what we did. It is also my wish that current and future athletes, administrators, governing leaders, Olympic sports, and others will find inspirational force and insight from our efforts. Never stop believing; take action and do the right thing. Serve others. Strive to inspire ambition in others. Be a servant leader, and the future will unfold with limitless possibilities and greater rewards than you can imagine. Most importantly, serve the athletes first.

Life is nothing without challenge. It's how we evolve and how we justify our existence.

During the summer of 2005, I was requested by the United States Olympic Committee and the United States Bobsled and Skeleton Federation to begin dialogue on the future of bobsled and skeleton. As of August 29, 2005, I began volunteering myself, once again, as the interim executive director of the USBSF through the 2006 Torino Olympic Winter Games, in order to provide a trusted, productive, and hopeful future that rekindles the Olympic dream and ideals for bobsled and skeleton athletes.

* * *

In retrospect, my involvement in skeleton, both as an athlete and as an organizer, has been one of the most challenging and rewarding things I've ever done. First, there was the mental challenge of simply overcoming the fear of getting on that cafeteria tray-sized sled and sliding headfirst down the hill.

This is especially true when I think about the first few times I went off the top of a run—that was pretty terrifying. It reminded me of the first (and only) time I went skydiving. It's pretty similar—you spend a lot of time preparing, and you've got to get everything absolutely right, because if you don't, you are exposed and at risk. So from an athletic standpoint, to go from sheer terror at the thought of jumping on one of those things to becoming good enough to represent my country in World Cup competition—that's a pretty exciting thing. Representing the United States as an athlete is an experience that I would not have missed for the world. If I were to compare skeleton with other physical accomplishments, I would have to say it ranks right up there with becoming an Ironman, climbing mountains, or skydiving. The skeleton sliding experience may last only sixty seconds, but it certainly provides an athletic thrill that lasts a lifetime.

Beyond the physical experience of sliding, I also found the privilege of serving as an organizer of the skeleton movement to be extremely rewarding. On the psychological level, it was fascinating to bring all of the various constituencies of skeleton onto the same page and take them in the same direction. It was a thrill to create a community around skeleton, a community that includes athletes, friends and family of the athletes, supporters, and other interested people. I think the objective approach and sense of inclusiveness we created in the skeleton world were critical ingredients in our success. I also found it extremely rewarding to overcome the financial and political obstacles that we encountered as we sought to bring skeleton to the Olympics. I found it more self-motivating and more inspiring the further along we went. This reminds me of a quote by Johann Wolfgang von Goethe: "The person born with a talent they are meant to use will find their greatest happiness in using it."

The ultimate goal, of course, was to achieve Olympic success in both men's and women's skeleton at a U.S. venue—the 2002 Olympics in Park City, Utah. I just feel lucky that I got to participate in the Olympics in this way, and it was more satisfying to be a part of the Olympics—and to exceed our goals—from the opening ceremonies, through the skeleton victories, and ending with the closing ceremonies.

I had the privilege of making so many friends and getting to meet so many people whom I otherwise would never have come to know. I found it especially moving that one of the members of the team, as I mentioned earlier, named his daughter after my wife Fallon, the "mother hen" of the women skeleton athletes, during those years. It was certainly a challenge throughout to balance the demands of skeleton, both as an athlete and as an organizer, with the requirements of work and family, but somehow it all came together in the end.

I have been fortunate in my lifetime to accomplish many things on a high level, whether in business or in sports or nonprofit service. I will say that in many ways the skeleton experience has been one of the most important things I've done, or perhaps the most meaningful and satisfying thing, because it brought together so many elements in my life that are critically important to me. First, family—I got to do all this with my wife, and my children were there to experience it as well. Second, I was able to take my business experience and acumen and apply a business model and plan to an athletic endeavor, and that was a richly satisfying experience. And third, as I mentioned, the physical thrill of skeleton compares favorably with the other great physical and mental challenges I had taken on in my life.

I was honored to find myself in the role of servant/leader, and the role I played in the skeleton saga reflects the values around which I organize my life— the more you give, the more that comes back to you. The combined experience of competing as a skeleton athlete and serving as a skeleton organizer has given me the ability and confidence to do even larger-scale things in the future, and for that I am extremely grateful.

What sort of larger-scale things? My involvement in sliding sports continues in a meaningful way. The athletes have decided they need and want me to return and play a role for them.

Finally, Skeleton, to me, meant an athletic challenge at the highest level, an organizing/business challenge that took all the experience and creativity I had, a chance to compete as an athlete on behalf of my nation and to represent my nation in the Olympics—and to do all this with my wife and children at my side. It just doesn't get any better than that.

Jimmy Shea used to kid me, "You think too much!" Well, maybe that's true, but I can say without exaggeration that skeleton has provided me, and many others, with the ride of our lives . . . and it's not over yet.

What you leave behind is not what is engraved in stone monuments, but what is woven into the lives of others.

—*Pericles*

Acknowledgments

First, it is of utmost importance the reader appreciates and understands that this story relates primarily to the period of time leading up to and including the 2002 Olympic Winter Games. These words, except as otherwise quoted, solely reflect my perspectives and opinion at the time. Because of countless actions and events since 2002, my perspectives during the subject time period in general and discussed herein, have evolved and are much different and forward looking today.

Second, the following unique and capable people were irreplaceable in their areas of expertise as they supported my efforts and made notable contributions to the success and glory for the United States of America leading up to and including the 2002 Olympic Winter Games: Dwight Bell, Taylor Boyd, Dr. Dan Carr, Trevor Christie, Ryan Davenport, Lincoln DeWitt, Kevin Ellis, Tristan Gale, Dave Graham, Greg Harney, Terry Holland, Terry Kent, David Kurtz, Zach Lund, Kevin McCarthy, Kirk Milburn, Gary Moy, Lea Ann Parsley, Jim Page, Eric Parthen, Kirsten Peterson, Heather Ross, Mitt Romney, Matt Roy, John Ruger, Jill Savery, Jimmy Shea, Chris Soule, Tricia Stumpf, Peter Viaciulis, my wife Fallon, my son Robert, and my daughter Browning. There were many persons behind the scenes, including other athletes, family members, friends, and certain members, respectively, of the Salt Lake Olympic Organizing Committee, United States Olympic Committee, and the United States Bobsled and Skeleton Federation board who contributed in the right way, for the right reasons, at the right time. These individuals made the entire experience and resulting history possible, worthwhile, and enjoyable. I thank, commend, congratulate, and salute them for their blood, sweat, tears, patience, understanding, and proactive thoughts, ideas, and actions.

Third, some of the following names are repeats from above, but I greatly appreciate them for their willingness to dedicate their time to be interviewed for this book: Terry Allen, Taylor Boyd, Danny Bryant, Ryan Davenport, Lincoln DeWitt, Kevin Ellis, Tristan Gale, Orvie Garrett, Dave Graham, Mickey Holden, Terry Holland, Tom Kelly, David Kurtz, Craig Massey, Kevin McCarthy, Pat Murtagh, Tim Rath, Jimmy Shea, Chris Soule, Bob Storey, Paul Varadian, Fallon Vaughn, and Peter Viaciulis. Thank you to Milli Brown, Kathryn Grant, and all of the other capable persons at Brown Books Publishing Group, for believing in this story and facilitating the resulting product. Thanks to Michael Levin and his editing staff for their invaluable additions.

Additionally, I would like to thank my mother, Mary Jo Vaughn Rauscher, for all she has done in preparing me for life and for her unwavering love and support; my friends Rusty Getter, Mark McKinley, and Carter Montgomery for their omnipresent support, interest, and help during the Salt Lake City Olympic Winter Games and throughout life—a special thanks to Rusty for the incredible DVD he created documenting our Olympic experience.

Can we do it again? As Todd Beamer commanded on September 11, 2001, and President George W. Bush resounded on the evening of the opening ceremonies in his personal visit with the U.S. athletes, "Let's roll!!"